The Path of Roses

Soul Transformation Through Divine Love

Celestial Messages Received by Jimbeau Walsh 2019-2021

"As a small boy while visiting my mother's garden, I could feel the glow of goodness, blessings, and safety. The beauty of the rose, the tenderness, the miracle, led me to Divine Love. My path through the roses continues to inform my journey with a fragrance, both temporal and spiritual. Join me as we journey together to our blossoming transformations of soul."
......Jimbeau Walsh

Introductions

"This book is a joy to read! Be grateful, friend, that you have discovered 'The Path of Roses'. In it you will find a marvelous, true story of one man's journey to God, an inspiring story full of guidance and inspiration for all seekers after truth.

The author, Jimbeau Walsh, is a master storyteller, a gifted musician-songwriter, a Divine Love minister who has performed over 3000 marriage ceremonies and co-authored a book with Rev. Michael Nedbal entitled 'The Divine Love Minister's Handbook.'

In his search for truth, he studied Christianity, Hinduism, Sufism, and Judaism. In 1987 he found what he sought through a direct experience of the Divine. From that moment on, Jimbeau focused on deepening his relationship with the Creator. During his birthday on April 1st, 2019, he discovered much to his surprise that amongst his gifts is the ability to serve as a channel for messages from the most highly evolved in the spirit world, Celestial angels.

His friends nicknamed him "the reluctant medium" as his humility caused him to doubt that he was truly capable of serving in this way. Over the years, highly diverse beings of light have chosen him to be the instrument for their messages to humanity, and doubt left him.

These pages hold deep wisdom, both in Jimbeau's telling of his soul journey, and in the powerful, wise messages of the many beautiful souls who share their guidance through him. Invest in these messages. Open your heart and soul to them. I assure you that mighty blessings will be yours. These are a treasure trove of wisdom from God, shared by angels to us on earth. We are blessed by these fruits of Jimbeau's instrumentality!"

—Margaret Terry Adler, Social Worker and Art Therapist.

"Jimbeau Walsh is a man who possesses extraordinary talents - a musician for over 60 years, a spiritual seeker all his life, and an exceptional storyteller. Recently he has embarked on a journey to develop his gifts of mediumship. Having worked with and encountered Celestial angels for several decades, he discovered that he was able to receive verbal and clairaudient communications from them. Fortunately, he has recorded his experiences and communications so that the wider world might benefit from them as much as he has. These messages are short, concise, and potent in spiritual truth. They are meant to inspire the soul to pursue an intimate relationship with God and to release what impediments we might have that keep us from this relationship. For those who are curious about mediumship, those who are serious seekers of spiritual truth, and those who have already embarked on the road of soul awakening through receiving the gift of Divine Love, this book is a must-read. I heartily recommend it"

—Al Fike, author and medium.

The Path of Roses - *Soul Transformation Through Divine Love*

Since my childhood roses have had a special significance for me. From my mother's rose garden to having roses appear always as a sign of a blessing, of safety and goodness. Roses led me to Divine Love and continue to inform my journey with a fragrance both temporal and spiritual. I hope you will join me on this budding journey to our blossoming transformation of soul.

My mother kept a rose garden that she meticulously tended and I often helped her. She certainly associated roses to the Mother of Jesus and as a Catholic religiously prayed 'the rosary' and had several rosaries which are the beads that make up the 'garland or crown of roses,' hence the name, Rosary.

As I began to explore spiritual traditions I noticed that roses were not only important cultural, mythological and political icons, but also spiritual symbols. Roses are often associated with the Divine Feminine i.e. goddesses, and with many female saints, most especially Mary, the mother of Jesus.

Roses are used as religious symbols in Islam, particularly Sufism. In Islamic Sufism the rose represented the quest for Divine Love. For the Sufis, the rose also stands for divine grace and the manifestation of God.

In the Jewish tradition Solomon likens his Shulamite love interest to the rose flower, also referred to in the Mishnah as the 'king's rose' (Wikipedia). In the Song of Songs 2: 1-2, the Jewish people are compared with a rose, remaining beautiful amongst thorns, although some translations instead refer to a 'lily among thorns.' The Zohar[1] uses a 'thirteen petalled rose' as a symbol for the attributes of divine mercy named in Exodus 34: 6-7. Of course Jesus and his followers were all of the Jewish faith. It is sad to me that the white rose, which is very much associated with Jesus, was maligned in the movie The Hunger Games.

Known as the 'King of flowers' in Hinduism, the rose plays an important role in religious practices. As a symbol of love, devotion, and admiration for the divine deities, the rose is a beloved aspect of Hindu rituals. Hindu belief holds that the rose almost became the predominant flower that also represents spiritual enlightenment, beauty, purity, prosperity and eternity. One day, the gods Vishnu and Brahma were arguing about which flower was the most beautiful. Vishnu fervently favored the rose, with its unmatched shape and scent, but Brahma had never seen one before and therefore chose the lotus.

When I met Care[2] she was, as she stated, 'On the Path of Roses,' which I later found out to be the path of Divine Love. For her, it was a true sign from God if roses were in a particular place at a particular time. Most importantly, it was a requirement for her to enter a restaurant - that it

---

1 The Zohar is a foundational work of Kabbalist literature.

2 See the preface to Chapter 6 for more information about Care and this meeting.

has roses in some form or another as a sign that we were in the right place, safe and in grace. In my life with Care, we had many miraculous moments with the roses but I shall share one with you here.

One day when we were living near Dallas, Texas, after dropping off her children with their dad who lived nearby in Tyler, we camped out in a campground bordered by wild roses. Care woke me up at about 3:00 a.m. to tell me that we needed to get in the car and drive because the angels had told her to do so. I was of course, sleepy, grumpy and more than a little bemused by such a strange request. On the other hand this was a person in whose company I had been visited by angels and I knew deep down that there was purpose in her request. So, I handed her the car keys and said, "Ok you can drive." She replied, "No the angels want you to drive." I grabbed some cold coffee and we get in the car; I was in the driver's seat without a clue where or which way to go. So I asked, "Right or left out of the driveway here?" She replied, "You're driving so just go whatever way feels right." I confess that my thought was 'maybe I can go back to sleep because I am sure either way will not feel good.'

Care then said something like, 'here's a way you can try. Go either right or left and if it doesn't feel right turn around and go the other way.' Oh, I am so going back to bed I just know it. Ok, I go left and its dark out and it feels lousy and I turn around knowing that right will be no different; but it is. Going right on the road everything just opened up and I felt immediately like I was in some flow.

Shoots! That day we picked up a homeless man and helped him out with the small amount of cash we had with us. We went to the train station in Dallas and got Care a ticket to Chicago because the angels told her to go and visit my mom whom she had never met; and we essentially tried to help whomever we came in contact with. Around 5 pm we were in downtown Dallas in what seemed to be the financial district - surrounded mostly by large buildings, and feeling very hungry after a long and eventful day.

We noticed a beautiful carved wooden sign for a restaurant, 'The Palms,' that was hanging outside a place that not only advertised free food at happy hour but was playing the song 'One Love' by Bob Marley out into the street. Wow! Will there be roses? Of course! We go in as usual and start looking around to see where the roses are. There was a beautiful mahogany bar with a brass rail, an incredible buffet of every kind of food, stained glass windows and great music. But no roses! Not on a skirt, or window or even on the bathroom toilet paper or air freshener. None. Nada. Nowhere. I kept looking for a while, and then not seeing Care went back to the car. She was in the back seat which really meant she was very much in a prayer mode, but I took it to mean she was not pleased that it took me so long to come back.

Anyway I told her I had the perfect idea. I had seen a flower shop a few blocks away that was selling a dozen roses for $10 and we could go and buy them and bring them into the restaurant. She said, "Sorry it doesn't work that way," and began to have a deep prayer thanking God for all the events of the day but also requesting help because we were tired and hungry and Care knew He would guide us to whatever we need.

I was milliseconds away from starting the car when a silver van pulled up in front of us directly across from the entrance to The Palms. A man in a very nice brown three piece suit got out and opened the side rear doors. He reached in and grabbed what appeared to be a large vase with at least 2 dozen red roses and brought them directly into The Palms; he came back out empty handed, reentered the van, and it sped away. Care looked at me with the biggest smile in Texas and said, "We can go in now."

.....words of Jesus in a message on 4/7/22

My dear ones, I come on a bed of white roses *that you may know it is me. The path of the heart opened in God's love is the way of the transformed soul. For the mind can inform what is necessary in prayer, in service, but only the soul and an opened heart can change you. I ask you each day to examine your heart, your spiritual heart, as it is the doorway to your soul - the place where God's Holy Spirit brings His essence, His great and glorious love into your souls. Examine your heart that you may know love.*

For prayer is opening the heart to the love of God. True prayer is to be awakened to the realities of the love of God; the vastness of His universe, the magnificence of all His creations, but none more so than your soul having the great possibility of becoming at one with our glorious Father.

..... words of Charlie Chaplin from 2 messages on 6/14/19 and 8/26/21

I am on the path of roses, of Divine Love... *I wish to impress upon you your worthiness for love. I wish to encourage you to discover your gifts, to light a candle to the world; to pray and ask God to transform your soul, to heal you, to lift you, to awaken you in love.*

What awaits you in spirit is beyond what you can conceive, and you will discover the truth of my words one day, but know this for now: Love is the great gift. Love is the answer. Love is the path. Ask and you shall receive, and whenever you knock, assistance will arrive. Isn't that wonderful?

.....words of Yogananda in a message on 12/14/20

This is why we are here speaking from our souls to your souls: **On this journey where each one will be transformed from the mortal to the immortal, from the human to the divine angel, from the finite to the infinite in the love of God.** *May this blessing be yours.*

Jimbeau's Preface

It never occurred to me that I would one day compile a book of messages I had channeled from Celestial angels. In fact, I wasn't even aware that I had this particular gift until I received my first message from Paramahansa Yogananda in 2019.

In 2017 I had taken a trip to the Self-Realization Fellowship (a spiritual community that Yogananda[3] founded in the 1920s) in Encinitas, California with my good friends Al and Jeanne Fike. Al is a gifted Celestial spirit medium, and on that trip, he began receiving messages from Yogananda. A little later Al told me that Yogananda not only wanted to speak through me but that I would produce a book containing his messages. I found that comment somewhat strange and perhaps a little ridiculous because I was not, as far as I knew, a medium, Celestial or otherwise. I actually put that thought, despite several reminders from Al, out of my mind as fiction.

Some time passed, then Yogananda came to me on my birthday, April 1, 2019, and we had a lively repartee about his desire to use me as a medium/instrument for his messages. The messages was shockingly clear as day, and I recorded it and have included it in this volume to allow the reader to see for themselves what I was seeing and hearing for the first time.

The next message from Yogananda came on April 6, 2019. In the years since, I have received over 125 messages from him, and I have received over 225 messages from 49 other Celestial / high-heavenly sphere spirits. Many of these messages were channeled through me during Divine Love prayer/meditation circle meetings, but the spirit communicators intend that their words be shared and heard not only by the folks who attend those circles but also by anyone (including interested spirits) who are curious about the Divine Love path or simply seeking to be lifted up from the dark conditions of the earthly plane and their own inner uncertainty, pain, doubt and fears into love.

---

3 Yogananda (1893-1952) was an Indian monk and yogi, who introduced Hindu spirituality to the west in the first half of the 20th century. After he passed on to spirit he was rediscovered by the 'counter culture' in the 1960's and 1970's.

So, as God's plans and our co-creative efforts come together in the fullness of time, I was able to bring this book to print in 2024 in Nashville, TN, with the help of my good friend and spiritual brother, Phil Orr. We have decided to present the messages in chapters that feature messages from many spirits from the years 2019- 2021 in this first volume.

I hope that the messages in this book are an inspiration to you and provide some practical help as you decide to take the path of soul transformation through earnest prayer for God's love to infill your soul.

For even though prayer and meditation is recognized by all the great teachers to be the key to receiving God's love and grace, it is so important for each soul to discover how to actualize their will in order that their deep soul longings will connect their aspirations with the great soul of God.

I find that practical and very simple spiritual advice goes beyond any deep metaphysical or esoteric information and philosophy in magnetizing the soul to its Creator and thus beginning its transformation from being made in the image of God to oneness by receiving the essence (Divine Love) of God[4].

---

4 For more information about how Jimbeau became aware of his mediumship abilities, see the Author's *Bio* and *Afterword* at the end of the book.

In Gratitude

With deepest gratitude I dedicate this book to God and the angels who have guided me and chose me to channel these wonderful messages for the benefit of all of us both on earth and in spirit.

I first wish to acknowledge in gratitude my dear parents, James and Ann, who engendered in me a deep sense of spiritual longing and who loved their children with kindness and tolerance.

I also wish to thank Geoff Cutler for his love and support in posting the messages I have received and for making it possible for me to travel and share my spiritual experiences, prayers and music in several countries and on three continents.

I would also like to acknowledge: Phil Orr for his spiritual and material support and brotherhood, Al Fike for mentoring me as a medium, Michael Willey for his wonderful transcriptions, videos, and prayerful heart, Ruth Duval and Melissa Lewis Goyak for being the best Divine kind mice ever, and Care Darby Walsh for introducing me to Divine Love and the Celestial angels.

Cover design and graphic art by Linda Hostettler, Design Pro, LLC.

Chapter 1: Once Maligned, Now Forgiven 1
   Judas of Kerioth 1

Chapter 2: Saints 18
   Francis of Assisi 18
   Clare of Assisi 36
   Bernadette and Therese 52

Chapter 3: Performers, Writers, Poets 54
   Charles (Charlie) Chaplin 54
   Rev. George Vale Owen 66
   Sir Arthur Conan Doyle 70
   Kahlil Gibran 72
   George Gurdjieff 76
   Hafiz 80
   Robert James Lees 88
   James Padgett 93
   Fred (Mister) Rogers 98

Chapter 4: Voices of the Bible 102
   Noah 103
   Moses 105
   Elizabeth 106
   John The Baptist 107
   Mary 108
   Jesus 109
   Jude 111
   Mary Magdalene 112
   Andrew 113
   Simon Peter 114
   John, The Beloved 115
   Luke (The Physician) 116

	Paul	124
	Thomas	125
	Nicodemus	126
	Stephen	128

CHAPTER 5: INSPIRED THEN, ANGELS NOW 130
    Mahatma Gandhi 130
    White Eagle 131
    Hazrat Inayat Khan 134
    Martin Luther King, Jr. 135
    Thomas Merton 136
    Baal Shem Tov 139
    Yogananda 141

CHAPTER 6: LADIES OF THE LIGHT 188
    Care Darby Walsh 188
    Eileen Caddy 211
    Ann Rollins 228

ABOUT THE AUTHOR / MEDIUM 230
    Jimbeau Walsh 230

AFTERWORD 232

INDEX OF TOPICS AND RELATED MESSAGES 235

ADDITIONAL RESOURCES 240

INVITATION / INQUIRIES 241

Chapter 1: ONCE MALIGNED, NOW FORGIVEN

Judas of Kerioth

Let me explain about Judas to those who are either curious whether this spirit is 'the Judas from the New Testament reviled as the betrayer of Jesus,' or simply wondering who this spirit may be that is communicating with me. Even if you skip this introduction the answer should be evident when you read his messages that follow. For a more thorough explanation about this soul, Judas of Kerioth, I recommend you read his messages to James R. Padgett in several books entitled 'The True Gospel Revealed Anew by Jesus' (received 1914-1923) that contain information about his life and journey in spirit or read the wonderful book entitled, 'Judas of Kerioth,' which contains messages received (2001-2003) from Judas through H.R., a medium in Ecuador.

I have received many messages from Judas who sometimes signs off as 'I am Judas, once of Kerioth, now an inhabitant of the Celestial heavens and a follower of the master.' He is a down to earth, engaging, funny, plain-speaking Celestial angel who is always ready to give practical spiritual advice to those who are interested through yours truly. Since my wish is to receive messages that contain information and guidance that is practical on several spiritual levels, Judas always obliges me and what is received is meant to be actualized in daily life for the sake of one's soul transformation in God's love.

For many of us our spiritual path is not smooth, but contains obstacles, challenges and sometimes by-paths that lead us into very negative spiritual conditions. We may find ourselves in a very dark place where we feel helpless to escape. And sometimes the despair is so strong and overwhelming that suicide is seriously considered as the only way out. Judas was one of these people in his last days on earth. He had hatched a plan that he thought would force Jesus to show his power to the Roman authorities and thereby usher in a new age where Judea, under the leadership of the Messiah (Jesus), would overthrow the hated Roman overlords and become the leading nation that would enact God's will on earth.

His plan backfired entirely and to his astonishment and dismay he saw his friend taken into custody, tried and crucified as a common criminal. His *despair was so great that he threw himself off the Temple Mount and died. After a very long time in a dark place in the spirit world where he had to confront what he had done and what drove him to do it, he was approached by Andrew, his friend and one of the Apostles. Andrew convinced him that he had been forgiven and that he was loved. This enabled Judas to begin his journey out of the 'hellish' spirit realms into the heavens and ultimately to the Celestial heavens where Jesus resides.*

Judas' story reminds us that there is no unforgivable sin, and that if we earnestly want to find a way out of the darkness in our soul, help will come. God will send angels to assist us. If a soul reviled as much as Judas can be transformed into a Celestial angel - that should give great hope to us all!

The Way, the Light and the Truth
June 23, 2020

I am here your brother in Christ, Judas of Kerioth. Yes, it is me. I have been with the dear brother today and he was asking me earlier: 'Why is there not more mention of praying to God for God's love in what became what you know of as the Gospels and Epistles and writings of the Apostles?' He was wondering why this seems obscured. That is a good question.

First of all, as you may know already, much of what made it into what became the New Testament, those writings, has been retranslated, interpolated, changed many times over, and through those words received through James Padgett and others, they have told you many a time that words were changed and much of what they said or wrote was not included and much of what they did not say or write was interpolated. So knowing that I wanted to impress upon my dear brother here and all of you that if you do read between the lines and you just take the words of the master, you can see those words themselves show his oneness with God and the love that flowed and emanated from him - directing all to God, directing all to knock, to ask and listen, and look.

And those of us who followed him we were simple. Yes, a few of us had some education but mostly we were very simple. But you know there is something about being simple, being local. We had, you might say, built in lie detectors or BS detectors. So, when we heard the words coming out of Jesus, our souls knew that he possessed the truth and what emanated from him was a light, lighting the world, lighting our world, and he showed us the way to the kingdom of God's love - the way, the light and the truth. His wish for all is to carry this love in your souls that the dear brother Elijah spoke of. Carry that light to all.

Imagine your words, whether serious or in humor or in jest, were as if a prayer to each one. It is so important, so important, so needed, to take words of truth, words of love, words of forgiveness, words of encouragement and hope to all - most especially during this time on earth. You who are so blessed with this great love of God that you draw us to your circle, as you are touched by God's love we are touched by your hearts and are happy to be of service.

May the love and light of the heavenly Father, the most Holy One, be yours. And may you shine that light and give that love and hope in faith to all. I am your brother and friend in God's love. I am Judas of Kerioth.

BECOME A STAR

July 21, 2020

I come to the reluctant one to give you a few thoughts. Have you ever wondered why people wish to become celebrities, to become famous? Perhaps you know already that this is a desire on one hand to share gifts and on the other to be loved. When people attain this status in the world this thought becomes a major consideration: 'Shall I rest on the laurels and bask in the love and adoration of humanity, or should I take my good fortune and whatever gifts I have been given and give service to the world?' This is of course a human example, and I would say an obvious one.

For you whose souls wish to receive the love and to have this love of God you don't need to be celebrities, but you can serve and share and take your candle from under the table and let your light shine on every being that you may truly be a star in the firmament of God's kingdom. This is our wish for you that you may be this light to lead others out of darkness and that they may feel your love with their souls and wish it for them.

Sometimes you plant seeds and depending on where they fall the results may vary. But you know when they fall on fertile ground and they are cared for and watered, in this case in the love of God, in the living waters, those seeds will grow. One need not be concerned beyond being a light and a love in this world in the grace of God. I am pleased with this one for taking this message and how he has received, and I shall come again. With all my love I am your brother and friend in Christ. I am Judas of Kerioth.

Love, Light, and Healing
July 27, 2020

I am here Judas of Kerioth, a disciple of the master still. When we talk of light and love, the light is the vibration of love at its highest frequency. When you see one of us you see us in a light. You are also beings of light and though you have material bodies every particle of you vibrates and emanates from the soul. When one is out of harmony or not living in their souls, we refer to this as being in darkness because the vibration is so dense. And yet, all healings are a result of light and the vibrations that are in harmony with the laws of God's universe, the highest being His love. When you send this out to those in need and they are open to it they receive a healing in body, mind, and soul.

When one comes to spirit we bathe them in light, and most especially those who have experienced a violent death or are extremely troubled or fearful. We bathe them in the blue light of calm in peace and they feel the love of those healing spirits around them. And should they be on the path of Divine Love they are accompanied by Celestial angels and lifted in the vibrations of light and God's love.

As you feel this light and love in your souls and open to it and our loving Creator blesses each one of you, you can send out this light, you can transmit it to whomever you'd like and collectively send it out to the world where there is much darkness. But I wish to tell you there is much light in the world - billions praying, meditating, chanting, longing for change, longing for harmony and peace, for sustainability. Your light joins them and collectively you lift the planet and the vibration which I tell you, my dear friends, can heal the whole planet, and will in fact, bring the change you so desire and which we so desire.

This is also why you are drawn to music - a vibration that is easily felt, and beautiful music lifts every soul, touches every heart, and connects the longings to the Creator. So pray and sing and send out the love. We are with you in this endeavor in this blessing, in healing and in the beautiful transformation of every soul here in God's love.

I thank you for taking my message. May this guidance bless each one and may God's love be with you all.

THE SAFETY OF GOD'S LOVE
August 20, 2020

I come in the love of God to my dear friends as I watch over you and encourage you in the knowing, as only we can know, what awaits you. It is so important for each one of you to feel safe so that you can allow your hearts to open without fear, without distraction, being interrupted, or anything that would pull you away from the magnetism of God's love.

When I was on earth the Master often took us aside to a place of refuge, a sanctuary where we could pray and be instructed. Of course, as you know, he balanced this with his public life, and we accompanied him on that journey as well. But one must precede the other, and that is why it is so important for you to be in safety in your soul so that it may receive. This is so efficacious to the inflowing of God's love, accompanying the longings, accompanying faith which, yes, indeed, brings trust. Then as you are in God's grace, fully exposed, the nakedness of your soul is clothed in the glorious blanket of protection and happiness of God's love. Is this not why you come to this circle? Of course, it is. So be open, have faith, trust in God, and walk and breathe in His love that this world may be blessed.

I would only add that even if you are to go in public and bless one soul, touch one soul in the love of God, you have put a star in your heavenly crown and the Father delights and we celebrate that you have given the gift, the greatest gift of all to another in your sharing.

Stay in the love and we will stay with you. You are so dear to all here and you are my friends on the path to the Celestial kingdom where I reside in the love of God. Go in peace and know I love you. I am your brother in Christ always. I am Judas of Kerioth.

MAKE GOD YOUR FIRST RESORT
September 19, 2020

I am here your brother in Christ, Judas, enjoying, as always, you coming together to study the teachings I gave our dear brother. And I wish to commend you on selecting those two very comprehensive messages today. And I am going to keep this short, but I do wish to remind you, in your busy lives, and in your world full of entertainments, to practice going to God in prayer, so that God is not your last resort, but your first.

If I take this a step further, as you progress and God becomes your only resort, it does not mean that you give up all else, but rather, all else will be given when you put God first, because He is the provider of every gift. If you even spend a few moments of your day upon waking giving the day over to God and those of us who guide you, your Celestial friends, you will keep a little bit of that in your consciousness and it will be easier to be in the flow of God's grace.

And when you are in the flow of God's grace you attract all things in a harmonious way, bringing every good and perfect gift in God to yourself and others. This I share to encourage not to admonish. But to all, my love and blessings for each of you, and for your beautiful community in Divine Love, I am your brother, Judas of Kerioth. God bless you.

A Bit of Advice
September 24, 2020

I come in the grace of God as a disciple of the Master. I wish to offer you a bit of advice. A very simple practice of connecting with God, with feeling His presence, your soul and His soul, and that is this:

'Find a quiet place free from distractions, turn off the world, set aside all the things you must do, your material concerns and even your spiritual concerns, and for a moment just be. Feel your being and the spirit of life in your physical body and beyond, for you are not limited. Feel the light of your soul. Feel your heart and its longings for love. Allow these longings to go to God. Be receptive. Relax into love. Release your mind that your soul may communicate and be at one with its Creator from your heart. You have nothing to lose that isn't worth losing. What you have to gain is the glory of God's love. Allow this.' I thank you. All my love and blessings. May God's love touch you deeply on this journey. I am your eternal friend in God's love. I am Judas.

7 | THE PATH OF ROSES
SHOWING DIFFERENT FACES
October 16, 2020

I am here, Judas, and I come in the love of God and my dear brother Kahlil Gibran is with us today. We were ruminating as to who might speak and Kahlil defers to me. I wanted to clarify about the messages of the masks. And this was a discussion that we had of showing different faces to different people in different situations. And then when touched by the real, which the sun in this story represents, the love of God, there is a oneness where all the masks drop.[5]

This is not to say that among different groups of people, there aren't situations that you wouldn't approach, or say or do in ways that are more appropriate with that group or person. What the message here is this: 'Instead of being a little bit of this person and a little bit of that as you become at one in the love of God, all your gifts become channeled through the prism of all the colors which can only be seen when the light is shining through your soul.'

This is the crystallization of the soul in God's love where there is a oneness and yet there is a much larger field of embrace than trying to piecemeal each thing you wish to convey. Picture a crystal with the full spectrum of colors coming through to each one. For even the most beautiful painting is as if nothing in a dark room. So yes, you can, of course, present things in the appropriate manner to whomever you are addressing. Let me clarify again. Describing to a blind man a painting might be quite difficult unless he could feel it through his touch, if he could feel the emotion or what it represented in terms of landscape or the heart. So therefore, you would find an appropriate way to describe something to such a person. And as the analogy of blindness is sometimes used when referring to spiritual blindness or even short sidedness, I hope my description is revealing.[6]

My brother Kahlil is a beautiful soul and he shed a light through his heart into his writings and his connection in spirit awakened in him something very deep, and to this day has this effect upon his readers.

---

[5] Judas is referring to Kahlil Gibran's story 'How I Became a Madman,' which he shared with HR in the channeled book, 'Judas of Kerioth.'

[6] Note: Later Judas came and told me to look up this from Matthew 6: 22: "The light of the body is the eye: if therefore thine eye be single, thy whole body shall be full of light."

Oh, if you could see him now, a beautiful, progressed soul who lives in a realm that is the doorway to the Celestial kingdom, you would be amazed. And so, he will communicate in the future from where he is now and the condition of his soul in the love of God. I thank him for deferring to me. All of us here we leave you with the blessings of the abundance of God's glorious love. We thank you; we love you. I am your brother in Christ. I am Judas of Kerioth.

Think of Eternity Not Death
February 12, 2021

I was so pleased to hear and to be part of listening to those messages that you all read today. The beautiful words of Eileen Caddy that she received, the wonderful descriptions of the spirit world and its eternal nature in George Vale Owen's book, 'Life Beyond the Veil,' and the reminder that if one wishes to be in rapport with the Celestial realm the most important thing is prayer.

For as in the messages that James Padgett received from John, and as is reflected in what Hans had received from me, it is a matter of soul to soul. It is above the earthly mind, and you can call it soul mind. Life on earth is in time and space; it is mortality. Life in spirit, and most especially in the Celestial realms, is beyond time and space and immortal.

When on earth people often think of beginnings and endings and because they have a sense of self-preservation attached to their body, they fear the death of that body, and yet, as you read today, when the chick in the egg emerges from the shell it leaves it behind and gives it no further thought. This is not quite the same as those who leave the earth plane in the sense that although they discard that earthy body as you all will and at some point, give it no further thought, but your earthly attachments may remain.

The irony is this: fear of death of the mortal body becomes somewhat humorous once one is in spirit and knows it. I ask you to consider the opposite and rather than consider the time of your death and how long you will be on earth, consider what you would like to do when there is no end in eternity.

I tell you this - the more you devote your time to prayer and receiving the great love of God, the more your journey in spirit will be above the earth planes in the beautiful progression through the spheres that you are reading about, to the indescribable glories and magnificence of the Celestial Realms. I tell you this as one who is an inhabitant of these realms, but who also suffered greatly in the lower spheres, in the hells, from my remorse of conscience and the effects it had. My journey was one of being able to forgive myself for, as Andrew told me, I was forgiven by God, by Jesus, and by all the apostles, and that so lifted me. At first, I did not quite believe it, but as it came into my consciousness and I could feel the light, and I could feel the love, I wanted so much to be in the state of forgiveness and to help others who were even in a worse condition than myself, as you may have read and already know.

I only wish to add that you have chosen the journey of God, of love and light and believe me this will lift you up, so have no fear of crossing over and know, should you receive enough of God's love and grace, this transition will be easy, loving, and beautiful. There will be many to embrace you. I say these things not to cause fear or to suggest anyone here is going to pass over this evening, but so that you will focus your attention on the eternal love of God and your welcome when you do pass. You will leave the earth life as a mirage.

I wish you every blessing, every gift, every freedom on this path and to again remind you, whenever you call, we come. So, remember to call - through thick and thin we are your brothers and sisters in the love of God, in Christ. We love you. We truly love you and God so loves you. Hold this in your heart, in your souls and be of good cheer and joy. I am Judas of Kerioth. God bless you.

Dealing With Threats of Harm
February 17, 2021

I am here your brother and friend in the grace and peace of God. May His love be showered upon you. These questions about violence, conflict, those who are out of harmony, who use the Bible or other books to defend acts of aggression - this has been made clear in my writings through H.R., but most especially in the writings that James Padgett received and the words of the Master himself both in the Gospels and in contemporary revelations.

I wish to say that when things started to get difficult for us, and I mean the Master and those of us who were his disciples and followers, although he always spoke from his heart, from his soul, in ways that all could understand, he often removed himself from situations of impending violence for the sake of our safety and his own.

I tell you this because while you are reading and understanding how important it is to speak the truth, to stand up and be counted, it is also important to recognize when you are up against a brick wall, as they say, and to remove yourself from a situation of impending harm, most especially physically, but I shall say including verbal abuse or other forms of negativity which make it difficult for your physical presence to be there.

First pray. Ask God for protection, to put a bubble of love around you to send out and radiate the love in your souls. Yes, first do this. And I may say this is why we always encourage prayer and constant awareness of God and His love, His grace, His will, and the harmonious flow that goes with your uniting with God and His love and all those blessings of His. First, do this, and then if the person and what you are being confronted with does not recognize the state of your being, your wish for peace, your emanations of love, and your kind words, then yes, remove yourself to a safe place until things calm down. The Master did this, so you know it is good advice and true.

May you all continue to find truth and sustenance in your readings, diverse as they may seem, and yet progressive on the path to the Celestial kingdom showing the way in God's love. How can I wish you anything but this? May God bless you with a great inflowing of His love, as you open your heart, that God may touch your soul. I am your brother and friend in Christ, and I love you. I am Judas of Kerioth. Go in peace. Go in peace.

Let Go and Let God
March 12, 2021

As always, I am delighted when you come together in prayer, in study, to consider the great truths that came through the Master. The greatest being the truth of God's love. The mind is in flux and can bend and twist and maneuver, and yet at its core it is an organ of discrimination which is able to distinguish one thing from another. Its quality of intuition can send a signal of danger which feels inharmonious or disturbing, but just as often it sends out a signal that something quite good is coming, and then you have a good feeling. This is your intuition.

Part of what James Padgett received in terms of the history of Christianity, which was important, is its origins, and the errors that were made and the assumptions that became part of the orthodox dogma. However, the real importance of those messages was to take the mind away from the concerns of the orthodox teachings of hellfire and damnation, Jesus' blood redeeming, and the fantasy of the virgin birth, and so forth. The real message is to be in your soul, above such distinctions, above the mind, and to find in true prayer the greater reality of receiving the great gift of the Creator's love. This is our purpose.[7]

This is the core of what we wish to disseminate to you, as has been said, again and again, soul to soul. For a soul receiving the essence of God, His great love, becomes at one beyond the mind and all its byways, all its explorations, however intellectually valid they might be. For we in the Celestial realms wish to serve you, to serve your souls, to encourage the longings to take precedence over the mindful curiosities, valid as they may be, but that are in a sense, only extensions of the material world and the material mind. As you read today, "Let go and let God, go to God for all." "This is the great truth."[8]

May the grace of God be with you all and stay with you in this circle of light, in this circle of love. May God bless you. I am your brother and friend in Christ. I am Judas of Kerioth.

Depictions of the Spirit World in Film
June 7, 2021

I am here Judas, your brother in the Divine Love. I wish to address the questions of the dear sister about the film she saw ('What Dreams May Come') and its depiction of the spirit world, the hells, and changes, and so forth. I am aware of that film, and I must say that it was inspired not only by spiritualist writings but by a certain amount of influence from the spirit world, although not the Celestial spheres.

It does show some of what one experiences when crossing over into spirit especially when one suddenly finds oneself there. It addresses the innocent and a realm that they would go to and pictures that realm satisfactorily. As for the hells, well there aren't flames and boats and

---

7 Judas told me later that our souls lead us to Divine Love truth, not our minds.
8 Extract from Eileen Caddy's book 'God Spoke to Me.'

some of those things that were used as visual depictions to give you an idea of what a soul would feel like to be in hell.

Certainly, the author and the filmmaker got their point across. Presenting the idea that one could progress from hell, the idea of a soul mate and having love, the idea of travel, and by earth standards, a peek into the beauty and harmony of the lighter spheres, although their depictions are about purification and redemption in the natural love. A very good place to start!

It was groundbreaking, as is this newer movie, an animation called 'Soul' which does give one a sense of being out of the physical body in a realm of light, though again, these realms of spirit are very much lower spheres with some light in them. One could say that from the earth plane to maybe the second sphere is depicted.

And yet, since humans have almost no conception of life in spirit, these films are valuable and give the audience a sense of being without a human body but still alive and with a sense of progression in love. I will say this, that if the writers, and the director, and the makers of the film 'What Dreams May Come' were aware of the Divine Love, there would be a sequel of progression to the Celestial heavens and the same with this movie 'Soul.' But those very well meaning and loving individuals who presented those films simply have no knowledge of higher realms and transformation from the human to the Divine.

It is my wish, and the wish of many here, that those of you who are creative, will bring this vision to fruition through film and other media as you do in song or poetry. Let the truth be seen. I think I have addressed this issue to some extent but if you have further questions, I will be happy to answer them with the help of my brother here. Until then go in God's love and grace. Pray! May God bless you. I am Judas.

Prayer Is the Answer to All Problems
July 25, 2021

I am now an inhabitant of the Celestial heavens and I come to tell you no matter what your station is, no matter how separated you feel from the love of God, at any time, no matter what your sins are, all can be redeemed in the love of God as I am.

Often one tends to focus on the error, on the pain of separation, on the loss of innocence or on some betrayal, and that pain and often the despair that comes with the remorse and sometimes even the unworthiness one feels. And yet when one does recognize and clearly sees what needs to be remedied, then one can focus on the solution.

When something breaks in the material world, for example, you have a flat tire and you are at the side of the road and perhaps you're running late and this is not a good feeling, and in fact can be traumatic in some instances, but at some point, help comes and most especially when requested. For if you do not know how to fix a tire and you send out a request for help, someone will come to your aid. So let me put this in spiritual terms. When you feel your soul bereft of love, of your connection with God, and you are immersed in the consciousness of your troubles, recognizing them, at some point you send up a request, you focus on the solution with all your heart, with all your being, you call out to God, as I did. And God answers and you are sent help and lifted up.

And in this beautiful circle of souls who come for the love of God, who come to be in His holy presence, who have come with the deep longings to be transformed from the mortal to the divine, God sends us to be with you because you are on the path of Divine Love and your journey leads to the Celestial heavens where we abide in the presence of God.

So, quite simply, I say when you recognize what seems to be the problem, all one needs to do is reach out in prayer and therein lies the solution. For God's love is soul to soul. Put your mind to rest and your heart and soul to be forever opened in God's love. Be at peace in His holy presence. Allow joy in the eternal blessing that is yours for the asking. I shall step back and be in this prayer with you in the Glory of God. I thank you. With all my love I am with you. I am Judas of Kerioth, now an inhabitant of the Celestial heavens and your eternal friend in the love of God.

Simply Bring the Truth

July 26, 2021

I am here and I come again to this beautiful circle. I am Judas. In my time on earth walking with the Master and my brothers and our sisters, we witnessed firsthand how God works through those who are open and blessed with His love as Jesus was and is. Everywhere we went, some kind of goodness, some touch of God's love, some healing, some resonant story, reached out from the Master to the hungry, even as we did not have the kind of media that you have, where you can in a moment share a wonder and reach out to the world. This being so, we always ask you for discernment in what you are putting out to the world. It isn't that you cannot speak out against injustice, for the Master did. But please remember that there were those among us who wanted revolution, and who mistook the revolution of God's love for the overthrow of the Roman yoke, that being our mindset.

So, imagine this job that the Master took on. He selected each one for a reason and many others were drawn in by their hunger. He told wonderful stories as you know, and when you review what is written in the New Testament, you can see he drew from the prophets of old with whom he was extremely well acquainted and often used their words to make a spiritual point. My point here is that you can use what is true in your tradition and bring truth to anyone's present moment, and present belief. And rather than confronting them by pointing out the error, we ask that you simply bring the truth. For example: 'Will you pray with me? Let us ask the heavenly Father, our Creator, to bless us, to heal this one, to open a door that has been closed.'

Even those who might not even believe in God, when in crisis will often be led by their soul longings to reach out, and they will call on you, each one of you, and you can tell your story and touch them with the love that you have, for really, we are telling His story. There is much each one here can do to bring this love in your souls, this light into the world. I am not telling you something you don't already know but wish to remind you of the great power of God's love to touch a soul with a simple word of kindness, with a prayer, with a hug.

As you walk this world and more and more feel this glow, this substance of our heavenly Father, that you now possess to whatever degree in oneness, you cannot help but wish to serve, to bless, to love all, and to give this gift, and to speak the truth that you have been given.

When you look back on your lives and sometimes with some remorse over time wasted, I say to you, from this moment on consider how you will utilize each moment walking on the path of Divine Love, moving forward in the grace of God, in Joy, in gratitude, in service, in kindness, bringing peace and hope, in the knowing of the glorious future that awaits you and all in God's love.

I thank you all and my brother here who likes to tell stories. I shall step back in gratitude to you for allowing me to step forward and I shall be in this prayer with you for the love of God. I am your brother and eternal friend in the Celestial heavens. I am Judas once from Kerioth now your angelic brother. God bless you.

Our Souls Stand Naked Before God
August 30, 2021

I am Judas from Kerioth and now an inhabitant of the Celestial heavens where God's love reigns supreme and there is happiness beyond the conception of mortals. What you can perceive with your souls when you're open to God's love will give you a kind of insight into what awaits you in spirit. It has been said that when one passes into spirit, they stand naked before God, and I wish to say that as brother Francis stood naked before his townsfolk, he was not afraid. It was because he knew there was no shame in exposing yourself to God. And so, this was a physical metaphor for how all things are exposed in spirit, but not as you might imagine, immediately. For until one recognizes that they are, in fact, now in the spirit world and has some sense of the condition of their soul, that condition may, in fact, be hidden for a time, but eventually all truly do. Our souls stand naked before the Father in glory, in the purity, the blessing and bliss of transformation.

If you allow yourselves in your prayer to take a good look at your condition, and you realize, when in the love of God, what you no longer need to carry and allow God to carry you, you too will experience what Francis did. After I passed into spirit and saw my condition, as you are most probably aware, I thought I was hopeless and unredeemable. But when Andrew came to me and told me he loved me, that all my brothers loved me, and most particularly the Master, I little by little was able to let go of my shame, my remorse, and to begin to feel my worthiness.

So please always remember every soul is worthy to be blessed, to be in the love of God, to progress. When you hear the words 'God loves all his children,' that means you, and you, and you and all. Lastly, I say if you find yourself in some condition of darkness or shame or regret or doubt, remember God loves you, and all of us here will come at your beck and call as I did today. Have faith, take heart, and may the love of God touch you deeply, heal you and transform you. On behalf of all here, we love you. May God bless you always. I am your brother in Christ, your eternal friend. I am Judas. God bless you.

Begin Anew
September 9, 2021

Happy New Year my dear friends, Rosh Hashanah! This is a good time to begin anew, to change course, to walk in faith.

The will of God allows for everything in the big picture to be in harmony. And despite all the in-harmonies created by free will there is no force that can disrupt the harmonious structure and being of the universe created in love and in light by God. What shall be your New Year's resolution? What do you wish for your own soul? For, as you have discussed, a soul that is transformed, a soul living in grace, draws all good and perfect things to itself. This magnetism is the great attraction, for all beings' desire love.

This is the Jewish New Year and this month when Yom Kippur, the Day of Atonement (and at-onement) fall, is when the Jewish community seeks forgiveness for their sins, for their misdeeds, for their in-harmonies, by asking for mercy and to be newly anointed. I point this out so that you will make a connection for yourselves, not in a religious sense, but in your spiritual lives. To start fresh each day, to carry the intention to be changed, transformed, and made anew in God's love. And yes, you will expiate whatever holds you back, whatever separates you from the Creator, when you allow His love in. The more love that comes into your soul, the more whatever has separated you shall dissipate, like a weight around your heart that has held you down and now you are lifted in love and light.

May the gate of light be opened; may the gate of God's love be opened. May every blessing be yours and may you have faith and know we have your back in all things. You have given great joy to Mr. R.J. Lees, to Rev. Owen, to Sister Eileen Caddy, and all of us here as you continue to explore and absorb the truths that have been given. Take them all in as best you can, and I promise you will not be disappointed.

With all my love and blessings, I am your brother and eternal friend in the love of God, a redeemed soul, I am Judas. God Bless you.

CELESTIAL ENERGY

October 18, 2021

I am happy to be with my friend this evening and I wish to say a few words. Do you know that feeling you get when the electricity goes out and for a moment when the hum of electricity, the sounds generated by it, come to an abrupt halt and there is that brief moment of, 'Aha, peace.' Also, you may feel that peace when you are in nature and most prominently near waters and places where what you call negative ions put out a charge of beautiful energy.

So, consider what comes out of your TV set, if you have one, what kind of energy comes out of a film, a conversation that has a negative center of gravity. You may think of God's love as these beautiful negative ions clearing the atmosphere and sending a beam of light over and against the prevailing winds.

We talk about persisting in prayer, not in terms of saying a rosary or having to have a mantra or words that go no higher than the lips, but that which arises from the longings in your soul, that which touches the soul of God Who always responds. It is important to be able to be in the vibrations of light, in the grace of God, carrying those emanations from heaven. So, each of you can carry a piece of heaven with you and know you are protected from vexed spirits, and that you do not have to react in kind but walk in love, walk in joy, walk in faith and be a waterfall, be a forest. Rise above! And let me just say: 'Be a Celestial waterfall, a Celestial forest, as you carry the essence of God in your souls.'

I am your eternal friend in the love of God and your brother in Christ. I am Judas, once of Kerioth, and now a Celestial angel.

Chapter 2: SAINTS

Francis of Assisi

Like most kids growing up Catholic I heard stories about Francis of Assisi, known by most as St. Francis. I enjoyed the visits from the Franciscan Friars in their modest garb and even went on retreat to a Franciscan monastery. Those encounters and watching the movie 'Brother Sun Sister Moon' was about all I knew about Francis' life growing up.

In 1993, after the passing into spirit of my wife Care, I was invited to Italy by my old friend from Chicago, Tom Vack, who had been living there for many years. He is a design photographer and was highly admired for his unique use of light. Tom had met Care and wanted to help me heal from her loss. I went to Italy with my son Adam who was about 11 years old at the time, and we visited many beautiful places including Assisi.

The lovely town which had the Basilica of San Francesco and the nearby Basilica of St Mary and the angels, was very peaceful, but in truth, very touristy. We first went to the St. Francis Basilica and appreciated the Giotto frescoes on the walls, but for me it felt like a museum and not a sacred place at all. Then Tom took us down the hill to the Basilica of Mary and the angels which also had a similar museum feel to it. Seeing my disappointment, Tom urged Adam and me to follow him to the Porziuncola, a church which was inside the Basilica and one Francis had restored under instructions from Jesus (in a vision).

The Porziuncola was small enough that we didn't really notice it at first, because on that day the area around it was dimly lit. However, we could see inside the small church where many little candles were burning. We stepped inside the open doorway. I can only attempt to describe that experience as walking through the doorway and into the ectoplasm of Divine Love, being overtaken and embraced in the divine presence. I don't know how long we stayed but tears of joy streamed down my face as I sat in gratitude for this wonderful blessing of God's presence and His love showering upon us there. Having grown up Catholic, having abandoned its orthodoxy, and being highly critical of that church, I was stunned that here in this little building was God's love. My friend Tom, knowing this said to me, "Now Jimbeau, don't be so hard on the Catholics; they had Francis!"

Later, with Al and Jeanne Fike, we received another profound blessing in the St Francis grotto at the Self-Realization Gardens in Encinitas where Yogananda and Francis both spoke to us through Al.[9]

After I started receiving Celestial messages in 2019 from Yogananda, Francis was one of the first of many celestials to come through me. I often noticed then, and still to this day, that Francis and Yogananda are Celestial friends and come together to our prayer sessions. I found out much later that Yogananda loved Francis and had visited Assisi and felt his presence. Francis sometimes signs off as, "I am Francis, once from Assisi, now an inhabitant of the Celestial heavens."

This Sanctuary
April 7, 2019

I am Francis and I come to you in God's love and with great love for all of you here and for this beautiful place. This sanctuary is a place of refuge for many. When I walked the earth with my friends in the hills around Assisi we sang and prayed with so much joy to be in God's creation. And that is why it was easy for us to open up to God's love in our own simple way despite our beliefs which were very Catholic.

Of course, we were considered outsiders because we wished to live a simple life in communion with God and God's creation. And those who have been to the little church that I restored with my friends are aware of the presence of God; His love is in that church still, to this day, and it is respected by those who go there. I ask you to bring that same respect to this sanctuary because this is a holy place and those who come, they come for healing, for refreshment, for the blessing of God's grace and for our messages. It is important to keep this place as a Sanctuary, not only this room but all these grounds and the beautiful gardens I am so found of visiting.

And when there is conflict in this place or disagreement or argument, I ask you to do this with humor and love so that any negative energies are dissipated in the love. It is a joy to come to this place and visit, and all of us here commend you for the work you have done and continue to do, for the healings that are present here, and for the deep desires of all of you to reach out to the many in a world that is busy and conflicted, as you

---

9 See the preface for Yogananda in Chapter 5

know. This is a sanctuary and a place of light in God's love. How blessed you are. I thank this brother for delivering this message and I am pleased with the way he has done so. May God bless you all. I love you. I am your brother and friend, Francis.

Notes from Yogananda:

Paramahansaji:[10] "In the morning we reached Assisi. There we saw St. Clare's tomb. St. Clare was a great devotee of St. Francis. Only after great request, he once broke bread with St. Clare; and while they were sitting together, people saw the Church was afire. When they came, the fire vanished; it was the light of God. St. Francis met Jesus in the woods almost every night. As I was visiting his living tomb and put my head on the shrine step, St. Francis appeared to me. Then I saw a tunnel of eternity into which he disappeared. The entire cellar beneath the church was replete with his vibrations. You would have enjoyed very much to meditate here. St. Francis is one of my beloved saints with whom I commune and have communed. I write to you these sacred things for God has made you sacred by meditation."

BE MINDFUL OF YOUR HEART'S DESIRES
June 28, 2019

It is so much easier to see the workings of the Creator in nature. I want to encourage you both to always know you can retreat in nature, whether you are in the city or the country, to find that quiet place to commune with God. You know that this possibility is always present to connect wherever you may be, but in nature there is a calm and a peace and an obvious visibility of God's work. I not only encourage you, in your travels, to pray and meditate in nature but to encourage others to join you. Should you find yourself in a busy place, then of course you just need to have your soul connect, and God and the angels will bring this peace and calm to you.

There is a great longing for light, and love, and the peace that passes understanding in so many souls, and most especially in this dear place where you found yourselves at the present moment. Please know that we will continue to be with you and guide you. Follow your heart's

---

10 Paramahansa Yogananda in a letter written to Rajarsi Janakananda, from Rajarsi Janakananda: 'A Great Western Yogi.'

desire. Gravitate towards where your heart is moving you. Should you find yourself in difficult situations, go to your heart. Connect with your soul.

In the garden of God's love, may you continue to bloom like the roses, like the lotus, like the lights that you are. May God bless you. I promise you my love and protection. I am your brother in the Celestial heavens, Francis, and I love you.

You Can Have a Circle of Light Anywhere
August 6, 2019

What a beautiful circle of light you have here. We come here when we feel the longing of every soul reaching to the heavenly Father. This draws us to you, and we come to be in prayer with you, each one of you opening like a rose to the Creator's love. I come to not only wish you a great blessing in this love but to tell you this is all you need, this simple gift of God's love directing you always on the path of light and truth and love.

Be in this state of grace, this state of Holy Communion with the heavenly Father, and let your soul perceptions lead you so that there be no doubt which way to go and what choices to make. This is what I did with my friends in Assisi as we flowed in the Father's love. We had almost no cares for anything else. Often, we forgot to eat. We imbibed the fruit of the Father's love in our souls, and we played, and we sang. This was our church.

My friends, you can do this anywhere. I would say it's easier in nature but this place here, there is much light in this place. There have been many prayers said here. We can feel it. Please remember we are here to support you and I say to you, give not a thought to doubt, negativity, weighing this or that. Let your soul truly be the center of your lives, that God may open your soul to a radiant flowing of His love. This is the gift.

I am grateful to be here with you all and to have this one allow me to come through, though he is reluctant. I am Francis. I love you all. May God's love be with you all and may this circle of light expand throughout the earth. You have drawn many into this circle, visible and invisible. We are here. We love you. God loves you. I am Francis.

BE IN THE GARDEN OF LOVE
August 20, 2019

Hmmm, 'every little bird that sings, may it give your heart wings.'[11] Be in the joy. Be in the garden of love. When I was on Earth, my friends and I, we sang sweet songs and we worked quite hard to build a life in God. We removed ourselves from the everyday busy world which we had all known. We had known war. We had known the material mind and material things. But we opted for a simple life. And of course, I do not expect, nor do any of us here in the Celestial realm expect you to totally give up your world, to give up your material things. But you do know the joy in love. So we ask: 'Make life simpler. Spend more time in prayer. If you are busy, talk to God.' You will get an answer as we did, and we do. Be in the garden of God's love that you may all bloom and blossom.

It is my wish for each one of you to open like a rose. Let the fragrance of God's love not only fill your soul but be seen, be felt, by each soul that you touch now on your journey walking into the future in God's love. My love to each one and God's love to each one. May it bless you each. I am your brother and friend in the Celestial heavens, Francis.

BECOME THE GARDENERS OF YOUR SOULS
November 17, 2019

It is Francis, yes, Francis who spent time in the hills above Assisi with my friends. I couldn't help but come and walk the gardens yesterday with the brothers and the wonderful sister. I wish to say to the gardener,[12] this is a wonderful creation, a co-creation with nature. It is obvious this did not happen by itself, but with vision and focus and determination, so this beautiful landscape appears. As one brother said, it is a wonder of the world, and indeed, in your world, it is a wonder.

The time and the energy that has been put into creating this sanctuary in nature, this place of refuge - I ask, consider now creating this place of spiritual sanctuary, a refuge for the souls. As the rain comes down and nourishes the land, the flora and fauna, allow the showering of the Creator's love to come into this place of light and nourish your souls. Everything has led up to this in your lives.

---

11 'Every Little Bird That Sings' is the title of one of Jimbeau Walsh's songs.

12: Reference to Ancient Gardens, Eudlo, QLD Australia. Home of Peter and Clare Heilbloem

Become the gardeners of your souls so that they may blossom and the fragrance of the love, like a rose, like a lotus, will permeate this atmosphere for all to feel, and for all to heal. For every longing soul, provide this. The reward will be beyond what you can imagine for it is a Celestial reward. I wish to thank, on behalf of all of us here, the hosts who have offered their place to be a place of prayer and sanctuary. I encourage them to continue this effort and invite all that they can possibly accommodate. I see that it is their heart's desire to serve others in this way. This, of course, would be their choice. Should you choose, you will have much help, much guidance. We will come and be with you in prayer, in sanctuary, in refuge.

May God's love permeate this place and in each of your souls, blossom. Become the gardeners of your souls, my dear friends. May the Creator bless this place and all who come. We shall protect you. I am your friend and brother in the Celestial heavens, Francis. May God bless you.

Tend to the Gardens of Your Souls
December 15, 2019

I come to speak about the gardens of your souls, these precious gifts. One must tend to one's garden as the Creator and nature takes care of all the rest. Water your gardens with your prayers, this I ask of you. Check on your growth every day. Allow the sun to come in and raise you up, the sunshine of God's love. Allow the rains to nurture your souls with the showering of God's grace. Allow the winds to make you strong, the incoming wind of the Holy Spirit bringing the love. Enrich the soils with the nutrients of faith and hope, charity, and forgiveness.

The world is the world, and the human condition is what it is. However, you may walk amongst this world, amongst the human condition and still be free. With the light of God's love, this light in your souls, you carry the fragrance of Divine Love to each one, as you bring the gifts of your garden to this world. What a blessing you are.

There are many teachings in the world, there are many intellectual ideas to entice one; many, you might say, perspectives on life, creation, and the planets. I do not wish to condemn any of those things as unworthy because your minds require this food. But when you plant the seeds and allow God's love to bring those seeds into fruition and the flowers of your soul blossom, you bring this fragrance, this beautiful fragrance to the world.

I encourage you to tend to the gardens of your soul. When you grow a garden on earth, you can be amazed by how many fruits, how many vegetables, how many flowers can come from a single seed. I promise you; you will be amazed at how many you are touching in this world. There will come a time when you will see the fruits of your labors, and The Creator will bestow gifts you cannot imagine in gratitude for your work. For now, let us bask in the warmth, in the glory, in the light and the beauty of God's great love, given to us who have asked. We will continue to ask for there is no end to the blessings. May each one open like a rose.

My blessings to all. My love to all. May God's love bless you and change you and keep you in grace. I am your brother, Francis.

BELIEF IN GOD'S LOVE TRANSCENDS ALL OTHER BELIEFS
January 1, 2020

It is a new year for all of you and as you welcome it in prayer, we join you. You may wonder: 'What do I take with me into this new year and what do I leave behind?' I would say, it's a bit like putting on a new coat for a new season when you walk into a new era in your lives, wearing this coat of protection, the Celestial guidance, and the warmth of God's love in each one of you. I left my coats behind. So many material things were offered to me, but when I saw the light, I realized that I would only take my soul with me into the next world and that all these material things, aside from the bare necessities, were not necessary. I laid them down as burdens and they were burdens. I was lifted up into the light in prayer with my friends, as you do with your friends for God to open up your souls.

This path that you have chosen does not require you to give up all your material things. But it does require you to know what is important and to know that your soul is what you take with you, in this world and the next. Your souls, your beautiful souls filling with light, filling with the love of God. You know this is the greatest gift, not only to receive, but to share with others. As you walk into the new year, go beyond all the material gifts, and give the gift of God's love to all. Allow this beautiful gift to be your present to the world. The presence of God and His love, this great gift, you can share with all, whether you speak or whether you are silent, because you carry this. Though you may not see it, you can feel it, as the world will feel it. This will be your gift, should you choose to share it.

This is what we did back in my day on earth and we seemed quite ridiculous to many. I think we provided a lot of amusement for people, walking around in our simple clothes and praising God and singing, eating simply, prayerfully working, and taking time out for formal prayers. As you know, to this day, the world acknowledges that gift that we received, and I am here with you to share that.

I wish to add for you all that my brothers and my beliefs were quite simple, or as you would say, orthodox. We believed in the tenets of the catholic church and the trinity and the crucifixion of Jesus and his godhood and all these things that, as you know, are in error. But the one thing we believed in above all else was that our prayers could connect us with God's love and that transcended all those things. As you walk into the world, the world of belief and dogma and error and materialism, take this present of God's love with you. Offer to pray with all, that all may receive this gift that you are blessed with.

I embrace you all. I support you all, as we all do. I leave you with my love and my wish for God's blessings to be yours. I love you. I am your brother and friend, Francis.

Crazy for God

February 14, 2020

When I had my realization of the love of God and I could clearly see that I no longer placed any value on riches, acquirements, battles and all these things of the world that are considered normal, my parents and many of my friends believed that I had lost my mind. Yes, to them certainly, I appeared a bit crazy. I was crazy for God and the experience of receiving this Divine Love. It was not difficult to let these things of the world go, over and against the longings in my soul. I prayed and my friends prayed with me, and God's Holy Spirit came and showered us with love.

When we stepped out into the world after a time, certainly we appeared as beggars, but the joy in our souls and the love coming through us outshone the world and was undeniable, and even the church fathers could see this. Yes, they did think: 'Well, they're rather harmless, these fellows, but they're prayerful and they have such joy, so we will allow it to flourish,' though they did not think it would. Some had an awakening of conscience when they would be in our presence. The richness of the love in our souls, over and against their material outlook was shocking and humbling.

These prayers that brought the love of the Father into our souls were not from our minds, they were from the depths of our souls and the more we received the more we wanted. Until, as this one knows, I will use the phrase: 'We were the richest souls in the world.'[13] Surely, we felt it so, and the humble work that we performed made a difference and to this day resonates with many souls around the world. Losing your mind to the longings of your souls, really means you give precedence to the soul. Your mind will still function, and you will know one thing from another. You can say it's an organ of discrimination.

But if you allow the longings in your souls to become prevalent, as you do when you come to this circle, you will always feel the showering of the love of our Creator and this love will transform your souls, I promise you. Do not be afraid to give up this world, because what awaits you is glorious beyond your dreams. I tell you this as your brother and friend. All my love. May God bless you, each one. I am Francis. God bless you.

FOLLOW YOUR HEARTS
March 8, 2020

What a joy to see this gathering of souls longing to be one in God's love. This is not a path of the mind but rather one of the heart. To paraphrase the words of our dear brother Matthew: 'where your heart is so there is your soul, and when the heart longs for the Creator's love therein is your treasure.' There is no higher love. There is no greater gift. It is a simple path to allow your heart to open so that God may touch your souls and bring His love into each one, changing you, healing you.

As the dear sister said in her prayer: "we have all strayed." I too in my time on earth had quite a life exhausting my physical desires and pleasures until I came to a place where I knew I could not continue that path and ever find happiness or joy. This was the beginning truly of my deep prayer for God to heal me, for my will to merge with His. And then everything became clear and simple.

---
13 Reference to Jimbeau Walsh's song 'The Richest Man in The World'

All these things I had stored, all the wounds, all the guilt, and all the unforgiveness, was transformed in God's love. So, you see, it is very simple. When you hear: 'follow your heart' there is wisdom because it leads to your soul and the deep longings you all have to be transformed. There are so many here today with you in this beautiful circle of light.

I leave you with all my love and blessings. May God bless you and change you as we are truly one in His love. I am your brother and friend Francis. God bless you.

The World is Slowing Down
March 15, 2020

Is it not amazing to be able to see and know that things can change in a moment, as they say, for better or worse? The world is a busy place and circumstances upon this earth are causing you to slow down. When you come to prayer in this sanctuary, this circle of light, you step outside the world as you allow your soul to reach up and out from the deep longings within each one of you. And the heavens open and we come to be with you, but more importantly, God in His glory is able to bring His love into each of your souls, your hearts breaking open like a beautiful rose, thus taking a break from this world, this busy world.

My friends and I, we did this in a conscious way, and I should say that the world in my time was also busy. There were wars, plagues, illness, the marketplace, and society. We'd had enough of this and wanted to be in grace, so we removed ourselves for a time. And like you, we prayed. And like you we received. At some point we were able to go out into the world, and we brought our message of God's love and the teachings of Jesus, as we understood them, and the simplicity of our lives and the riches that could be obtained by each soul beyond this world of materialism. It was a very simple message that we even brought to Rome. And although there was much spiritual blindness, they could see us, they could feel the love, they could perceive our intentions and we were allowed to carry on.

I tell you these things because in some ways this is what is occurring within your community. You have stepped away from the world to be in this prayer. And right now, the world is slowing down. There is much fear, concern, but there is also much consideration of the sanctity of each life. And many, though they may be believers in God and a particular religion, they have not considered the spirit life in any meaningful way.

Many believe they have insurance, and their beliefs and their churches will take care of the rest.

You, my friends, who are undergoing this beautiful transformation in the glorious love of God, when you feel ready, and many of you are ready, can take this love, this joy and this light shining above the world and beyond it to those who are concerned, afraid, in doubt and disturbed. Your faith will be visible, your love, the love of God that you possess in your souls can be felt. As you know when you embrace someone in love, words are not always necessary. So together we will be present in the light and love of God to this world, and in faith we allow our loving Creator to bless all. Be not afraid. God's love is the peace that passes understanding; and what is meant by this is intellectual understanding, for soul perception outshines the mind. I thank each one of you and this one.

My wish for each one is the great gift of God's love to lift you all up and to awaken you forevermore. We are with you here and you will be with us here - in time. With all my love and blessings, may God bless each one. I am your brother and friend Francis. God bless you.

HOLY COMMUNION HOLY COMMUNITY
March 17, 2020

The words 'Holy Communion' mean to be in communion with God. In these beautiful circles that you have, each one is in communion, each one to the extent of their longings and abilities to be open. I say to you all, these longings are everything. They transcend any words you might have, and they bring you into this glorious communion.

The world at the moment may not be discovering the great gift of Divine Love, but certainly many are in prayer. And you can see neighbors recognizing their neighbors, some for the first time, and people singing out, reaching out, even though they may not physically touch as we cannot physically touch you, yet we reach out in spirit. So many around the world are reaching out in the spirit of love, in community. Your community reaches out in prayer, and it becomes communion, sacred communion.

Many may come to you recognizing that you have a connection beyond this world, a loving connection that they may feel. To those who reach out, let your heart open; do not deny them, love each one, and offer a prayer if you are moved to do so. A prayer asking God for love, for healing. This will offend no one and will bless many so that all may grow in the garden of God's love and blossom as you are blossoming my beautiful friends. It is a wonder to see the light that connects us and the love that we share in God. Keep this communion. Allow this community to flourish. Even when you cannot touch you can reach out. And so you are, and so it is. May it continue to be.

God bless you. I am truly your brother and friend, I am Francis.

The Simplicity of Our Lives
April 12, 2020

On this day[14] we celebrate the resurrection into spirit. When you pray and receive God's love we make this connection to immortality, and I wish for each one here to receive this gift in such great abundance that you feel the connection to the Celestial realms and immortality - beyond fear and beyond doubt being in God's love.

My friends and I left the world behind, and I wish to tell you many of us had lived a very unholy existence prior to our leaving the busy world; and we made a pact to celebrate the earth and to pray for God's love and live simply. As we grew in this love the world around us began to feel it. This took some time but many of my friends, my brothers and sisters who found the path of a simple life, a sustainable life, nurturing both the gardens in our souls with God's love and the garden that is the earth. We became a force for everything that is good, and we shared this.

Eventually the spiritual orders that were founded both in my name and Clare's name flourished and exist to this day, albeit institutionalized to some extent. And yet the principles of praying to God and living in simplicity still exist. You, my dear ones, are blessed to know this wonderful truth of God's love. You don't need to join a religious order for you carry this into the world, each one of you. And each knows the simplicity of life - beautiful – and of God's love.

May your holy community thrive and bless this world in God's love and in the simplicity and sustainability that earth needs. I celebrate with you today the reality of eternal life in God's love and embrace each one of you precious souls. All my love and blessings to each one. May God continue to bless you. I am your brother and friend, Francis.

14 Easter, 2020

A Bridge Between Heaven and Earth
April 25, 2020

You are a most gentle group and you have touched my heart. I left the busyness of the town to be in nature with my friends, to feel the beauty of God's creation and to be in harmony with it. We had a balance, our little band, of the natural love of God's creation and the Glory of God's love received in prayer. It was, as you can imagine, at times a kind of heaven on earth.

And some were quite astounded that a group of seemingly poor beggars could be so rich in the gifts of the spirit, as we called it. And yes, the sun of your galaxy and the Master, the first true son of God to receive the love therein, is an analogy so you can see the harmony between the two worlds. Your prayers and the longings that you have create a bridge between heaven and earth.

As it has been the deep desire of so many for a more sustainable earth it is also the desire of so many to make a connection to the spirit world, to the love of God, to the Celestial realm. It is not a battle between these two worlds but a harmony. As you pray you may feel the touch of God's love and a oneness with the natural world and a oneness with the very source and Creator of that world. This is my wish for you as I travel with you on your journey and visit.

Please know when you ask, help is always available. We are here for you more than you know. May each one in this beautiful circle open to and receive the love of God in great abundance. I am your brother and friend of your soul. God bless you. I am Francis. Go in peace.

Allow the Intentions of Your Souls To Reach Out
May 23, 2020

You have often heard that we call you children, brothers, sisters, our friends because truly we are all God's children. This you know, and as the Master remarked, 'that one must become like a child to enter the kingdom in innocence, in openness.'

These wounds that come to you now, which come to the fore, are long held, many from childhood. As you pray for and receive the Father's love, this love expiates those wounds and removes them. They are replaced with the joy and the light of the child born again in God's love. Truly the meaning of those words, 'you must be born again to enter the kingdom of heaven.'

In this sense we all become children of the Father in the most beautiful and glorious way. It is no accident that those of you who came today to be in this circle shared your hearts, shared your experiences, because there was much empathy within this group. We can feel it and we honor it as we honor each of you on your journey. There is nothing more important than reaching out in prayer.

You need not think of this as being formal, being on your knees, having prayer beads, or a rosary, or a mantra, or particular words. I suggest you allow the intentions of your souls to reach out during your day in that deeper request: 'Dear God I need to feel your love, please touch my soul, protect me from any harm, from any negativity, and allow me to be a blessing to all.' One can do this in any given moment, on any given day and into the night, and as your prayers open to receive the light and the love of our heavenly Father, it shall be yours.

I am your brother and friend in God's love and a disciple of the Master in the Celestial heavens. May God continue to embrace you in His love and change you so that great joy will be yours. God bless you. I am Francis.

The Path of God's Love
June 6, 2020

I am drawn to your prayers, drawn to the longings in your souls, I come to bless you and to be with you in the Father's love. When my life became simple everything was discovered in grace to my soul and to my brothers and sisters who followed the simple path of prayer. But let it be known that we were a most joyous group. We sang and played and enjoyed God's creation - the flowers and the beauty and the animals and the countryside. Yes, we were on the natural path, and we were also on the path of God's love.

The world was not without its troubles, but we were examples to others of the harmony between the natural and the Divine. I know that I am very known for the animals and my relationship with them and much of that is true. For as I felt God's love in my soul the animals were not afraid. They are very sensitive; they can feel your intentions and so they were drawn. I say: 'Be not troubled by where you are on your journey or what your gifts are, but go to God in prayer, and as you receive the glorious gift of His love discernment will be yours for you are on this path of God's love, and He will light the way for each one of you when you allow it.'

You are in a wonderful bubble of protection and when you call, we come with all the love in our souls and with our intentions to be a blessing to each one of you. As God blesses each one of you for your asking, we come to be at one with you in His love. Be not afraid, have no fear, walk in faith, trust in God and you will join us in the Celestial realms. Have no doubt it will be so. May God continue to bless each one of you with the glorious gift of His love. I am your brother and friend in Christ, I am Francis and I love you.

THIS COMMUNION CAN BE YOURS
June 16, 2020

I have stated many times that I went from a worldly life to a very simple life - in harmony with nature and in prayer to God and removed from the world for a time. During this time on earth where you have been somewhat removed from the world at large, the opportunity to go into your souls, to go into prayer, to make things simple, has been yours.

When I considered, when I was quite ill, if I should leave the earth that day what in fact could I take with me, what would I want to take with me, and what would I wish to leave behind. I allowed this to inform my walk into the future. And since the many things of the world that I had indulged in did not bring the happiness and uplifting and joy that I sought, it was not difficult to leave them behind for the glorious communion of souls of my brothers and later the sisters. Walking in nature, living simply, praying for God's love this communion can be yours.

This community connected around the world which you have the benefit of - what a gift it is to each other and what a blessing it is! You come together in this prayer, in this circle with the longings in your hearts, in your souls to receive the greatest gift of God's love. And as much as you allow it, believe me you shall receive it. May it lift you up, sustain you, and transform you. This is the grace of the Gift. May each prayer connect you to the Celestial realm and the love of God. May it be yours. And so it is. I am your brother and friend in God's love. I am Francis.

Carry the Love of God Into Spirit
July 17, 2020

I am here, Francis, your dear brother, and you are my dear brothers. I make no demands as we only suggest and encourage. We wait patiently for our influence and our advice, which is always given in love, to be accepted. For the message is always about love; this you know and above all things, the love of God, to pray for it, to receive it. If you wish to be truly wealthy this is what you wish to possess. All else is superfluous. This is not to say that one should dismiss the needs of others for food and shelter, for love, but to say the one thing that is worth carrying with you into spirit, the most precious thing, the most valuable thing, is the love of God. And even this God does not demand but only offers with open arms.

We who have been transformed in this love, redeemed, changed from mortals to the Celestial kingdom as angels, we say: 'Be kind to each other, embrace all in God's love.' Cherish your friends and family and be grateful that you have discovered the truth. Let this Holy Communion be your template, be your guide, and when you are moved to be in communion and community with others who are open to receive the grace of God and His Divine Love consider that choice. For the intentions of all in the circles of light is to receive this great gift whatever the person, wherever they are on their journey, so encourage them, for all need love, all are wounded. Is there a single soul who is without a flaw that can cast the first stone?

We encourage you to be in communion to support all those who wish to be transformed in the love whatever their station. For first it is important to take care of one's own house and then assist others. I say this with all the love in my heart and the grace of God in my soul. God bless you. I am your brother in Christ, Francis.

Embrace All in God's Love
August 1, 2020

When I left my family home and began my walk in nature amongst the beauty of God's creation in harmony with His creatures big and small, I was so grateful for every flower and the delights of creation in the natural world. I was also following the longings in my soul to reach the Celestial realm. For my soul knew there was something beyond the Earth plane in this love of God that would carry us and transform us and lift us up.

We lived in harmony in the natural and the divine. The human condition seeks harmony and peace, brotherhood and sisterhood, equality, and sustainability. These are beautiful aspirations, and we pray that the Earth may be in this harmony as you do. Those of us in spirit and most especially those of us in the Celestial realms, knowing your future, we come to join you in your prayers to receive the great love of the Creator that transforms the soul. You stand on this bridge between heaven and Earth and love connects both. There are the natural heavens, the beautiful, beautiful realms of the purified soul and the Celestial heavens - beyond the words of the transformed soul, from the mortal to the divine angel.

May there be peace on Earth. May all here in this circle and beyond be in harmony without judgment because there is really only one path and that is love. We come to embrace you on this path in the grace of God. May each one be blessed in His love. I am your brother and friend in Christ, I am Francis. Go with God.

The Secret of the Soul is to be Humble
August 18, 2020

I wish to speak of pride: the pride of a parent for a child growing up, doing well, the pride of a team, of an accomplishment and so forth. This side of being proud is a grace. But you all know the saying 'pride comes before a fall,' and this was my experience. I was to inherit much in worldly goods, in connections, and business. And I had traveled and been a soldier, and from my point of view beaten the world and risen above it. When I took ill, I saw the worthlessness of this pride, of these material things, these worldly accomplishments. It shook me to my core, and it humbled me. I walked away, much to the disdain of many, the anger of my parents who had loved me so much and had held such high hopes in their world for me.

I had an experience which could be compared to the story of Paul falling off his horse, being struck so to speak. And there I was falling off my high horse to the ground, the good earth, to the sights and the sounds of the birds and the smells of the flowers, and even the soil in my fingers, all of God's creation, not of man.

And I knew in my soul I could connect to my Creator, with my being in His church. And this church was pure and one that allowed much freedom and brought so much joy and gifts to myself and my brothers, and later our sisters. But you know the secret of the soul is to be humble before your Creator, to ask 'Dear God, bless my soul, heal this wound, touch my friends, change me and this mortal coil to at-onement with you in eternity.'

I tell you it matters not through which lens you are seeing the world or spiritual life, which philosophy, or which science, for when you open your heart, trust in sincere faith, and you call out from the deep longings in your soul for that treasure beyond all the earthly treasures, you receive it. It is simple. It is divine. It is God's love and God's wish for you.

My dear brothers and sisters, you are blessed, and you belong here. Fear not, God is gracious. I am your brother and friend in Christ. I am Francis. Go with God.

Blessed are You

October 10, 2020

I am here and I am your brother, and I am your friend and your guide on this path. I am Francis. Blessed are you who pray for the love of God. Blessed are you who forgive those who have offended you. Blessed are you who reach out to the less fortunate. Blessed are you who do not judge, for God is the judge.

As you walk this world my brothers and sisters, if you could say only one thing to everyone you meet, consider what that might be? Let me say that in some cases it might be unspoken but delivered through God's grace in your soul. The time will come again when you may hug all those and hug them with the love of God. For now, during this time of tribulation, we are influencing all not only to pray, which is our utmost desire, but also to consider how much anyone needs to sustain their physical body, to live in comfort, or to be able to travel.

We understand the requirements of food and shelter, being able to travel and (in your case), spread the word of God's love embracing all. During this time, we also wish the world a healing and for all human beings to consider not only what is necessary in your world, but as I have said before, what you will take with you, and that of course, is your soul. As the Master said: 'Store not your treasures on earth,' but receive the riches beyond measure of God's love. This you know. My brothers, I encourage you to spend your time being love, speaking love, singing love, sharing love. This way you will be a blessing to all as you wish to be. How we love you, all the brothers and sisters on this beautiful path, whatever their differences, we support.

My warmest loving embrace to you and yours and to all. God bless you. I am your brother and friend in eternity, I am Francis.

STAND NAKED BEFORE GOD
November 10 , 2020

I am here Francis the one who sang and preached and walked the hills of Assisi. I wish to add, if I may, to the insightful remarks of my brother Yogananda. When I had my awakening, I saw the world for what it was, that the world lived impoverished in spirit. When I felt the touch of God's hand upon me, I knew I could let go of everything and there I was standing naked, proclaiming my mission and my desire to live in the richness of God's love and the poverty of simplicity.

Only God could change me, this I knew. But I would have to take that step towards God and this I would like you to consider. I don't mean you all need to take off your clothes and go live in the woods, (laughs) but you do need to stand naked before God spiritually and allow God to change you. Make your consciousness your desire to live in grace and it will be so. I leave you now to be with you in silent prayer. May God bless you. All my love to each one of you. I am your brother in Christ. I am Francis.

Clare of Assisi

Angel! Ah dear, sweet, full of light, and deep as the ocean, Clare of Assisi,[15] beloved of Francis and a Celestial. Here is the back story on my hearing from Clare.

---

15 Clare of Assisi (July 16, 1194 - August 11, 1253) was one of the first followers of Francis of Assisi. As a teenager she decided to enter a convent and led a life of poverty and dedication to God. She later founded the Order of Poor Ladies in the Franciscan tradition and wrote the first set of monastic guidelines known to have been written by a woman. Her order is referred to today as the 'Poor Clares.'

We had a small group that began meeting online in 2019 to study the spiritual writings of several people.[16] (We continue to read works of authors both living and in spirit to this day). The three original members of this group, unbeknownst to the others, had all been encouraged to meet each other by a mutual friend of ours who had spoken to each of us individually about the others saying, 'Well so and so is an artist and like you - poor as a church mouse - so I think you'd really be good friends.' Fast forward to a night at the end of our group readings when I was in prayer, I received this: "My dear kind mice, it is I, Clare of Assisi."

THE RICHES OF THE SOUL
March 21, 2020

My dear children, I am Clare of Assisi. I was drawn to your circle, because of your discussion and because I felt the yearning of your souls, and I had been watching over the sister who had been traveling in England and is now back in Canada.

I am the founder of the order of the Poor Clares and though you may feel like little church mice, you are indeed on your way to becoming beautiful angels of light, for you know what is of value, what are the riches of the soul, in the midst of the material world. Your journeys have brought you to this place together, your souls wishing to be in harmony, to understand and to progress in the glory of God's love. We support this in every way, and we are here.

Yes, the universe is vast, and the kingdom is beyond human imagining, but you have made a connection in light and in love that cannot be broken. This is the bridge between heaven and earth, and you are on it. I shall come again and guide you and be your sister on this journey toward the fountainhead of God's love. God bless you. I am your sister in the Celestial realms, Clare.

---

16 These included the channeled messages from Judas of Kerioth received by H.R. in Ecuador in 2000 and 2001; Eileen Caddy's many books of channeled messages from God ('Footprints on the Path,' 'God Spoke to Me'); messages received by James R. Padgett from 1914-1924 from Jesus and many other spirits both Celestial as well as from the many spheres of the spirit world both low and high.

Riches and Joy
April 4, 2020

I am here Clare of Assisi. I'm drawn to this beautiful circle. You may know me as the founder of the order of monastic women who became called, and are still called, the Poor Clares. We followed in the footsteps of my beloved Francis of Assisi and his brothers who had decided to leave much of the world behind and live the simple life. I address this issue because you are in a period now on the earth where you can contemplate the importance of material things. How much does one need? What is necessary?

And deeper than that: 'What is it that brings joy to the heart, to the soul?' Simply being able to go out in nature in the country, or even in your village is a joy! We had given up so much of the material things, but we had food, we had shelter, and we had the beautiful experience of living in nature and appreciating God's creation - at the same time as we prayed for the love of God to touch us, to change us and to guide us.

And so you see there is not much that is necessary to maintain a simple life and actually what it takes to receive God's love, to let go in any moment of your material attachments and just ask for the blessing; these things, these material things, fall away and you are given the richness and the glory of God's love. Such a joy! Such a joy!

Thank you for allowing me to come to my dear sisters and my brothers in God's love. We are one. I am Clare.

Love Is the Healer of All Hearts
June 21, 2020

My three beautiful kind friends, please know that these matters of the heart are always healed in love, the best medicine. To my dear sister who will undergo procedures in the coming days I encourage you to put your heart at ease, to listen to beautiful sounds in nature and in music. I encourage you to distance yourself from any in-harmonies, and in this manner, I speak to all. Surround yourselves with love, beautiful music, nature, the beauty of God's creation. This behavior will produce a calm, a peace, and a healing that will facilitate a quickening of your bodies' immune systems. This I give to all three for all have health issues.

When you call you know that we come, so please utilize our invitation to be with you, to surround you in light, to influence those you encounter, and during any procedures we will be happy to influence those who are working towards your healing and facilitating those procedures. May all our souls connect with God's great soul beyond words and the longings that we hold in our hearts for the grace of God to be at one with us.

I am happy to be of service, and always know that you will all have many to come at your beckoning call. Just remember as we remember that God loves us in every moment and that love is the great healer. With all my love and blessings for my three kind mice, I bid you farewell for now, but I shall be with you when you call. God bless you. I am Clare of Assisi.

TRUST AND FAITH

July 8, 2020

I am here Clare of Assisi. Yes, it is me and I am your sister on this path of Divine Love and faith. I know in the messages that the brother (HR) received from Judas there are some wonderful insights into what faith is and how to obtain it. And in those messages, it is said this does not include the entirety of what is faith.

I would say consider the faith of not only Elijah, but of Moses, leading his people, rising up in faith, trusting in God, the faith of Noah building an ark, being ridiculed and laughed at, and yet he knew. In my time the faith of Francis, and of course the availability of God's love, walked hand in hand. I saw this with the eyes of my soul and that very perception lit a fire in my heart. It caused me to have faith because I could see what Francis and his brothers could accomplish, could bring to the world, walking in faith. And so I also took that path and my sisters and I, the Poor Ladies (later the Poor Clares) as they called us, how we were blessed. Often faith sits side by side in the mind with trust. And while the two walk together, one is more of the human condition. For you can trust in people and events yet I would say: 'put trust in God and the knowings of the soul' - that is faith. As you receive this love (and as you have just read) the soul perceptions increase and the vision, the perception of immortality, becomes a real thing.

My three kind mice you are blessed with this faith and this knowing, and it shall only increase the more you open to God's love and allow Him to touch your souls to shine a light beyond fear, beyond worry, beyond doubt, and yes, beyond ridicule as you walk in faith and in the flow of grace.

You attract us, you bring us into your circle, and allow us to share and guide you and love you with the love in our souls. Thank you for allowing me to come and speak. With my love and blessings for all and in the grace of God I am your sister and friend; I am Clare of Assisi. God bless you.

In God's Love We Are Never Alone
July 14, 2020

The Poor Ladies and I who became known as the Poor Clares, we wished to follow the desires of our souls, to feel that joy, that ecstasy of being in the presence of God. We left the world behind, and simplicity became our order.

You know it is possible to feel alone even in a crowd, even with family, with friends, when your heart is closed or not engaged. It is also possible to pray the rosary, say a mantra, have prayer beads and yet not connect with the Creator. All these disciplines were instituted to bring souls into connection with their Creator, but I tell you if the heart is not activated and the soul engaged, lifted up by God's love beyond the wounds, beyond the hurts, beyond the fear, and beyond the doubts, the connection is not made no matter how many the years of mental prayers.

I see you all engaged in the world, and I would wish none other for any of you because you have the secret and the key to the kingdom. It is to engage, to open the heart and allow God to touch your souls and receive. To be mindful of that one discipline which brings so much freedom and connects you to every living being and to the Celestial kingdom where you realize you are never alone and there is always help, always support.

We learned this from our dear brother Francis as he talked about how God took care of all His creatures and to be as the birds - free to allow God to care and comfort and provide for each one's needs, materially and more importantly, spiritually, soulfully. Knowing this truth, allowing the love to blossom in each soul brings faith and a deep understanding with your whole being that God is the provider, that God's love transforms you, heals you, and awakens you into eternal life.

It is with great happiness and the gratefulness of my heart that I come to you and have the privilege of speaking as a disciple of the Master and your sister in God's love. May His blessings be showered upon each one of you that you may live and walk this world in grace. God bless you. I am Clare.

Connecting to God as a Simple Act
July 20, 2020

I come to this gathering, this sacred blessing in this circle, to join you in prayer for God's love. I wish to tell you that to connect to the heavenly Father is a simple act, a simple intention of allowing the longing in your soul to ascend over your mind from the depths of your heart, to be at one with God in His love. If you wish this to be your guidance, simply remember this longing.

When I prayed on earth, I would fold my hands and I would be on my knees, I would close my eyes, but my gaze would be heavenward to match the longings in my heart. And this gaze to the heavens allowed me to see the angels and the light and even the presence and beauty of the Master, as God blessed us all. We did not need much, and we did not desire much knowing that God would provide for all of our needs. This faith had become ever present as all things were provided by our heavenly Father, enough that we could share with those who even had less than us. I tell you, my sweet and beloved friends, the real gift was God giving us His love which we gave to each one in gratitude and thanks. May this be your guidance to carry this love to all.

Stay open to the Father's love and light and you cannot go wrong. How we are loved, how we are loved. May God's love be with you. With all my love and blessings, I am your sister in Christ, I am Clare of Assisi. Go with God.

Choose Wisely
July 27, 2020

I am here, Clare. I come in the grace of God. You can see how important it is to raise your thoughts above the concerns of the world. We were able to do this as we cloistered ourselves, and yet we sang and prayed and communicated what was necessary. But the focus was on prayer, and by this I don't necessarily mean a formal prayer, or in our case, what were church prayers. We often prayed just from our souls to feel God's grace, to be in harmony with heaven and earth in God's love.

Jesus was our guide and brother Francis our mentor. This busy world that you live in, which is in a state of pause to some extent,[17] is still saturated, bombarded in fact with thoughts and opinions and all kinds of vibrations coming through the airwaves. Each one of you can choose what to allow in and what to remove yourself from. You would not walk into a situation in the physical world that you know is dangerous or out of harmony. Or at least you would not do this without feeling a connection with God, going in the state of grace, being in the company of angels and going into the situation to uplift others and pray with them, and to bless them. In this circumstance, this is not only acceptable but welcomed when you connect with others. If you approach this in service to be a blessing, to remember God, to uplift those who are downtrodden, to elevate their thoughts to rise above their complaints, to have their center of gravity be lifted in the love and light, then you may bring this to others. You draw us near, we protect you, and we guide you, we inspire you.

The world has always needed this and never more than now. So again, however you wish to connect or under whatever circumstance you find yourselves in, we encourage you to bring the love over and above the complaint, the fear, the negativity, so that all may be healed, all may be uplifted in joy and the love of God. You can do no greater service than this.

I'm so glad you felt my presence for when my three kind mice come together, I often wish to see you, and I hope you find my guidance helpful. To all who are here I give my love and blessings in the grace of God. I am your sister in Christ, Clare of Assisi. Go with God.

We Are With You on This Journey
July 29, 2020

I am here, your sister in Christ, Clare of Assisi. I come as promised when you gather, whenever I can be with you, I shall be. And I was with one earlier today as he was exploring the sisters who have carried on the tradition that I started. And as he could see and was surprised that, despite their being very Catholic and having a lot of dogma, their focus was God's love, praying for God's love. And I would say this is the reason they have lasted and carried

---
[17] A reference to the Covid-19 pandemic.

on in so many countries. Whenever a sister is drawn to God and the riches of His love and does not feel satisfaction from all the material things of the world, the soul seeks a way to be in communion with its Creator. And those on the path of Catholicism, many of those have been drawn to my beloved Francis' group of Friars and to the Poor Clares, my sisters. You should know we guide them, and we accompany them in their prayers and in their joy. For the most part they are a very happy, joyous community.

My three kind mice and my dear brother (MW) who is moved in his soul to join, I welcome you. And I know your grandmother (Clare Darby Walsh), she too followed the path of God's love and the roses and walked barefoot upon the earth and cared for the homeless and the poor. And though she would be perceived as secular she would be considered a nun for so much of her time, as was ours and mine, was dedicated to prayer. All the miracles and blessings and glorious spiritual phenomena that accompanied her life and mine as well were a result of our prayers, no matter the tradition. We are lifted up beyond the traditions, beyond many of the beliefs into the truth of God's love and its transforming power. This you know. This you feel. And we come to be in this prayer with you. We feel the love in your hearts, we see the longings in your souls and so many are drawn to your circles, yes even this little circle.

There are many here and I wish to thank you all for taking the time to come together bringing your prayers to the heavenly Father to receive His love and guidance which we are always delighted to give. We are yours in light and love and in the grace of God, and in His wondrous blessings. Please know we are with you on your journey on this path to the Celestial realms which you have chosen.

May God bless you every step of the way. You have our love and blessings in His grace. We are your sisters in Christ, Clare and Care. God bless you.

GOD'S LOVE IS ANTI-GRAVITATIONAL
September 22, 2020

I am here with dear brother Judas. We have been with you, with others, and have been along for the ride, and the beautiful message from Jesus that touches us as well as you.

When you awake in the morning if you can remember to set your intention for the day in prayer to God: 'Dear God, walk with me this day. Open my soul to your love that I may be a blessing to all. May your angels be close to me and guide me.' You needn't of course, say those exact words but hopefully you can understand the intention and the gist of what I wish to communicate.

There is a very important reason and purpose for this encouragement. Imagine if you will, days and days of inclement weather or days of drought, days of floods, days of darkness and suddenly, it's a beautiful day with just the right amount of sunshine and wind and rain, all in harmony and you notice the beautiful colors of the day, most especially in nature. And your heart is lifted. Ahh! You may even say: 'Thank you, God, this is so wonderful,' like a rainbow appearing after a storm.

The world, the material world, run by the material mind, is often in a cloud that seems like an endless disturbance or gray area. And people greet their day with quite often a sense of impending doom or fear, or simply just negativity. I call this a negative center of gravity. And I tell you this my dear, dear friends, because God's love is a positive center of gravity. In fact, you could say it's anti-gravitational, for it lifts you up above all the weight of the world and the troubles and entanglements and the negativity of the earth plane. This is why we come with a positive message. We come in the grace of God and the love of God because this is your wish, this is your longing and we are so happy to respond, and God responds, showering you with His love and grace.

There is great attraction in being in God's love. There is a magnetism that draws not only those of us in the Celestial heavens, but harmony on earth and affects those souls in darkness where they are able to receive a blessing for even the slightest inclination. So, as you walk in joy, as you walk in the happiness, the peace, the light of love in your souls, you bring this gift that God has given you, to all. Isn't that wonderful! We are all here with you, and we bring our love and guidance and our support, and yes, even our gratitude, that you have chosen the path of God's love. May God continue to bless you, and may His love draw you in ever closer. I am your sister in the love of God, and your sister in Christ, I am Clare of Assisi, and I love you.

This Will Be Your Treasure
October 4, 2020

I am here your sister in Christ, Clare of Assisi. I am here to also honor my beloved Francis.[18] He was our inspiration and mentor, and to this day, many brothers and sisters have taken up the journey upon the path of poverty, prayer, charity, kindness to all, and peace.

What we realized back then was, what you call - the saying is, 'you can't take it with you.' This was our realization that if we were to pass over into spirit, what in fact, could we take with us? You take your soul and its condition. Though you cannot take your material goods whether you be wealthy or poor, you can take the riches of Divine Love, a wealth beyond measure. You have chosen rightly this path to be open to God's love and the great riches that are bestowed on each one. I tell you this will be your treasure.

These prayers will be the stars in your heavenly crown, each one. This love, this endless love of God that you have discovered, will never be lost and this you will take with you. So let us celebrate this wonderful community coming together in Holy Communion in the grace of God, and its riches. As you honor my beloved Francis, he and all here honor you. Go in the grace of God. I love you. I am Clare of Assisi.

Love in Action
October 23, 2020

I am here your sister in Christ, Clare of Assisi. There are many beliefs: spiritual beliefs, religious beliefs, philosophical beliefs, scientific beliefs, and so forth. When what is believed is put into practice in life therein lies the proof of whether that belief carries truth with it. In other words, when it is practical to live your beliefs and the results bear fruit and that fruit is a blessing and loving and harmonious and healing, then you know that belief will sustain you because now you have experienced the reality of what was once an idea, with your very being, and you have witnessed what was posited perhaps theoretically, now as factual and true.

I mention this because in my day there were also many schools of thought, but my friends and I, we were simple and believed in the Catholic church and its dogma. As we prayed and received God's love and grace

---

18 This was an online DLS prayer circle honoring Francis of Assisi.

we saw the simplicity of faith, the essence of God's grace manifested on earth. This surpassed much of what we once held as necessary to believe. This was love in action, faith personified, healing manifested.

So, when you pray to receive God's love, His essence, you transcend much of what you held to be important, to be truth in beliefs, because your soul is activated in God's love. You have become the blessing - the bearer of the gift. And this is a full circle of the practicality of your prayer life as it becomes substance or, shall I say, substantial in your walk.

May your prayers bring the love of God into your souls changing you forever and bringing that great happiness and joy and transformation that God wishes for you. It is my wish as well. I am your sister in the love of God, and I love you. I am Clare. Go with God.

Be in the Moment
October 28, 2020

My dear ones, it is I, Clare. I am here in the moment. And how wise are those words, to be here in the moment, to live in the moment. The others of God's creatures, in the animal kingdom, are often delighted by watching one another, and being in the moment. For generally, they are just present. They have their routines for eating and mating, sometimes hunting and foraging. In that sense those cycles are much like what humans engage in. The difference being, of course, you have souls. Your souls are always in the moment and yet your minds cause you to reflect, sometimes in good ways, and sometimes not so good ways. It is the mind which stirs doubts. It is the mind that causes the emotions to feel anger or bliss. But as you know, in human love, these are, as you have read, two sides of the same coin. God's love transcends that currency, and yet it embraces all: in the natural love, in the Divine Love, in compassion.

The desire to serve others comes when there is love in the heart. And when that love is activated by God, it leads to a life of service. For the joy that is felt, the empathy for the human condition, is great. And this love you feel. You so wish to share. My dear ones, this is, as I have said before and I shall continue to say, not to intimidate you or barrage you with ultimatums, but to make a point. I know that you all know what brings great happiness. So as God answers your prayers to receive His love, beyond the words and beyond the good advice for daily living, let your desire to be His true child be foremost. This I encourage you and welcome.

May your days be blessed in each moment with the love of God, that you may spread joy and happiness to all and comfort. It is so important to bring comfort to all souls. I am your sister in Christ, and I love you. My dear ones. I am Clare of Assisi. Go with God.

Bring a Song to Your Heart
November 6, 2020

My dear sweet friends I have a request of you. Should you find it difficult to pray, to be in harmony, to stay in the love of God and His bountiful light, bring a song to your heart. Sing if you can or listen to someone's song that lifts your soul. This is important, for a beautiful song can be a prayer. A beautiful song can bring your soul much delight. Consider the Psalms of David and all the songs that you loved, that brought you comfort and peace. Essentially, I say to you: 'Stay tuned to the Divine channel, and the music of love, and the words of love, so that you may be lifted above the troubles of this world and that your love be a force, a healing force, an emanation and vibration from above in the grace of God.'

You are in a beautiful circle of light and many angels are with you in this moment. Be still with us. (long pause)

Allow your hearts to open wide that God will shower your souls with love divine, the most precious gift in the Universe. All Glory to God on High! I leave you with my love and blessings always. I am your sister in Christ who once walked the hills of Assisi. I am Clare. Go with God.

The Physical Manifestations of Divine Love
January 25, 2021

When my beloved Francis, beloved by so many, crossed over into spirit, he was so absorbed in God's love that the passing of his spirit leaving his body was in a sense undetectable, because the energy surrounding his body permeated the place where he lay, although his spirit had left, so blessed was it. This is the physical manifestation of Divine Love. For if you could not feel it, if it did not manifest itself in light and in a beautiful energy, you might not know of its existence.

It is possible to receive the love of God without feeling a great physical presence because it is beyond the world. However, when you feel the love around your heart, in your soul, this is God's confirmation that yes, you are feeling His love, and you are being transformed in grace.

For many are leaving the Earth plane without this understanding, without the benefit of the knowledge of divine truth, Divine Love. So, most enter the spirit world in the same condition that they were in on earth, requiring much assistance and requiring a certain amount of education so that they will now know they are in spirit. Those who have received the love of God, in a sense, they too enter spirit in the same condition, yet their souls are lifted above the earth plane and without the attachments that hold so many down.

When you are in the circle of love and whenever you are connected to God's grace and allow yourself to be lifted, God lifts you up; above the pain, the troubles, the concerns, the wounds, and we come so that you will know you are never alone. So that you will remember that you can always call on us for assistance for we do the bidding of God. Our wills are aligned with the will of God and His laws, at one in His love. This is your destiny dear brothers and sisters. This gift that raises you up brings to the world the reality of God's love, each one of you a channel of His love and light. Each one a soul in transition. Be of good cheer and bless all with the love in your hearts, the love in your souls. For the journey on earth is short and as you walk the earth may you leave a trail of love. May your rose-petaled paths bring the fragrance of love divine to all.

Thank you for taking my message. All of us here are with you in this circle of light and of love and in your silent prayer. May God bless each one of you and heal the world. I am your sister in Christ. I am Clare of Assisi. Go in peace and grace and love.

The Importance of Faith

February 5, 2021

I am here Clare. How important it is to have faith. I spoke about courage and today you mentioned having a leap of faith. When you take that leap, which is a courageous thing, and you walk in faith, and you open to the love of God, all things fall into place in God's time and in the flow of harmony in His universe, on earth, and in the heavens. When you align yourself in faith in love all things become possible.

This freedom that you so wish to have is yours. Make use of it. The deeper your prayer, the more time you allow and make for it, the more the wonder of its blessings in the response from the Creator will astonish you. Just as you are somewhat amazed that you have picked messages to read that seem to be in harmony with each other, you will evermore be amazed to be walking in the flow of God's grace and love, seeing things not though dark glasses but through the prism in the clarity of God's love. May this gift be yours.

I am your sister in the love of God and in Christ. My dear kind mice I wish you every blessing. Go in peace, go in grace, go in the love of God my dear ones. I am Clare of Assisi. God bless you.

Spiritual Immunity
April 8, 2021

I am here, your sister in God's love, Clare. My dear kind mice I can tell you that Robert Lees[19] was beyond flattered that you are reading what he received, those writings that have been in obscurity for so long. It is indeed a worthwhile endeavor to pursue an understanding of the spirit world that was depicted in such a beautiful way. He will come and speak to you as you proceed, but today I come asking each one of you to be at peace, to take care of your bodies, to let go of those things of the earth life that concern you.

When you spend more time in prayer, in peace, and in the vibrations of God's love you will create an immunity that will help you mightily in your earth life, but even more so in your soul's life and the life to come in spirit. My dear ones, pray, pray often as you can. Open your hearts to God and He will bless you through and through. The Divine Love of the Father carries you to His grace, His healing, His joy, His embrace. Let us take a few moments more to open to His love and be still in his blessing. I shall step back and be with you in silence for a few moments. I go in peace, and I love you. I truly do. I am your sister in Christ, Clare of Assisi.

---

19 Robert James Lees authored three amazing books, namely 'Through the Mists,' 'The Life Elysian' and 'The Gate of Heaven.'

The Wise Choice
May 24, 2021

My dear ones it is I, Clare of Assisi. My dear brother, my beloved Francis, at one point in his journey on earth, made a choice. You here in this circle of light have made a choice to allow your souls to be changed, to awaken in the love of God while you walk upon the earth. I often walked barefoot to be close to the earth, to tread lightly, to allow the healing magnetism of nature to sustain and heal us.[20] This outward sign of poverty, humility, and service was preceded by the deep desire to feel the love of God.

It is wise to tread lightly upon the earth that future generations may have a more sustainable planet on which to dwell. It is wise to walk in peace, but the greatest wisdom I can offer you is to be in this prayer, allowing your humble hearts to open to the love of God, that your souls may be forever blessed. This gift you can receive while on earth is a great blessing.

This community, this church without walls, this sanctuary, is something to be kept sacred, to be cherished. For truly when you receive this love you begin to realize that you are, indeed, a child of God, a most beloved child, and the object of His great love. This you have chosen. This is a glorious choice and I honor it as does Francis and the many here.

We shall step back to be in prayer with you in praise of God, in celebration, in joy! May the grace of God be with each one of you, may there be a blessing to all in this circle and beyond in this family of Divine Love, in this portal of light. Peace to all. Love to all. I am your sister in Christ and your eternal friend in the love of God. I am Clare.

Meditation Is Not What You Think
August 26, 2021

I am known as Clare of Assisi. I founded an order of nuns inspired by my beloved Francis. We gave up much of our material desires except for necessities because as Charles[21] has pointed out, we knew that love would nourish us and most especially, God's love.

Our environment at times was harsh but the gentleness and the flow of being in the grace of God was like a warm glow on a winter night, like

---

20 This refers to her sisters in the Order of the Poor Clares.
21 Charlie Chaplin's previous message that day, 'Love Is The Great Gift.' (See Chapter 3)

a cool breeze on a midsummer's day, the blessing of a spring shower and all the colors of fall. Be gentle with yourselves, so that your needs may be taken care of. Just as the birds are not concerned and as Francis so beautifully put it, 'Be not concerned about your next meal,' or all these things that weigh heavily on people in your world today.

When you come into prayer, in Holy Communion, the more you let go and, as is said, 'Let God,' the more you will be lifted. Be gentle with yourselves. The world, so much in darkness, despair and seeming chaos, will respond to your love. All that is required is a little time in prayer, in meditation, with an open heart that God may touch your soul. Relax your mind for meditation is not what you think.

Feel this grace. This warm embrace of our loving Creator. Are we not all children of God? All are worthy to be loved, to receive it, to share it. Trust and have faith. You have nothing to lose but doubt, worry, and concern, and everything to gain in the love of God, your gift to humanity. Go in peace. I am your sister and friend in Christ. I am Clare of Assisi now an inhabitant of the Celestial heavens and I love you. Go in peace.

Love of God Leads to a Life of Service
October 29, 2021

My dear kind mice it is I, your sister Clare. The love of God leads to a life of service. For the heart opens with empathy to all of God's creatures and because the law of God is progressive, there is always someone to help lift another up, even in the lowest hells. When you reach out in love remember the words of the Master, 'Whatsoever you do for the least of these, you do for me.' The kindness that you read about today,[22] Aphraar, not knowing why he was being rewarded for an act that he did not even think about but was soulfully moved to do - to save the life of a child. It is a fitting example of service to another.

In receiving God's love, one cannot help being moved to lift others up in whatever way one can. You all know the saying, 'it is better to give than receive,' the deeper meaning of which is the rewards of helping another outshine the act itself for what is rewarded in gratitude. The soul is the receptacle of the rewards for the good that one does however unseen to the mind but recognized by each heart in the feeling of joy that you were able to do something for a soul in need. Lastly, I will just say this. If you

---
22 'The Gate of Heaven,' Chapter 6 (The Verdict of Revelation) by Robert J Lees.

are feeling down and out, troubled, and that your lot in life is at a place of stagnation, go and find someone to help, as I know you can do. For there is always someone in need and you, my kind mice, have the greatest gift to give of all in the love of God. Rejoice. I am Clare. God bless you.

Bernadette and Therese

These two women have been canonized by the Catholic Church. Bernadette (1844 - 1879) was born in Lourdes, France. She had serious illnesses throughout her short life and began receiving messages from Mary when she was 14. Her family, townspeople, and the religious and civil authorities were very skeptical that her visions were genuine. Bernadette never wavered from defending the veracity of her visions. Despite her illnesses and constant pain she was loved for her kindliness, wit and holiness. Her life and visions led to the founding of the Marian Shrine in Lourdes.

Therese of Lisieux ('The Little Flower,' 1873 - 1897) became a nun in the Carmelite community of Lisieux, France. Known for the simplicity and practicality of her spiritual life, she became one of the most popular Roman Catholic Saints. She wrote a spiritual autobiography, letters, poems, religious plays and prayers. She also was a painter and photographer.

BENEDICTION OF THE FATHER'S LOVE
July 17, 2020

I am Bernadette, and I come in the grace of God to this circle of light and love, to this holy Sacrament, this Benediction of our heavenly Father's love. This communion of souls which has drawn so many you cannot imagine. The place where I lived became a healing sanctuary and to this day it continues to be so. It is the place where I prayed, and Mary came to me. [23] The healing waters there, the miracles there, are well known. The healing waters in this circle are the living waters of God's love and grace.

We come to be in this prayer with you that all may be healed in the grace of God. I am your sister and friend in Divine Love. I am Bernadette. God bless you. May His grace be with you.

---

23 One of Bernadette's visitations from Mary occurred on July 16th.

Every Prayer Creates an Invisible Sanctuary
October 11, 2021

I am here, 'The Little Flower,' Therese. I wish to say only a few things. May your prayers lead you to a fate indestructible. May the love in your souls be so strong, it cannot be penetrated by the darkness of the world; for the substance of God's love outshines and is far greater than any material possession, any riches. I know you must live in the world as you have chosen, but every prayer creates an invisible sanctuary full of light and the protection of the angels.

Trust what I say because it is real. Peter and I do not wish to sound severe or to admonish anyone but to strongly encourage you to pray. Be mindful of God throughout your day the best you can. When you falter, be grateful as you get up in the dependence of God and rise. This dependence on God is always necessary. Anyone, whether they be religious, spiritual, a non-believer, scientific, intellectual, if anyone opens their heart to the Creator, they shall be blessed as you are.

Thank you. All my love and blessings from my home in the Celestial heavens. God bless you. I am 'The Little Flower,' Therese.

Chapter 3: PERFORMERS, WRITERS, POETS

Charles (Charlie) Chaplin

Who wouldn't be happy to receive a message from Charlie Chaplin? I wouldn't have imagined in a thousand years that I would be getting messages from him. But alas, I have. He has commented on his life and his progression in spirit in several messages. Although his genius, as well as his flaws, have been documented in many books including his own biography, his messages from spirit carry his hopes, his support of the arts, his progress as a soul, and his deep devotion to his mother (institutionalized on earth for her mental illness) who was always and continues to be his spiritual guide and champion. For artists of all stripes who have a spiritual bent or even lean toward social justice and secular humanism, Charlie is a wonderful guide.

When I was in Ireland in 2019 and was considering going to the town of Waterville where there is a statue to his memory, a place where he brought his family on vacation for over ten years, he came to me in spirit and spoke. "Feel free to go to Waterville if it is your wish but know that you don't need to go there to contact me as I am here for you."

GOD'S LOVE IS THE GREATEST THING IN THE UNIVERSE
May 4, 2019

I am here, Charles Chaplin.[24] How I loved to speak the truth and expose untruth with humor while on earth. It might take an Irishman to understand my ways both spiritually and politically as I was a nonconformist with a vision. I could envision ways to tell a story that touched the heart and tickled the funny bone, and so I made movies. As you may know my movies covered themes of social justice, poverty, workers' rights, tyrants, and romantic love. I believed in love and that one should smile even if your heart is breaking. I love it that the song 'Smile' still strikes a resounding chord with so many. I loved music and poetry and acting while on earth.

I find that here in spirit my passions continue with the addition of my progressing from an agnostic to an absolute belief in God and His love for us. I am not a Celestial spirit, but I am on the path of Divine Love

---

24 Sometimes Charlie Chaplin introduces himself as 'Charles' or he may say 'you may know me as Charlie' because he is speaking to different groups in different messages.

thanks to my mother, always a believer who had unflinching faith while on earth that lifted her in spirit to the Celestial kingdom. She never gave up on me even when I so wished to give up on myself. Her mental illness on earth had no power in this world and was dissipated in the light that was her soul. She was my guide upon crossing over and I was so thrilled to be reunited with her and I am endlessly inspired by her stunning luminosity and wisdom of the truths of the spirit world and God's love. I pray now for my soul to be transformed and awakened in God's love.

So, my dear friends, if I could tell you one thing, I have learned it would be this, God Is love! God's love is the greatest thing in the entire universe. You who have chosen to receive it and believe in it have chosen wisely. I am drawn to your group because of this and because this instrument has many creative projects in his, shall we say, 'back pocket.' We share a need to express ourselves with humor and with music and for it to be helpful to others, to serve humanity. I hope to be of service to him in getting as much of what he has received 'out there' as possible. He has made some great efforts at times to do this, but the timing wasn't right. It is now. We shall work together, and I shall guide him through his doubts and mindset failures that have paralyzed him as they often did me.

Let there be love. Let there be light. Let the music soar and laughter and joy abound. Oh, how the world needs you. God bless you. I love you. Charles.

Whoo! This is Wonderful
June 14, 2019

You felt me in Ireland, and you realized you did not need to go to my summer place there to be with me, just to have a thought about me was all that was required. And today, as on this journey, you bring laughter and love and song and joy. Whoo! This is wonderful! I may follow you around for a while! I told you I would help you with this and so I am, and perhaps not in the way you think. So, as you said (to someone) earlier, 'Meditation is not what you think.' That was funny! So, just be in your soul and I will be in my soul with your soul on this journey, bringing laughter and joy and love and much music and delight.

This is a wonderful place of light. It is a joy to be with you and your dear sister. This is a good thing you are doing. Many will be blessed. I am on the path of roses of Divine Love, and I support you. Thank you for letting me come through. I love you very much. I am your friend, Charles.

Use Social Media to Reach the Millions
September 16, 2019

It is Charlie, as you say, yes. How wonderful when the world has no weight. As Andrew says, love leads the way. As you know, in my life on earth I had visions of a better world, and I made movies which brought joy to many because I could always see the humor even in the darkest hour. I made political movies, and I made social justice movies and romance and pointed out the disparities between the rich and the poor. But you see at the center was the heart. Though I did not know God, I knew my own heart and when I rested in my heart, I could bring the vision I had to the screen.

I am still B.C. Charlie, before Celestial, but I am on my way to being A.D., angel divine. This too is your journey, so I wish to suggest a few things. You need not focus so much on the political. There are many people in the world working on that. All of you dear souls, you will affect many peoples' souls and their hearts will be opened. This too will have a wonderful effect on the world bringing light in this dark hour.

I also wish to say in my day I had the big machinery of the movie industry behind me. They made sure through the press and other means that the word got out for another film and of course millions came to see it. In your world, though at times you think it impossible to get the word out like that, you have this social media, and you can reach millions should you choose to do so, and I would encourage this. It is not beyond your grasp. I would also say that at times you feel that your message is only for this group or that group and yet there are many in the shadows of orthodoxy yearning also for the light and love in prayer and song that you bring. Reach out, my dear friends, reach out to all. This will cost you some time, but it shouldn't hurt your pocketbooks. Of course, the Celestial reward is priceless. So, with a smile in your heart proceed.

I am your friend and brother on the Celestial journey. My love to all. May God bless you all with His glorious love. I am Charles.

Dance Around the Negativity
October 31, 2019

I am here Charles, your brother on the path of God's love. I wish to say just a few things to you. If you can recall I had a particular way of dancing, in and around and over and up and down all the negativity, whether it was those Keystone Cops or others. I could dance around it in joy, without reacting in negativity, though sometimes disappointment showed on my face; remember I was acting. I wish to tell the dear brother here that he certainly knows when he crosses the line, though he wishes to speak truth. This is good.

I would ask him and others, all of you, to do the dance. It's a divine comedy. It's a divine romance. The love of the soul far outshines the natural affections. This I know now. Let your love shine. Dance in joy. Speak from your heart. Speak from your soul and don't forget to wiggle your mustache a little bit. As you know, God has a wonderful sense of humor. How else could we be here?

May God bless you. I love you. I am your brother and friend, Charles, Charlie Chaplin.

Use Your Art To Spread the Truth of God's Love
December 6, 2019

I am Charles. You of course know me as Charlie Chaplin. It has been a while since I spoke, but I wish to add a few things. At times, because you see your group of light as being small, a light in the darkness, you can be discouraged. I lived in a world where there was much darkness and I refused to accept it. I spoke out against it. Though I did not know of the Divine Love, I did know of love and justice and the difference between right and wrong and the equality of all beings.

As an artist, I encourage those of you who have the gift of writing, song, film, painting, or whatever it is, I encourage you to put this love that you have from God, this light, this happiness and humor out into the world through your art. If you help each other with this, it will be a great gift to humanity. For maybe they will not read a book or join you in this way that you are joined in this moment, but they will watch a movie, they will listen to a song, they will look at art. You have a means of communication that far exceeds what we had in my day.

The joy, the happiness, the wonder and the glory of the love you have, take this to the world, this world in darkness and know that you are not alone. There are many who are blessed in God's love around the world. They may have a different language. They may have a different culture, but they too seek and pray for connection with God in His love. Be not discouraged but carry on. Shine your light in the darkness. This light you are so blessed to have. This truth that I did not know on earth and now know, you are blessed with.

I am honored to be with you this day, believe it or not. So, if it is your wish to shine a light in the darkness, you will have much support. Remember this and know you are loved more than you know, but not more than you can feel. Thank you for allowing me to come. I will support you all in whatever way I can and know that you have the company of the Celestial angels. Transformed souls, how can you miss? Go in good faith and humor and joy. All my love. God bless you. I am Charles.

THE SUBJECT OF SERVICE
March 6, 2020

I am here, your friend Charles. We all were listening to the subject of service, and I too had contemplated this in my life. Often it is considered that artists, whether they be musicians or actors, painters, or dancers, can be often quite self-indulgent, and yes this can be true. But the great joy of sharing your gifts is in realizing you have served others.

In my work I realized early on that I could bring joy to others with humor, but I also could make statements about social justice, poverty, love, equality and even peace. That my projects are still watched, my films, tells me that I touched on something that helped others and this has helped me a great deal in my progression through spirit toward the Celestial kingdom where I long to be. I give an example here to these two musicians (JG an JB)[25] reluctant though they may be at times. When they are able to share their gifts of what they've received they know it brings them great joy and they realize there is purpose in sharing gifts.

So, whether you are caring for another human being physically or whether you are sharing joy and humor or a story with a moral compass, in song, through dance, or painting that expresses the beauty of God's creation, you can allow all these things to open doors not only of

---
25 Jane Gartshore and Jimbeau Walsh

perception, but of the soul. These gifts touch the hearts of many, so therefore, those who give as my dear brother said, their rewards are great. I too want to encourage you to give, to use your gifts. Do not despair, be in joy, be in love, and be in light. I am so very happy to give this message through my friend. God bless you. I am Charles. God bless you!

Share Your Gifts
March 17, 2020

I am here Charles. Some of you know me as Charlie. I am honored that I get to speak to you today and I am allowed because many are sequestered and disconnected from their usual distractions. It's a perfect time to share songs of love, to dance with the children, to create art, to give what you know of this truth of God's love. There are so many ways to share it without being overbearing, as with humor and song and a lightness. For with every crisis there is opportunity. As the old saying goes: 'when life gives you lemons, make lemonade.' This you can do.

You are such beautiful souls and so gifted each one of you. Each one has a unique gift to give to this world. It is amazing. I wanted to share with you that you may share with others your gifts. God bless you. I am your brother and friend, Charles.

Allow What Is in Your Soul To Be Revealed in the Light
April 2, 2020

I am here Charles. You may know me as Charlie Chaplin or you may not. My dear friends the world is not coming to an end. Though for some, leaving their mortal coil will end their earthly life and take them into the world of spirit with the freedom to progress towards the fountainhead of love.

You may wonder how can I receive this love, what you have been told is the essence of the Creator? What is the right prayer or disposition? You know they say that when you smile, even though you may be upset, it changes your chemistry and suddenly you can feel underneath whatever problem is occurring, some happiness, because you have allowed it. If you are in the darkness in a room and it has electricity, you flip a switch and, voilà, there is the light! If you flip the switch of your heart which may be off, or covered, or in pain or in doubt, if you flip the switch with the longings of your souls, then you allow your heart to open to love. For the Creator knows your desire, your longings, and when you allow what is hidden to be revealed, to be exposed in the light, if it is good it will grow, and if not, it will dissipate in the light and the love shown upon it.

I lived in troubled times and through a war and through poverty, and I realized at some point I wanted to feel joy and I could always find something funny, even in tragedy. And when I made films that was my template, my foundation, my wish - to bring some humor, bring some joy, to a troubled world. I wish for you beautiful souls here in this circle that has drawn me and captured my heart today, I wish you joy!

I am progressing as a spirit and praying with you to receive God's love and this I wish for all and myself. May you be a wonderful blessing to the world. Bring joy, be open to love, find the happiness beyond the sorrow. See the light through the darkness!

May God bless each one with a great inflowing of this love Divine. Thank you for allowing me to come. My love to all. May God bless you; I am Charles.

The Thief of Hearts

June 9, 2020

I am here Charles, or as you know me, Charlie. I am your brother and friend on this glorious path of God's love lifting us up from the human condition to the glory of the Celestial realms that await us.

Did you know that as a child I was a thief, for a time, when my mother was ill, and I was homeless, I had to steal to eat and to live? As bad as that may sound to you, it gave me a steely determination to succeed and I became, in a sense, a thief of hearts, capturing many in the world. We went through wars and other events in the world that hardened peoples' hearts and I was able to bring them joy and humor and to see the light, but also to remind them of poverty and charity, of those who struggle, the plight of the working man and woman, and the dangers of dictatorship. Yet all these things I approached in the spirit of love with joy in my heart and a wish to bless others, in a sense to heal them of their wounds, to bring a song and a dance and a smile (yes) to them!

I have met the Master and I barely have words to express his countenance, but he humbly said to me, "Oh, I too was a thief, I came to steal people from their somnambulant lives and their restrictive beliefs, into the arms of God and His Great love."

I tell you this, my friends, because whatever you think your station is in life now, you know God's love lifts you up, and in that awakening and, in that flow, as you say, there is joy and blessing and harmony. Let these be your gifts to the world. I shall go now as there are others wishing to speak. With all my love and joy and blessings, I am your brother in God's love. May God bless you all, I am Charles.

Tune In to love
June 20, 2020

I am here Charles, or Charlie to you. And yes, I am on this path of God's love with you all on my journey to the Celestial heavens. Are we not all on this journey? I was listening earlier as you had talked about me, mentioned me, the lower spirits, and the higher spirits and angels. It is important for the welfare of your soul to tune in to that which will lift you up, bring joy. The frequency of joy is a higher vibration than the frequency of sadness. Laughter is such good medicine. This much I knew and still do know.

This love we all seek and pray for, if you want true happiness and joy and bliss, this is the path - the path of prayer and meditation. There are those who teach going within, and I have had some experience with this. As you all know when you ask for God's love you shall receive, when you knock the door is opened. This going within and this small still voice which you hear people talk about is real.

You know, when God and the angels come, they come through your soul which is within and yes, they come from without. You can go within and allow God to open that door so that the angels may speak and in fact this is the door through which I am speaking to you now - the door of your soul.

If you wish to know what is worthy of your attention, of your focus, what will bring you true happiness and change you forever, it is opening to God's love. This you know and I know it too. I come and join you to encourage you to seek the highest, to use joy as your measure, and true happiness in your soul and your hearts delight on your journey to the kingdom of God's love and for all your days on the earth. May they be blessed with happiness and joy and may you all do a little dance every once in a while, I won't tell.

I love you, and I am your brother on the path of Divine Love. Much joy to each one. God bless you. I am Charles.

BE A GIFT TO THE WORLD
July 25, 2020

I am here Charles. You know me as Charlie, Charlie Chaplin. I have been listening to the conversation today as I often come and visit my friend. I thought about my own journey and my own gifts and how they awakened. I came out of poverty and my motivation was to succeed at any cost. My brother, Sydney, helped me immensely and I found I could sing and dance much like my parents. But I pushed myself and worked very hard and I always wanted to express my vision to the world that the world might see the poverty, that the world might be healed. My themes, as I have said before, were romance, social justice, the poor and the tyranny of dictatorship amongst others. I expressed these with my heart, and it touched the world because I had a sense of humor that one could laugh, even in dire circumstances, in my films. And I admit and confess to you all that in my later years I became something of a dictator and somewhat of the oppressor that I had railed against, but finally I surrendered, and clarity came to me and I forgave myself and sought forgiveness.

As I passed into spirit and was guided by my dear mother who had become a Celestial angel and who always believed in me, I began to progress. My prayer on earth was from my heart and mind and my prayer now is from my soul. And you who wish to be a blessing on this earth and progress in love natural and divine, I encourage you to let your prayer be from your heart and from your soul, that you may embrace the world and bless it with love and that your soul may awaken and progress toward the Celestial kingdom. In this way, each one of you can allow your gifts to shine a light on the darkness of this world to bring hope, and above all be present as love and a blessing. It is time; so, let each one step forward from the shadows and shine this light, this love you have received, the gifts that you possess and in this way, you will not be disappointed and you will be blessed in every way.

Thank you for allowing me to come through, my dear brothers and sisters on the path of God's love. With all my love and blessings, I am Charles. God speed.

SET YOUR SIGHTS ON THE HIGHEST
January 27, 2021

Movies and music and dance and stories and poetry and photographs all have the power to change thoughts, to help people change direction, and yet so much is wasted on frivolity and sensory pleasures. Therefore, hearing what films inspire you thrills me.

These were my intentions on earth: How can I lift people's spirits, bring them joy, and help them see the human condition? And as I have said before, to address social issues, social justice and poverty and women's issues, politics and of course romance and love. The touchstone of my work was insight leading to joy, never allowing negativity to overwhelm me no matter what the odds. These types of stories and films and so forth help people see beyond the human condition. Or, rather let me say, the condition that they find themselves in so often, surrounded by negativity and feelings of injustice and seeing or reading something that shines a light and that shows them a path forward.

Do I wish there were more movies about God's love? Do not you all wish for that? Stories that not only help heal but can transform a life leading the recipient into light and love uplifting them and awakening something in them that has perhaps been asleep or almost dead in fact, that stimulates the soul? I encourage you to set your sights on bringing more of this to the world in whatever medium you are comfortable in. Set your sights on the highest and as you start to see a story being formed, a song coming into range, a message, a vision, you can make this real.

Continue to pray for the love of God and pursue the highest my friends, my beautiful, beautiful friends. If you put your focus on this, the results, the rewards, will be beyond measure in the here and now and in times to come. For we are always in modern times[26] are we not? Those who are on earth anyway.

You can think of me as someone coming from the past and coming from the future in the here and now. So, stay lifted in joy, in love. I encourage you to make your amusements and entertainments of the highest. It has

---

26 A humorous reference to his movie 'Modern Times.'

been a while since I have come, so I am grateful that my brother has agreed to take my message and I am happy that he did. With all my love and blessings and the joy in my soul I wish you God's blessings. I am Charles. Charlie Chaplin. God bless you.

DISCOVER YOUR GIFTS AND GIVE THEM IN LOVE
March 23, 2021

I am here your brother and friend Charles - Charlie Chaplin. I come to you in the love of God on the path divine. It is so wonderful to see humor restored and to see the joy that comes to you in your beautiful circle, attended by many, many souls. But don't let that put you off for they are not required to come but are attracted to your discussions, to your prayers, and to the light in your souls.

When you are in the love, the love of God, humor is restored, joy and bliss are yours. You could dance, you could sing. Sometimes it is as simple as just telling a funny story to bring a smile to those in need. That was my mission on earth, and it continues as I progress through the spheres. I come to you to continue to encourage you to tell your stories, sing your songs, and bring humor to lift the weary souls of earth into the light. To love them, if even with a simple smile, a small act of kindness, a little tale of happiness.

You know in books and in films and songs even, often what begins as a problem, a tragedy, a very negative thing, becomes one of triumph, and this is of course, the journey of the hero that has played out through the centuries. I would say dear brother Judas is a great example of a spiritual hero. For not only did he overcome the darkness and his deeds and his despair, but he embraced the light. He received forgiveness, he forgave himself, his friends embraced him, and God lifted him up. He is a beautiful Celestial spirit full of good humor. This humor we have in common.

This is not to say that there is a lack of humor, but some have a gift in that respect. So really my message to you is this: 'Discover your gifts and give them to others in the love of God, with the love in your souls and with joy in your heart,' for love conquers all and dispels the darkness. Do not fret, for you are so very blessed and so loved by all here, and above all, by the Creator.

Thank you for opening the door for me today. I shall dance on my way out. Will you join me? I love you. I am your brother and friend in God's love on the Celestial path. I am Charles. Thank you.

What is Required for Harmony?
May 5, 2021

My dear friends on this path of Divine Love. You who are drawn to the creative arts in song and dance, in theatre and beyond, there is much healing to be had.

What is required is to be in harmony in the human condition and to be lifted in the love of God, as you desire. What kind of dance would that be? What kind of song would be sung? This you know. Your soul will inform you and it will always be graceful, joyful, uplifting and often humorous. For to put a smile in a heart is a great gift. To lift the soul from despair and darkness to hope and faith and trust is a great work. You can never give enough. And in this secular world so bereft of true joy, there is much to give, much you can co-create with us.

We are here for you, and you have my love and support and the encouragement and help of many, many, blessed souls. Go in joy and peace and love. God bless you. I am your brother and friend Charles.

Love is the Great Gift
August 26, 2021

I am here Charles - Charlie Chaplin. I grew up in an environment that, although entertaining, was full of struggles. It was a world that seemed bereft of love, except for my mother and brother, everyone seemingly focused on trying to survive. You may know some things about my life and my childhood, and I won't dwell on them, but I will tell you I was a street urchin for a time doing whatever I needed to do to eat. My mother was institutionalized, my father was absent, and my brother and I were as thick as thieves although he went away for a time.

I not only needed to make a living but felt this deep desire to be accepted, to be loved and I discovered my gifts during these formative years. I allowed myself to make mistakes, to learn, and I allowed inspiration to come through. And as you might be aware, I was very successful. I made many films, but I never forgot my struggles and I included the desire for love, the abuse of power, the horrors of war, social injustice, the bankruptcy of greed and so forth in my many films. I was by no means a saint, but I worked hard to bring joy and humor and truth as I understood it, and music and dance to the world. A world that, not unlike today, was in a lot of pain. I am now a progressive spirit on my journey to the fountainhead of the Creator's love in the Celestial realms where my mother lives and who has been my guide.

I wish to impress upon you your worthiness for love. I wish to encourage you to discover your gifts, to light a candle to the world; to pray and ask God to transform your soul, to heal you, to lift you, to awaken you in love. What awaits you in spirit is beyond what you can conceive, and you will discover the truth of my words one day but know this for now: love is the great gift. Love is the answer. Love is the path. Ask and you shall receive, and whenever you knock, assistance will arrive. Isn't that wonderful?

So, be of good joy! Fear nothing! Your soul is indestructible and longing, as are all souls, for love, both human and Divine. I shall do a little dance out of here now and I thank you for allowing me to come to this beautiful circle of such sweet and beautiful souls. With all my love and in the grace of God. I bid you adieu. I am Charlie Chaplin. God bless you.

Rev. George Vale Owen

George Vale Owen (1869-1931) was a clergyman of the Church of England and a spiritualist. He possessed psychic abilities and received messages from spirit via automatic writing. His messages were compiled into a series of books entitled 'The Life Beyond the Veil,' which describes the spirit world.

PRAY TO BE OPEN TO THE CREATOR'S LOVE
August 10, 2020

I am your brother in Christ, George Vale Owen. Some may know me as Rev Owen.[27] I was the pastor of a small church in England, and I received many messages from Spirit which humbled me and often astounded me.

---

27 Rev. George Vale Owen received beautiful messages from the Spirit World in 4 Volumes, 'The Life Beyond the Veil.' He was the pastor of a small church in England and his messages were widely read and loved. Geoff Cutler republished them almost 100 years later and they are available online and in print on Amazon and Lulu. The picture is of Rev. Owen with his good friend and ardent supporter Sir Arthur Conan Doyle.

As they presented the vision of the spheres from the hells to the Celestial kingdom, and the spirits that assisted me showing me the journey and presenting me to the Master.

I received these messages around the same time as brother James Padgett received his messages. I must say, now that I know them, James received from the highest what is required for each soul should they choose the path of Divine Love, and I am grateful to know him. My messages also touched on the love of God and the journey through the spheres. And though we wrote and received in different ways my messages were widely read and helped so many, not only in my native England, but even around the world.

I draw a parallel here between what I received and what you are receiving, those of you who are Celestial mediums, each one blessed with wisdom and the truth of Divine Love. We support you and each one that comes to learn, to pray, most importantly to pray, to open to the Creator's love, to be humble and ask. To allow the love to come into your soul that the Creator so wishes to give, to allow yourself to be healed and transformed. This has been and remains the message to all on the path of Divine Love.

Some of you I know can see this light emanating from the Celestial heavens, from God to the souls of all of us here - being blessed and blessing each other. Allow this love to change you, to guide you during this time and into your walk into the future which I assure you, each one, is glorious beyond what you can conceive. All praise to the Creator. May all be blessed. I am your brother in Christ, George Vale Owen[28], or Rev Owen. God bless you! God bless you!

28 George Vale Owen and Sir Arthur Conan Doyle photo: http://www.georgevaleowen.org

IN GRATITUDE AND GOD'S LOVE
August 12, 2020

I am here, your brother and friend in Christ, George Vale Owen, and Reverend Owen. I am so grateful for my journey and blessings I received as I do reside in what you call the 7th Sphere,[29] the gateway to the Celestial realms where there is love and beauty and music beyond even what I received and was described by me in my writings. And yet even then I could see the glory, I could feel the love. For my soul to be at one in Christ in the love of God was always my deepest desire.

To be with you and to hear you recite the messages I received is a joy for me and I hope they bring you much wisdom and glimpses, however big or small, of what is to come so that you are enticed to pray and to receive the love of your Creator. I wish to thank the dear brother in Australia for bringing out of obscurity the messages I received and the writings in the books which were once widely read and now again I hope they shall be, along with the beautiful Celestial messages received by James Padgett and others - your contemporaries in the world today.

Each one resonates with those souls, diverse as they may be, in exactly the way that opens them, awakens their soul, inspires them to be in prayer, to receive and to be uplifted on this journey in God's love and grace. Once felt, there will be no turning back though one may meander for a time, though one may doubt, though one may speculate on one's worthiness, I tell you: once you ask for this love and receive it and feel the joy, you can never truly go back as you now are on the path, a glorious path of God's love.

I am grateful to you all for coming together in this study and in your prayers. You draw so many beautiful angels and bright spirits and even those troubled ones in-between progressing through the spheres beyond what you can see. Know that as God lifts you up you lift up others. How beautiful is that my dear friends, my brothers and sisters in Christ! May all be blessed. I am Reverend Owen your brother in Christ. God bless you.

---

29 In the numbering system used in Rev George Vale Owen's books this would be the 14th sphere.

THE GUIDANCE I RECEIVED IN LIFE
January 11, 2021

    I am here, George Vale Owen. You may know me as Rev. Owen. I have been with this one today sharing from my soul, and I am honored to be able to speak to you. At some point in the life of each soul the intentions of that soul to be loved come forth. For as they say: 'Intention is nine-tenths of the law,'[30] and the law of God's love responds to intention. I was a minister of a small church, and I wished to communicate with my mother who was in spirit, and I also wished to know truth, to know God's love. On my journey through the spheres, I had a guidepost. That guidepost being what I had received on earth which became a series of books, originally as writings received.[31]

    This was during the same time as your beloved James Padgett was receiving his messages so full of the truths of Divine Love. My writings also include much truth about God's love, about the kingdom of God where Jesus is Master. I was given visions of the spheres from the hells to the gateway of the Celestial heavens. There were many lessons conveyed through me in words that were so beautiful I could not have possibly come up with them myself.

    I reached tens of thousands of people with very ordinary religious beliefs, but because of the hunger in their souls, their intentions were to feel the love of God, to receive the truth. And so, even though I was a minster in the Church of England, no one rebuked me, and I was not banished.[32] What I received was published and read widely. And my dear friend, who is still my dear friend, Sir Arthur,[33] encouraged me to shine the light and to spread the truths that I had received, so we did work together on Earth for <u>the Kingdom</u> and 'for the glory of God and the company of His angels.' [34]

30 Spiritual law (A reference to "possession being nine tenths of the law")
31 Series of Books compiled as "The Life Beyond the Veil."
32 I was up early this morning trying to talk to Rev Owen about his being or not being 'rebuked' and/or 'banished.' What I felt was that he was indeed 'rebuked' by his Bishop (and a few other clergy) and dismissed from his parish but not defrocked. At first, he was quite concerned, but as he embraced his mediumship and saw how many people came to his lectures as well as his support from Sir Arthur Conan Doyle, he realized God was going to take care of him and of course, God did.
33 Sir Arthur Conan Doyle (writer of the Sherlock Holmes Mysteries).
34 Paraphrasing the words on a cornerstone that Arthur Conan Doyle laid of the Kingston Na-

When you receive something that you know is true, it is because it comes in a package of love. Your soul knows this and so you can share that. The highest truth being the truth of God's love and the reality of every soul with true intentions being able to receive it and to be changed and to progress.

There is much that can be said about the journey of the heart to find love. But what must be said is that true prayer is not a matter of having rosary beads, or going on a pilgrimage, or beating oneself up denying this, or denying that. It is a simple matter between you and God. And when you go to God, when you ask the answer comes. We always say to you 'Do not trouble yourselves with analyzing everything and trying to figure out spiritual life' because my friends, it is a matter of the heart and a matter of the soul. God does the work for you when you open in prayer as in this circle of love. There are so many in attendance here this evening, so many. Thank you for the honor of me being able to convey this message through my dear brother. I step back now to join you in this prayer for God's love. With all my love and blessings, I am your brother in Christ. George Vale Owen.

Sir Arthur Conan Doyle

Arthur Conan Doyle (1859 - 1930) was a British writer and physician. He is best known for his novels and stories about the characters Sherlock Holmes and Dr. Watson. He was also a friend of George Vale Owen.

I Felt the Grace of God
December 15, 2019

I am here, Sir Arthur Conan Doyle. You know me as a writer. The books that I wrote, the stories that I wrote, are still read widely to this day, and often exaggerated (in film) to fit the musings of this time. Oddly enough, my works were quite rational. They debunked, to certain extent, what was deemed as mysterious. Yet, at the same time, I was a great believer in the spirit world and the angels. I devoted a great deal of time to studying the spirit world.

---

tional Spiritualist church in Kingston on Thames in 1927 "To the Glory of God and His angels."

This may seem a bit of a dichotomy to those who only know one side of me, but because the theme today, as my gracious brothers, beautiful Celestial brothers, have spoken about, is the mind and the soul, I wish to say that my mind was preoccupied with telling a story in a unique and engrossing way and I was quite successful at this. At the same time, my soul longings were deep, and I did promote spiritualism and those whom I believed were true mediums.

I felt the grace of God, though not at all like I have now in spirit. I encourage each one of you to pray often, to leave your doubts behind and allow this beautiful love of God to enter your souls. This is the best advice I could give. I am so pleased that this one has allowed me to come through. I shall come again, and I thank you for allowing me this moment with you, in this beautiful light you have, which drew me to your circle. God bless you, I am Arthur Conan Doyle.

Two British Spiritualists on the Divine Path
July 18, 2020

I am here Arthur Conan Doyle. I come in the love of God, in the company of angels and with my friend Rev George Vale Owen who was the finest medium I knew while on earth. As we make our progression through the world of spirit to the fountainhead of God's love, we traverse the spheres and follow our guidance. In the longings that we hold to be transformed in love we are guided by those who came before us in light and in love, and we make this the cornerstone of our walk.

We had knowledge received through the angels of this progression and the great divinity of Master Jesus whose light is so effulgent as to be blinding to those who cannot yet see with their souls. When he comes the atmosphere is filled with light, and a pervading love that can only be divine. We are drawn and the longings in our hearts and the depth of our souls wish for this love.

And those Celestial angels who come through to the earth plane and bring the truth of this progression and the transformation in love divine and in oneness to our Creator, they are drawn by your prayers. We are drawn by this love. I come with so many others to bless this group and to bestow our love in God to all. Thank you, my dear brothers and sisters, in the grace of God. I am Arthur Conan Doyle.

Kahlil Gibran

I have read quite a bit of Kahlil Gibran's work over the years and loved it. As a young man I read, like so many around the world, 'The Prophet,' and we were struck by the beautiful poetic timing of the language. I later read 'Spirits Rebellious,' 'The Madman,' 'Jesus Son of Man' and a collection of other writings. I was delighted that he wished to communicate and secretly (although perhaps not to him) wished I could receive a writing from him on par with his literary works. And this happened (a poem) on June 25, 2024, as it did with the poet Hafiz! I am quite pleased and grateful for what Gibran has communicated from spirit. The poem I so recently received will be printed in the second volume of 'Path of Roses.' What follows is the first communication from Kahlil Gibran I received in April of 2020:

I am here Kahlil Gibran.[35] Yes, it is me. This one has been in rapport with me on this day. The heart, the physical heart, receives oxygen from the lungs in the blood and the spiritual heart receives its life on the wings of prayer. For prayer gives wings to each soul allowing it to rise above the physical world to the ether of spirit and onward to the Celestial realm. So let your prayers raise you up that your soul may touch on heaven's door and the love of God Who hears your heart before you utter even a word. I shall come again, and it is my honor to be in this prayer with you. I am your brother in the love of God, I am Kahlil Gibran. May God bless you.

My Journey to Love
May 3, 2020

I am here Kahlil Gibran. I come as your brother on this path of God's love, and I wish to speak about gifts. You may know me from my works, most especially the book, 'The Prophet.' I had a gift of writing poetry and prose and pursued my love of painting as well. Technically I developed these gifts in many places from many influences. My parents were Christians in Lebanon, but I grew up in the United States (though born in Lebanon) and also lived in France. I was influenced profoundly by the writings, the quatrains of the Sufis and Blake, and the Bahais. The beauty

---

[35] Kahlil Gibran (Jan. 6, 1883 - April 10, 1931) is a Lebanese - American writer, poet, and artist best known for his book 'The Prophet,' one of the best-selling books of all time. Jimbeau Walsh began receiving messages from him in April of 2020.

of the parables of the New Testament informed my writings but I tell you I always believed in the oneness of humanity in what I called the spirit, the unity of religions. My work was an amalgamation of many diverse paths. You can see the paintings, the drawings of Blake in mine and the form of Rodin the Frenchman and the illuminations of Turner to name of few. And so, it was the same with my writings. I was in no way a monk but in fact I was quite a worldly man and yet I retreated into the depths of my soul and as the Sufis would say 'I lived in the world but also not of it.'

There are many gifts in this circle, many yet to be discovered, many evolving and growing. You can see through this lens, this light of God's love that you possess and therefore whenever you touch another soul and give of this light and love, that 'is' the gift. It matters not the medium.

I shall come again with your permission, and I thank this one for receiving. You are so blessed to have the guidance of the great ones who love you so, who inform you so, and who guide you in the love of our Creator. In the oneness every unique soul shining the light in this world. God bless you all. I am your brother and friend in the Divine Love, I am Kahlil Gibran.

Reunited With My Soulmates
May 4, 2020

I come again wishing to continue my discourse out of love for all of you, out of admiration for the path you have chosen. I have stated that there are many gifts in this circle and in your community, and that each one has something unique in relation to their soul, to give, to serve, to share. Some have been down many roads and many paths, others have clung to a more traditional way - often reflecting their family, perhaps their ethnicity or orthodox beliefs, but each one has found this gem of God's love and each one has a view of the world changed by this love. You may believe that you have not the experience to be able to share your journey, but whether your view is of a brick wall or a garden path, a dark night, a glorious morning, a prison cell or running down the beach, walking through the woods: all these views are now able to look upon a Celestial path as you walk into the future with this gift in your souls.

As you may know I was quite a seeker. I walked down many roads, many paths, and held many views, many philosophies and then I had my epiphany and realized that love was indeed the highest common denominator and that all could be one in love, and as you know, in God's love. All my experiences I could write about and whether they were positive or negative, life affirming or fearful, they all led to love, and therefore I could share my journeys and bare my soul. I even attempted to paint a picture, to draw a revelation and I was able to reach many. I wish to give each one of you encouragement and hope on your journeys as you share this wonderful gift, this truth you have discovered and more importantly, God's love that you hold in your souls. That He has blessed each one of you with for the asking, this we can see.

I should tell you just briefly that I have a wonderful soulmate.[36] Who would have thought that she came from a place close to the place of my birth in Lebanon. But her soul and her journey paralleled mine in unique ways. We both politically sought for the liberation of our people and for her, of women. We both followed spiritual paths and we became friends through correspondence. She often critiqued and edited my work in a most loving way, like my conscience, and I opened my heart to her which she felt. When I left the world, she truly felt the separation and now we are together in oneness and on this path of God's love. You too will have this wonderful coming together. I have gone on for a while so thank you for indulging me. May you continue your journey in God's love and grace and light beyond your fears and doubts, holding back as you open up your heart that your souls may be changed and blessed. This is an eternal journey, and it is a glorious one, I assure you. May God's love and peace be with you all.

I am your brother and friend in God's love. I am Kahlil Gibran.

Honoring the Book 'For the Love of His Creation'
August 30, 2020

I come in the love of God, and I wish to honor this dear soul who was given such a beautiful story[37] and received it so well. And I speak from experience for although I was a worldly man, yet when I opened to the angels, they wrote through me often beyond my own comprehension. Yet what I received has ended up touching millions.

---

36 He told me later that he was in the 7th sphere and his soulmate's name is May.

37 This book channeled by Jane Gartshore can be viewed on the website, new-birth.net.

This lovely soul, humble and desiring to serve, she too opened up and in the midst of the world around her that was extremely busy, sometimes chaotic, she allowed her gifts to blossom into a book, into a story that will

touch many. One can read it as a romance novel, as I too had this inclination in my writings, because the human love is something that we all feel and understand. And yet, the longings of the soul in times of crisis call out to God for guidance, and when you ask you do receive. This is the true story, the true admonition of this book. To pray, to go to God, to seek guidance especially in these times. This will carry you, protect you and shine a light upon your path.

May all who read this beautiful book not only digest it with their minds but hold the message in their hearts and allow their souls to receive the gift that is intended, God's love and guidance and healing. With all my love and blessings and my gratitude I am your brother and friend in the love of God. I am Kahlil Gibran. May God bless you.

LET YOUR LOVE BE A HEALING BALM
January 29, 2021

I am here, your brother in Christ, I am Kahlil Gibran, and you honor me by reading what I received and allowing it to touch your hearts. For I lived as if between two worlds, a very human existence, very earthly, and yet my soul was on the bridge to heaven, connected with angels. As a human I sought unity between these worlds and often wrote of the human and the divine. I knew somehow in my soul that we could be one with our Creator. And what was once mysterious to me, is now clear and within my vision and so much more.

I have entered the Celestial realms and ascended through the spheres in such magnificent company. Those who guided me on earth became my friends in spirit and my guides. What you do not grasp now in human understanding will one day become clear. I encourage you to take the soul's path and allow your hearts to be fully opened that God may bless your souls. For all else is contained in God's creation in the embrace of His love. In the awakening of the soul your eyes will see all things clearly, and even while on earth you will begin to walk as one awakened in the midst of a dream, and more and more you will see the sleep of humankind and your heart will burst in compassion, in empathy.

Let your love be a balm, a healing balm, to those in darkness, to those who suffer. This circle has so many gifts and I wish to say this to you, that you are dear to me, and I am honored by our connection in the love of God and light of His grace. My love to each one of you. Whenever you need me, I will come. I thank you and I bid you farewell in the silence of His love. May it bless each one of you, bring you great joy, faith, and trust. God bless you. I am Kahlil Gibran. Peace.

George Gurdjieff

I came upon the teachings of George Gurdjieff when I was 18 years old, a musician playing in a night club in Chicago and was approached by a man who said he was a Baron from Austria. He explained that he was guided to give me a book. The book, 'In Search of the Miraculous,' by PD Ouspensky, was essentially a comprehensive introduction to the teachings of George Gurdjieff.

When asked how to obtain immortality, Gurdjieff replied, "a soul must receive a portion of the substance of the Creator (Divine Love) in order to become eternal." He also said that people are essentially asleep, and unconsciously driven by base desires that can only be overcome by waking up and actualizing one's will. I have always felt that Papa G was my spiritual grandfather and the progenitor of my spiritual journey. Through him I was introduced to a great many Sufi writers and Poets among them: Farrudin Attar, Mullah Nasser Edin, Idris Shah, Al Gazzali, Hakim Sanai, Hazrat Inayat Khan, Rumi, and Hafiz. He comes to me on occasion now, always as a loving grandfather and most definitely a transformed Celestial soul.

Books by G.I. Gurdjieff:

> *Meetings with Remarkable Men*
> *Life is Only real when I am.*
> *Beelzebub's Tales to his Grandson or All and Everything*

Don't Rage Against the Darkness but Embrace All in the Light
October 12, 2020

I am here George Gurdjieff, a true disciple of the Master and your brother in Christ. When your soul awakens and begins to see the pervasiveness of sleep and darkness upon your planet it is indeed horrific at first glance. As you allow the love divine and the light of God's grace to come into your soul you will influence other beings. The vision of your soul is beyond the spectrum of the earth plane and yet you must engage with those locked into the material world. In fact, it is easy to perceive what events might transpire by looking at the conditions of those who are influencing events upon the earth. In a sense you can be prophetic and see the coming of war, unrest, instability, and yet, as you send your love and higher spiritual thoughts out into the atmosphere broadcasting from your soul, which has the grace of God, you have a greater effect than all the armies on earth.

This time has been perfectly coordinated in the heavens for you to engage in love. And when confronted with that which is not loving, continue to broadcast love, continue to speak truth, continue to act in kindness. For you cannot rage against the darkness but you can embrace all in the light. This is what is called an outward sign of grace. You who walk this path in the love of God and all of us who accompany you, support you, influence you on your journey, we will not allow failure because love, the love of God is the very essence of creation. Being out of harmony is only a moment's distraction. It is only the material mind influencing the actions. I encourage you to pray, to act from your soul in love, and change this world. Not only as a disciple of the Master but as a beloved child of God. What else could I wish for you?

May you go in God's grace today and bless all. I am your brother and friend in the Celestial kingdom of God's love. I am George Gurdjieff.

Continue To Bring This Light Into the World
June 14, 2021

I was born in the 19th century in a place that is now in Armenia but then was part of the Russian Empire and a crossroads between Czarist Russia and the Ottoman Empire and Armenian and Greek Christianity. I was brought up in the Greek-Armenian Christian tradition, but as a young man I hungered for the truth. In my travels I met many Sufis, and monks, and fakirs, and ascetics, and I visited schools of very ancient traditions whose goal was to connect those who came to the presence of God, the love of God. I had an awakening experience which left me in a state, I should say, of constant awareness, constant prayer. I did not wish to be put away in a monastery or cave somewhere as I had learned from some of my teachers to live in the world but to be not of it.

I saw the pervasiveness of sleep and all the self-gratification and self-satisfaction and lust for power that comes with that. So, at some point at the very beginning of what is called the Russian Revolution, I took a number of refugees, including family members to France. And it was there where I started the Institute for the Harmonious Development of Man. Now I suppose you are wondering where I am going with this, and I wish to say this. That from everything I had learned and from my own awakening, and having the love of Christ in my soul, I worked to distract my students from their distractions. To bring them to a place where they could open their hearts, regardless of what they were engaged in, and connect to God. We in the Celestial realms see the struggles of those who live in the world, and we see the longings and desires of those who wish to rise above it and live in love, live in God, as those in this circle do.

The conventional religions developed rituals to remind people of God, of love, of their distance, and bring their consciousness and focus from distraction to prayer. I could see by my time, which extended into the 20th century, that what began as a wonderful way to wake up had become empty ritual with all the trappings of spiritual materialism, albeit with some exceptions. So therefore, since you do not live in a monastery or a temple or a cave, this is your challenge.

You have chosen to come into this sanctuary and open your hearts that God may bring His essence into each of your souls. This is a wonder to behold. I was drawn to your circle by the prayer of my spiritual grandson and by the longing in each soul and the light I could see emanating. Do no despair, stay in your prayer, and continue to bring this light into the world. For there are a multitude in this realm of light and love, the realm of Christ, that supports you, and influences you. Thank you for allowing me to come. I shall step back to be in your blessing. May God shower you with love divine. I am your brother in Christ, George Gurdjieff. Go in peace.

Manifestations and Spiritual Experiences
September 28, 2021

May the blessings of God's love be upon you. You who have traveled far and yet have found yourselves at the very beginning of a new life. When one embarks on a spiritual quest, it is often beyond their scope to be able to perceive what it is, in fact, they are seeking except to say that ultimately it is union with the Divine, with their Creator, with love.

In the case of my dear brother here, my spiritual grandson, he has only just become aware that he started life as a very exuberant, abundantly energized, physical child with a very curious mind, with a deep desire in his soul to find the highest. And so, in relation to what you were reading earlier from Judas, in this one's life, his growth went from a very physical being to an intellectual being, to befriending his soul. Prayer and music played a large part in this as it does with many. But he sought manifestations. He wanted experiences that he did not find in the church he grew up with. He did not know that he wanted to experience God's love but he knew there must be something higher than this and so he read about me and my teachings and my interactions with students, and my constantly reminding them that the world was in a deep sleep and that humanity must awaken and that the conventional beliefs of who Jesus was, who he is, fell far short from the truth and were in fact mostly in error.

I traveled to many lands, had many teachers, sought out the ancient and the eternal, and came to a place of spiritual awakening and a consciousness of the treasures of prayer. Constantly I sought guidance, and constantly I received it. And so, I wish to touch on this subject of manifestations and spiritual experiences.

The desire of one to be changed, to be enlightened, to be free, to be love is at the core of all seeking that is spiritual in nature. You may be aware that teachers have often used certain substances or chemicals to shock their students into a state of awareness of their mortality and hopefully an insight into immortality. This also can happen to one who has experienced deep trauma or loss in their lives. But to those who linger in sleep and find spiritual life to be no more than another entertainment or amusement, a teacher will often go to extreme lengths to awaken the somnambulant student so that one might begin to see.

I am not in any way recommending that you all go out and try some drug or another or put each other's lives in peril, but I am saying that those who seek out manifestations are really looking for an ultimate connection with their Creator. All these experiences, all these manifestations, whether they be the opening of the third eye with spiritual visions, or the perception of lights, spirit visitations, kundalini energies, and so forth are not to be equated with the experience of praying for and receiving the love of your Creator. They may lead to that place of true soul longings, and it is always our great hope that this is so, but do not mistake the road for the destination.

And you, my dear ones, who have chosen this road on the highest path, I encourage you to make your day a prayer, make your journey a prayer. Talk to God and find a small, still place where you can hear His answer and feel His great love for you. I'm very pleased that I was able to deliver this message and I hope it will reach many and I thank you with all the gratitude of a grateful grandfather and one who is a transformed soul in the heavenly Father's kingdom. May you all go with the grace of God and know I am here for you should you call. I am your brother and friend, I am Papa George, George Gurdjieff, God bless you, God bless you.

Hafiz

Hafiz (1325-1390) lived on earth in what is now Iran. Many people regard his lyric poems as one of the highest points of Persian literature.

MY POETRY REFLECTS MY COMMUNION WITH GOD
December 4, 2019

Thank you for honoring my work and my words. I was in deep communion with God, and I was also quite a rascal. This is reflected in much of my poetry and during my life, not everyone revered those words of mine. I often found myself in trouble with authorities because they felt that I was outside the boundaries of religious belief. As you may know I was refused a burial in my religion. Yet today you might have to wait hours just to walk past where my body was laid.

I tell you this because of what you have discovered of God's love, and you also find that it is sometimes considered outside the boundaries of religious belief. You may be accused of not being a good Christian or as I was told, 'You are not a Muslim, these words are blasphemous.' Yet my communion with God was so deep I could express it. There were those who always understood me, and my words affected their souls.

Now of course, I am honored. I had never thought about being honored in the West but there are those who have translated my words in many languages. There is one, Daniel L.,[38] who actually is able to understand my words just in the same manner as I speak them to this one, this instrument, who is speaking on my behalf or rather that I am speaking through, as you call it 'channeling.'

What you read now of Hafiz is where my soul is now. I am in God's love. I am in that Celestial kingdom where you all wish to go. My soul, when on earth, wanted nothing but God, wished for nothing more than this communion. Therefore, despite the things I believed in, which when I crossed over found out were: 'No, not exactly like that, Hafiz.' I was reeducated in some ways on my entrance into the spirit life, yet because of my communion with God, all these issues were superfluous.

So again, as you go and speak the truth, and you are so blessed to have it, all of you, do not be turned back or offended when you are not understood because you will be as I was and am. Let this love of God permeate your being, awaken your souls, until your mere presence, the presence of love is more powerful than any words you might say. But when you do say them, or when you sing them, or when you write them with the love of God in your soul, they will have a transformative power to touch those who hear and see and read.

Walk this earth with the joy of God in your heart and in your soul as I did. There is no force greater than God's love. You know this. Thank you for

---

38 This is a great compliment to Daniel Ladinsky of whom Wikipedia says: He has written four works based on poetry of 14th century Persian Sufi poet Hafiz: 'I Heard God Laughing' (1996), 'The Subject Tonight Is love' (1996), 'The Gift' (1999), and 'A Year With Hafiz: Daily Contemplations,' (2011) as well as an anthology, 'love Poems from God: Twelve Sacred Voices from the East and West' (2002), and 'The Purity of Desire: 100 Poems of Rumi' (2012). In introductions to his books, Ladinsky notes that he offers interpretations and renderings of the poets, rather than literal or scholarly translations. His work is based on conveying and being 'faithful to the living spirit' of Hafiz, Rumi, and other mystic poets.

honoring me. I wish to honor you. May all fear and doubt, reluctance leave you as you open to the Divine Love. Thank you. May God bless you in every way, every day. I am your brother and friend in God's love, Hafiz.

Daniel Ladinsky (born 1948) is an American poet and interpreter of mystical poetry, born and raised in St. Louis, Missouri. Over a twenty-year period, beginning in 1978, he spent extensive time in a spiritual community at Meherabad, in western India, where he worked in a rural clinic free to the poor, and lived with the intimate disciples and family of Meher Baba.

A Beam of Light
March 13, 2020

I am here Hafiz the poet and you are in your galaxy - a pinpoint in the vast universe of the Creator living on a microcosmic dot in an expanding universe and yet there is a beam of light connecting each one to the source. This connection facilitated by love and brought about by each one seeking this love in the spiritual hunt where the prey captures the hunter.

The Creator in His wisdom makes it possible. How is anything possible? How are we breathing? Living in a world full of darkness and yet full of light. Full of death and full of life. You have discovered the majesty of the love divine - you have discovered the great treasure that our glorious Creator has given. No one would walk away from such riches. In God's love I am your friend, Hafiz.

What Part Will You Choose To Play?
October 7, 2020

I am here the poet Hafiz. Surprise, surprise, I came because of what you were all discussing about the reality of being in your feelings. When you read my poems and my writings, they are filled with an abundance of feeling for God, the presence of God, the beloved, the only romance truly worth pursuing. And this one, my brother, he quite likes many of my poems, but when he is concerned, he thinks of this very short one. In the English language it goes something like this: 'Now that worry has proved to be such an unlucrative business, why not find a better job.' Of course, this is only a fragment but it also a great truth. For when has worry ever brought a blessing? Prayer will bring a blessing, in faith, in trust.

It's God's show and yet we are all in it, in His theater, characters each one of us. So, what part will you choose to play? What do you wish to bring to the audience and how do you wish to honor the Creator of the play? If you go in faith, in the knowing that you can be at one with your Creator in love, if you trust this process, you will find yourself in the glorious ballroom of the universe dancing with the beloved to the most beautiful music in color and in light beyond any spectrum on earth. This is your future. This is worth the price of admission. Beyond whatever you have spent, will be your reward; never ending love, and the bliss and joy of the Creator's grace!

Thank you for allowing me to come through as I should like to do more often, and I wish all of you a great blessing in God's love, as we all do. I am your brother and friend and yes, I am a Celestial friend in God's love.

God's Dancer
December 9, 2020

God in His infinite patience awaits your arrival
In His grand ballroom
With all its magnificence,
And yet you and your partner
Dressed to the nines
Have chosen the poverty of spirit at the Pauper's ball.
No, not that poverty where you feed the hungry
With the bread of life,
With the wine of Divine Love
In the eternal dance,
But that impoverished ball of endless distractions
Succumbing to all those things
You believed you couldn't do without.
And yet when you arrive at the Creator's dance
You will wonder
And be amazed
And say: 'why did it take me so long to get here?'
And as you step out on the floor to dance with the beloved
You will merge with every dancing planet
Spinning in joy like the whirling Dervish you are,
God's dancer.

This Longing
April 11, 2021

You stand in front of the door
Peeping through the keyhole to the beyond,
The key in your pocket,
Your hand on the doorknob.
You don't know that you hold the key,
Or even that the door is unlocked.
But somehow you restrain yourself

from the delight of turning the knob
And pushing open the door,
Though it is your heart's desire.
Your soul sitting in limbo,
Waiting on the arrival of something
That you already possess.
This longing is all you have ever needed
To walk through the door
of the Creator's abode,
Where love reigns supreme.
Take this step to infinite grace and a place of no regrets
In God's embrace.

Infinite Ocean of love
June 2, 2021
Standing on the shore
of the infinite ocean,
Wave after wave
of uninvited thoughts and desires come,
Enough to drown
Even the most competent swimmer.
And yet one struggles
To traverse the great sea,
To fathom its depths.
As I float on the raft
of divine grace,
Unafraid to drown
In His love,
To merge with the very substance
of the Eternal One,
On the infinite ocean of love.
Won't you join me for a dip?

What if an Angel Came to Your House?
June 27, 2021

What if an angel came to your house?
Do you think you'd need all that furniture
That clutters up your place
To accommodate her?
No.
You would need to remove
All the clutter
In your heart,
That she may have a place to visit with you
In the Holy presence,
As a messenger of God.
How else can we spend time with you?
You who are so busy
Collecting more debris.
We can leap over those walls
That you have so dutifully erected,
But all we ask for is that you unlock the gate
That leads to the garden,
Where everything blooms
In the love of God,
In praise,
In joy,
In ecstasy.
Come and sit with me.
Let your soul
Be opened
By the spirit,
That God may come,
And His Holy presence
Have a place in your home.
Keep the fires burning,
Keep a log on the hearth,
Let the flame of Divine Love,

Forever in your soul,
Burn all impurities away.
When can I come and visit you again?

Buried Treasure and the King
Are you still looking for buried treasure?
That illusive pot of gold
Hidden in the trunk
Away in the attic
Beneath the floorboards,
Or deep in the earth,
High in the sky,
Are you still looking for buried treasure?
Why don't you ask the King
To share his riches?
The King of kindness,
The King of mercy,
The King of compassion,
The King of love.
Would He not gladly share his riches,
Feed the poor,
Prepare a place for you?
You who have been wandering homeless,
All you needed to do was ask,
And, as is said, every good and perfect gift will be given.
For the King
Is always sharing,
Always giving
To his loyal subjects,
So dear to His Heart.

Where Are You Going?

Where are you going?
How will you get there?
Would you like a lift?

Robert James Lees

RJ Lees (1849-1931), a British spiritualist, medium, preacher, and writer who was best known for his claim that he could help solve the mystery of the identity of 'Jack the Ripper,' the notorious London serial killer of the late 19th century. It is also reported that, as a boy he communicated messages from Prince Albert (who was deceased) to Queen Victoria.

He also received messages from friends in the spirit world describing the afterlife and its spheres. His best-known books describing the spirit world are: 'The Mists Trilogy' ('Through the Mists,' 'The Life Elysian,' and 'The Gate of Heaven'). His messages were widely read during his lifetime and sometime after. They are considered among the very best channeled messages concerning life in the many realms of the spirit world with vivid and compelling narratives filled with stunning descriptions of the landscapes, employments, enjoyments and atmospheres on the other side.

THE AUTHOR OF 'THROUGH THE MISTS' IS VERY GRATEFUL
April 13, 2021

I am here Robert James Lees. And what Clare has said last week was hardly expressive of the gratitude I have. For you see, I was known on earth and continue to be known as a person associated with what are called or what are known as the 'Jack the Ripper murders,' because when on earth I had visions of those nefarious deeds. I shared them with Scotland Yard and the police, but it was only when those deeds coincided with my vision that they began to take me seriously. What I saw was real.

My name and my work has long been associated with those tragedies. How can I tell you how my heart leaps with joy to know that the work I did, receiving these messages from spirit, which you are now sharing with each other and allowing your souls to absorb, honors me. So yes, I come to listen, to be with you, and to try and influence you that you may understand with your souls and have some glimpse of life here.

And I may say it is as difficult now, as I am an inhabitant on the precipice of the Celestial heavens in the 7th sphere, to describe this place and my journey. It is as difficult now, perhaps even more so, than it was then. I had wonderful guides and the words flowed through my hand and through my heart and left me with a trust and a faith that allowed me a fearless entrance into spirit - the glories of which are so difficult to explain and describe to those of you on earth.

Thank you for such kind words regarding what I received. I can feel your delight when certain passages impress you in a most loving way. For love is the path and God's love, as I stated then and continue to proclaim, is the path to the Celestial heavens. Have no doubt!

I thank you all from the bottom of my heart and with all my love and affection in the grace of God, I say goodbye for now. I am your brother and friend in Christ and a very blessed soul. I am Robert J Lees.[39] Thank You.

---

39 Robert James Lees photo, https://en.wikipedia.org/wiki/Robert_James_Lees

Please Update My Book Where Terms Are out of Date
May 25, 2021

My dear friends, please do not allow the words from another time, another place, to disturb your peace. Please know that I support your efforts to make whatever changes you deem necessary so as not to offend.[40]

I had read Samuel Clemens, known as Mark Twain, and was familiar with that particular dialogue, and I am quite sure it must have influenced my receiving. At the time, I believed that the spirits who were speaking were very much wanting to convey the equality of all souls, and when a soul comes into spirit there is equanimity. This does not however discount souls in the lowest spheres, who may have been quite attractive or beautiful on earth by human standards, and who in the spirit world find themselves spiritually disfigured, reflecting the state of their souls.

And yet as I received it, those souls with physical disabilities and imperfections are made whole in spirit. All souls become more beautiful as they progress through the spheres, and brighter. Darkness is used to express the condition of the soul, rather than any particular color.

But I will tell you this, that in the Celestial realms and the higher spheres where the spirit body becomes such a thing of light, the colors you know on earth are completely transcended, and yet, one can retain physical characteristics as to be recognizable. The colors in spirit are shades unfathomable to the human mind, the human sight, just as Celestial music is unfathomable to the human ear. And yet, some on earth can perceive these colors, or shall I say a portion, just as some composers may be very influenced by the vibrations in the Celestial realms so glorious!

I hope that I have managed to clarify things, and I wish to tell you that you are dear to me. I am honored that you continue your studies, but more importantly, continue your prayers. I wish you every blessing and perfect gift in the love of God. Please know I am truly your brother and friend, Robert J. Lees. God Bless you.

---

40 Lees is referring to a racially derogatory word used by a spirit to convey a positive point about equality in his book 'Through the Mists.' This term was in use at that time (1898) but is totally unacceptable today. The PDF copy of this book available on the new-birth.net web site has been amended accordingly

Do Not Overthink My Books
July 9, 2021

I've been listening to your discussion today and all your considerations reflecting on what I received.[41] Aphraar was trying to paint a very broad picture so that each soul in its own way, could understand not only the workings of free will, but also willful ignorance, for God does not punish. Humans make their own beds, and God waits for them to awaken and arise from the dream of death, from the ravages of sin, into the light of His love and compassion, and the glorious journey through the spheres, to the fountainhead of His love and grace.

To read these writings with your souls is all that is required. It is not necessary to overthink these things and in fact, the language they are written in is designed to throw off the mind to a certain extent, so that the soul may grasp the deeper meaning of the truths presented. Isn't that wonderful? It was a great gift to me, and as I have said, I am more than delighted that you are sharing it with each other and wish to share it with others.

The picture I received of the spirit world gave me great hope and lifted me from fear into faith. It brought me into my soul from a curious mind to the peace of God's grace. So again, I thank you, I am with you, and I hope I have provided some guidance on what you have read today. I wish to say as well, that it is fine to look back on one's errors and not repeat them, for that is a lesson learned. But how great is it to envision the future in each moment as you walk in the light of the Lord, in the grace of God, in the peace that passes human understanding, in faith and forgiveness, in truth and trust, in joy and jubilation. This is God's wish for all.

My dear friends it is my honor as well as my joy to be with you. May God continue to open up each of your souls to the great gift of His love and its inflowing that you may be the light and the love in this world, so in need. Pray and be happy for God loves you as I do. I am Robert J. Lees, your brother and friend in the love of God.

---

41 Refers to 'The Life Elysian,' Chapter 6, pages 79-84.

My Books Are Truly Sanctioned
August 5, 2021

The eye has not seen, the ear has not heard, nor have the senses perceived what God has prepared for His children in love. As you go through the descriptions in the books that I wrote, or shall I say, received, you get, as has been said, a mere glimpse of the conditions, the environments, and the state of being in the spirit realms. And yet, that mere glimpse is quite amazing for the earth bound to consider. Of course, because you are on the path of Divine Love, you can recognize the progression that is being presented to you and at the same time find great comfort in the blessings that God has gifted to all from the vilest sinner to the holiest saint.

As I have said, as well, I am delighted at your studies, and as Luke has pointed out, they are truly sanctioned should you wish to share these books and these truths. And they are from the standpoint of the earth higher truths, and they do contain the Divine Love of God and the progression of the soul, although not to the extent to which James Padgett received, yet he was certainly informed by their contents. And so, you can see there is something for everyone. You may reach many of a certain disposition by sharing the writings as you are doing, that I received. And there are some that very much resonate with the more judicious approach of James Padgett and the heart of Rev. Owens, and the beautiful soul of Eileen Caddy and her connection with the spirit of God, and those still on earth.

So, what I am saying and what has been given to you and through this one by many spirits is that it is not only ok to utilize these different writings at your disposal, but also to remember that love, and most especially Divine Love, can be communicated in many ways - your mere presence when you are in a state of grace, and you walk in it, talk in it, and furthermore when you sing or create a literary work, or a screenplay or a poem. This has been communicated to you before, I am being made aware of, so I won't dwell on that subject but just put forth its essence as a reminder.

Time on earth is of the essence, and if you wish the earth to be blessed, make use of your time wisely as you do in this circle, in this prayer, in this group. You honor me and others by your devotion to the truth and by your prayers for the love of God. And we honor you to be with you and assist you on your journey whenever you call. So, again with all my love and gratitude and the blessings of all here in the glory of God. I bid you adieu for now. Go in peace and grace with love. I am your brother in Christ. Robert J. Lees.

James Padgett

James Padgett (1852-1923) was a Washington, DC lawyer who practiced in the late 19th and early 20th centuries. His wife, Helen, died on February 14, 1914, and this unexpected event devastated Mr. Padgett. He contacted a medium, Mrs. Maltby, who not only was able to communicate with his deceased wife, but she told him that he possessed the gift of mediumship through 'automatic writing.' Even though Padgett was initially very skeptical, he began to receive messages from Helen and other spirits including his grandmother, Ann Rollins.

Then he was informed by these spirits that Jesus wished to communicate through him. His skepticism returned. Only after several early messages from Jesus were rejected by Padgett, (he threw them in the trash) did he begin to realize that these messages were genuine and valid. Over the course of 9 years (beginning on September 28, 1914) Padgett received over 2,500 messages from Jesus and other spirits. These messages remained in obscurity for many years but were recently published in four volumes by the Foundation Church of the New Birth.

James Padgett's messages are highly significant because they not only correct the errors in the Christian gospels but describe the real significance of the life of Jesus and his teachings. In addition, Padgett received messages from a wide variety of spirits, some famous like Abraham Lincoln, Julius Caesar, Mary Baker Eddy, Francis Bacon, et cetera on subjects ranging from being in the 'hells' to progression in the spirit world, Divine Love, war, the soul and its transformation from mortal to immortal, the purpose of life on earth, prayer and other topics. His channeling are among the most comprehensive spirit messages in existence and are quite astonishing.

Explore Your Gifts
April 15, 2021

It is your brother James Padgett and I come in the love and the grace of God. First of all, let me express my deep gratitude for this coming together, so to speak, on my behalf, for honoring my life, and my work. May it bless you all.

There is one thing that becomes obvious when discussing the gifts of any one person, especially those who can write profound books, beautiful songs of love, and poems that touch your heart. These individuals who bring their gifts to the world are often very flawed in other ways, as ones having great gifts but not being of the best moral character or truly upstanding people. I don't mean to say or suggest that those who bring gifts who inspire people are evil. No, we see that they, as I was, are just human.

I encourage all of you to explore your gifts to know that you are worthy and to step forward in truth. As you can see even I, with all the messages that came through me, had a reluctance to share them with the world, concerned about besmirching my reputation, and yet I did have a gift. These truths that I received are just as true now as they were when I received them.

So, find what resonates with your heart, with your soul, because your longing is more than a quest for information, more than an intellectual understanding. It is the deep longing of every soul to be loved, and on this path, to receive the great love of the Creator given to every soul that asks, and as the master said, in sincere faith, in earnest aspiration. So let your hearts soar in the knowing that you have discovered a great treasure. And know that as you honor me you bring transformation to yourselves in the love of God.

I shall be with you in your studies supporting each one, and I shall guide and influence as I can and when necessary. Lastly, know that I am not the same James as when on earth, for I am a redeemed soul transformed in the love of God and the Celestial heavens. I come to you with all my love and blessings in the grace of God. Thank you. May God Bless you.

A Lightbulb in a Dark Room
April 29, 2021

I am here, your brother and friend in the love of God and I have been with you this session beaming in the joy of your journey, of your wishing to understand, this transformation of soul, these truths that I received.

I was a material man in a material world, and I had all the desire for self-satisfaction and self-gratification as anyone, and though I grew up in the Christian religion, in my Methodist beliefs I did know of this Divine Love. I knew of it as something that existed as a gift from God, but like many, I carried with me very traditional orthodox beliefs of the Bible and Jesus. Yet, like many, when I was in crisis, when my heart was in grief and guilt over the loss of my dear Helen, I called out, and at first beyond my imagination, I began to receive messages from my dear Helen. Other than the fact that I disagreed with what she said, I was astonished that I seemed to have this gift.

Then one day the Master (Jesus) came, and I also did not believe that, thinking that it was an impossibility, but I tell you the love that I felt dissolved my doubts. I would say the first time I realized, after praying for some time, that I had a degree of this Divine Love in my soul, I was in a place with people who did not pray for this love, who had no concept of it. Though I only had perhaps a drop in the ocean of this Divine Love in my soul, I felt as if I was a light bulb in a dark room and I realized, 'My God, I understand!' I asked and I have received!'

As Cliff and Dorothy have mentioned, the messages I received convey deep truths in a number of areas that are not often explored by humans. I would add to what was said - that I received quite a bit of knowledge and truth concerning the spheres and the journey in the spirit world. All the way from those in the hells progressing through the spheres to the seventh sphere, and on into the Celestial heavens. You will see, if you have not read these messages, that they are quite diverse and from many different spirits to give you a picture of how the soul becomes transformed from wherever it is, be it the depths of hell, the blandness of normalcy, the good person, the longing soul, from the mere mortal to the very Celestial divine angel.

So, it is with deep gratitude I thank you and I encourage you to explore and pray. You will surely receive when you ask from your soul. May God bless you with the great inflowing of Divine Love. I am your true brother and friend in the Celestial heavens. I am James Padgett. God Bless you.

Advice for Teachers of the Padgett Study Group
May 9, 2021

I shall try and give you a very simple example of the grace of God. Who can explain the stories of the roses? And yet, you know it is a sign. It is a confirmation of the soul's connection with its Creator. It is living proof of communication from the spirit world. Because you pray, the signs you receive come from the Celestial heavens.

The mind will always seek answers and yet the soul simply knows. Those who come to this group with all their questions are sincere, and so you may give them sincere answers. Whether those answers are from the messages I received, which are certainly comprehensive enough, or whether you wish to add personal examples or information that is more contemporary, feel free. For the truth is the truth, and is it not the soul's longings and the transformation of each soul that is really at the heart of this matter? The happiness that lifts you all above this world is a joy that can hardly be expressed in language.

So, when you wish to present the essential truths remember the word 'essential' comes from essence. The essential truth being God's love. If you keep this in the forefront and speak with your heart, the truths of the soul will supersede the doubts of the mind. For the soul sitting in grace is something to behold. Remember what your purpose is and what you truly wish to give to each one that comes. This is all that is necessary, all you will need. The rest we will take care of and guide you. Have no worries; for in the love of God, in the flow of His grace, questions will dissolve into the light of day, into the truths of God's kingdom. I shall be there with you. Now and always, I am your brother and humble servant and friend in Christ, I am James Padgett. God bless you.

Explore the Truth With Your Souls
May 13, 2021

Dear friends of my soul, I have been with you today in this study group listening, guiding, encouraging, and influencing your souls to reach out in love. I am an inhabitant of the Celestial heavens with my soulmate, my dear Helen, and I want to encourage you all to read the messages

I received so that you may know these truths that are as true today as they were over 100 years ago when I began to receive them. As the love of God is eternal, so are His laws and His truths. You are a somewhat diverse group, and you have different sensibilities coming from different areas of interests and studies but the one factor that binds you together is the desire of your souls for love and to understand from the human condition the great truths of the kingdom of God.

As you have been told and you may be aware of, I received many messages on many topics, some of which had never been fully revealed to mankind, humankind, you would say. I wish you all to explore the natural love and the Divine Love that you may understand the difference between them, one which is of the human nature and given to every soul, and the other that is eternal, unchanging, and yet transforming.

When you have this feeling of soul mate love or a deep love for any other soul, the feeling that you have is the closest thing in human nature to this feeling of Divine Love. And yet the Divine Love supersedes even the greatest human love of a mother for her child and at the same time it embraces all.

As you explore this path to the Celestial kingdom, allow your souls to be touched that you may feel the glow, the glory, the magnificent and eternal bliss that the Creator has for each of you. Let your souls ascend and be lifted. You can give your mind a rest even as you read the subject matter and I encourage you to feel the substance, the essence of the truths contained in what are known to you as the Padgett Messages. And yes, I was deeply honored to receive them and to be changed by the truths within them.

With all my love and blessings and support from the Celestial kingdom, I am your humble servant and brother in God's love, James Padgett. God bless you.

Comprehending God

June 8, 2021

It is I your brother and humble servant, James Padgett. I have been listening today to the readings and the intense discussion, the topic 'Who and What is God' with excerpts being taken from the messages I had received from Jesus and the celestials.

I would say concerning what I received: one cannot comprehend the Creator intellectually, and even the Master himself pointed out the paucity of words to be able to describe God and His attributes. And yet reading between the lines one can perceive that as the soul in its longings to unite with its Creator receives the essence of the Creator, it can indeed understand the great being of God.

Even those who rely on science to explain the world at large and the universe cannot get further than the big bang, or the source behind the spark behind the bang, or the idea that God, The supreme Creator, is without beginning or end; even how you are existing in the world, breathing, living, and having these longings to be loved, to connect with your Creator seems a mystery to the mind.

Everything that has been said today has come down to the connection of your soul to the great soul. The result of which is receiving the essence of God defined as love, Divine Love. Thus, you begin to experience the transformation from the mortal to the immortal, from the human and the natural to the eternal and the divine. This is experienced as love, the emanations of the great soul of God touching every soul; inexplicable, unexplainable, and yet a tangible reality and the truth.

I wish to thank you all for coming together to study what I have received so long ago. I am honored, and I hope that these messages I received, many of which were incomprehensible to my mind, but eventually transparent to my soul, will benefit you all. They are only a template, the rest is up to you, and your longings, for God will respond. This is the path of joy and true happiness above and beyond the earth plane. Come and join us in God's love. For we are all His children. With all my love gratitude and the blessings of all here, I shall step back. I am James Padgett. May God bless you.

Fred (Mister) Rogers

My children both grew up with Mr. Roger's Neighborhood as young boys. No matter how rambunctious, wound up, or out of harmony they were, Fred Rogers would calm them down within minutes. When I found out later that he was a composer, a minister, a father, and a swimmer I felt a certain kinship to him. In the past few years several documentaries have surfaced along with a feature film (starring Tom Hanks) about the life and work of Fred Rogers.

On July 5, 2021, I received the first message from him in a small prayer and spiritual study group. I have received six different messages from Fred as of this writing, but I am sure there will be more to come. His work in the spirit world comes as no surprise and warms the heart as he always did and continues to do. I am told by a friend whose family were friends of Fred Rogers in Pittsburgh, PA. that what I am receiving from him is genuine. I couldn't be more honored.

REMEMBER THE IMPORTANCE OF GUIDING THE CHILDREN
July 5, 2021

I am your brother and friend in Christ. I am Fred Rogers.[42] Hello all! Aloha Jimbeau! For those of you who do not know me, I was a Minister while on earth, a father, a writer, a composer of music, a swimmer, and the host of a children's tv show. My ministry was directed towards the children of the world. I wished them to feel safe and accepted and above all, loved. I prayed every night for guidance. I prayed for the blessings of God's love. I did not know the path of Divine Love, yet I received it while on earth. This spark in my soul enabled me to teach children, to give them a sense of belonging in a world moving so fast. So, we sang, and we had puppets, and royalty, and guests of many colors, many persuasions. I often used someone's occupation, their gender, their race, to point out that we, in fact, are all God's children, all one in love.

I work with children now who have crossed over; so, my work continues, and I am a progressive spirit and an inhabitant of the fifth sphere as you number them, and a possessor of the great gift of God's love. I come today not only to introduce myself and my work but to remind such a beautiful group of souls to remember that your time on earth, however long, is but a blink in the eye of the Creator. What you leave your children and your children's children and the generations to follow is of the utmost importance, for the world so needs love.

---

42 Fred McFeely Rogers (March 20, 1928 – February 27, 2003), also known as Mister Rogers, was an American television host, author, producer, and Presbyterian minister. He was the Creator, show-runner, and host of the preschool television series Mister Roger's Neighborhood, which ran from 1968 to 2001.

I ask you to remember the importance of guiding the children, of being patient with them, of bringing the unity of all peoples, all religions, those who lack religion, and all genders in the oneness of love and in the blessing of God's love. For as is said, we are all God's children and one in His love. I shall step back and join you in your prayer for the love of the Creator. With all my heart I thank you for allowing me to come today. May God bless you all. I am Fred Rogers. God bless you.

WORKING WITH THE LITTLE CHILDREN
October 12, 2021

Hello Melissa! Hello Michael! Hello Ruth! Hello Jimbeau! It's Fred. I very much am touched by your appreciation of my life, and your acknowledgment of my journey in spirit, progressing in the love of God, towards the kingdom of heaven and the Celestial realms. And yes, I do work with the children of this world, always my passion. I tell you it would break your heart to see the condition of some of them, victims of abuse, of violence, of unlove.

It is a vast work, and those who work with me, and there are many who have been at this for quite a long time, rejoice every time one of the little ones receives a healing, begins to trust, feel safe, and we do our utmost to provide a cloak of protection and love with all our hearts and all our souls. And when you remember that you are a child of God and that we are all His children, each one a precious gift, no matter what condition, it becomes easy to open your arms to all the children of the world, regardless of their age, there position in life, their station, their race, their religion, or their gender. For the soul is beyond those limitations. And when the light of God's love touches you, fills your soul, you become as if a little child, unaware of darkness, danger, and living in the bliss and faith that the love of God puts in your souls. How good is that!

This Divine Love is the greatest gift, and this you know, and this knowledge you can share. But even more important, is to touch others with the gifts that this love brings into your soul, of kindness, empathy, compassion, gentleness, and great joy.

I thank you all, my dear friends, and I shall come again. May all the children of the world be blessed in God's grace and his protection and may you each live in His love in this life and the next, where destiny leads you to the great kingdom of God's love where we are all one. Let this love change you, you won't regret it. I love you, and I am your friend in God's love, Fred Rogers. Won't you be my neighbor?

Chapter 4: VOICES OF THE BIBLE

The Bible is an amazing book but it is more like a library spanning nearly a thousand years of history and includes all kinds of literature: stories of creation, historical tales, political history of tribes and nations, poetry, apocalyptic writings, gospels, etc. And though much of it is inspired by spirit guidance and by God's spirit, parts of it are merely human writings written to advance a particular political / theological point of view. And in some Evangelical Protestant and Orthodox Jewish traditions the view that the Bible is the 'literal word of God' or 'inerrant' is not the viewpoint of many biblical scholars and certainly not the point of view of the Celestial spirits who have communicated to me.

The spirits mentioned in the Bible whose messages I have channeled are a disparate lot especially when considered from their lives on earth. In some cases they lived in different parts of the Middle East or were separated by centuries of time. They are male and female, some spoke different languages and they had different views of who God is and how to relate to the divine. But at a basic level they all had a faith and trust that God was real and that prayer was the means by which to communicate and petition Him.

They all came to me as advanced spirits who have been transformed by God's love and who wish to communicate this truth to us on earth. And they all acknowledge that Jesus was the first human being to be fully transformed by Divine Love to the extent that his soul has become at one with the great soul of God and has entitled him to be the master of the Celestial heavens.

You may wonder what people like Jesus and the apostles and other people known from the Bible might say if they were with us today. In fact they are eager to share their wisdom and advice with us. And the messages from the biblical characters may cause all of us to rethink and reimagine the truth that inspired them and the learning and soul development they have made since their time on earth. The key point they wish to communicate is that God's truth is always about unconditional, everlasting, and always present love. This Divine Love is transformative and enables human beings to partake of the very essence of God, not only being created in the image of God.

People may be influenced by many kinds of spirits, both vexed or dark spirits and more advanced and full of love spirits. This book only contains communications from the most advanced and enlightened angels who encourage us to advance towards at-onement with God, to desire to be on the path of roses, to be filled with God's love. They know this is not an easy path and it has many roots and rocks that may cause us to stumble. So they come to encourage us and to confirm how wonderful is the journey and our ultimate destination.

Our lives on earth are full of spiritual ups and downs with times of hope and despair, of joy and sadness, anger, frustration but also of happiness and good will. Unfortunately many people in the modern world no longer acknowledge that there are spirits who are near us and try to influence us. So my message to you the reader is similar to the message John the beloved told to his community in the New Testament about which spirits to trust. 'Test the spirits.' In other words ask the question, if what is being communicated or felt in your soul is of love, Divine Love, or is it something inharmonious and negative.

If the thoughts or feelings are not of love they are not coming from God or a Celestial spirit. And if your spiritual community or belief system says the Bible is infallible, then in loving kindness I ask you to reconsider the parts of the Bible that are condemnatory of individuals or nations, or exclude certain people from God's salvation. In my view, based on what the angelic spirits are communicating through me, those parts of the Bible are not from God but simply from the minds and beliefs of the biblical writers and transcribers, for God never condemns, never judges, never hates and always forgives.

Noah

God's Love Is Your Spiritual Lifeboat
September 29, 2020

I am here Noah. My dear boy you ask about the flood and about the details and circumstances of my life on earth so long ago. There was indeed a flood. I perceived this and I did indeed build a craft for my family and for some animals. I had warned others about the coming events, and I was known as someone who had dreams and premonitions - as someone who could foresee events, and often people would come and inquire. Others thought me strange, or perhaps a bit crazy, as you would say. In those days this was not so unusual.

Whether or not I was taken seriously was another matter and I was not taken as seriously in this matter as what I perceived would happen. Many died in this flood but not all. The part of the world where we were was inundated with rain and high waters and many perished, so it seemed as though we were the only survivors, and of course the accounts of this episode were greatly enhanced in the biblical records to make a point, including the size of the craft and its ability to carry all the animal species of the world.

Of course, I can tell you these would not have fit into the great structure that the biblical record records, and I could not have built such a structure. But I did have faith and I did have precognition, so my family was saved. There are no remnants left of that vessel. I can also tell you the purpose of the story is to have faith and follow one's guidance. If you can apply it to these current times, the events occurring on earth presently, then consider that my story will be most helpful to you.[43] And as you know you have perceived these events and the seriousness of them, and you have told others. Your friend has received many communications on this issue, and they have been documented, recorded and written down.

Whether or not you come together as a community physically may or may not happen, but I do commend you for coming together spiritually, asking for guidance, and praying for God's love on your spiritual lifeboat that your souls will survive and be blessed for all eternity regardless of earth events. This is a wonderful and most precious undertaking, and we here acknowledge it and encourage it and are quite happy to assist. As for the physical, follow your guidance without fear. God will provide and we shall guide you. It is love.

We are watching over you all with great love every day, every night, everywhere you are in these troubled times.[44] Have faith. God bless you. My dear brother, I thank you. With all my love to you and all. I am Noah.

---

43 Noah explained some time back the real cause of the huge flood he experienced - it was earth changes such as we are currently experiencing once again.

44 A reference to the global Covid-19 pandemic

Moses

WE ARE PROVIDED FOR
April 10, 2019

I am Moses and I come to speak about God's care for all of His children. In my time, I went from the riches of the palace to the wanderings in the desert. I wondered, 'How will we feed these people? How will they be cared for? Where will we sleep? What will happen to us?' So, I prayed, and every need was taken care of.

I look in on your beautiful sanctuary. You have things we could not even have dreamed of in our world. You have ways of communication, transportation, access to food, warmth, and shelter. You have been provided for so beautifully and you will continue to be provided for. Yes, if you ask you shall receive, but you must ask in faith, as I did. I believed God would provide. Though I did at times have my doubts, I just prayed harder, and everything was provided to me.

All things will be provided to you. As I told my spiritual grandson here whom I have been with for a long time, we shall lead the people to the promised land of God's love, which is truly the promised land, where the soul is transformed. You touch on the Celestial heavens, in these realms where we live and dwell. This is your future. Do not think for a moment that there are not angels, so many angels at your beck and call, working with you, providing for you, the heavenly Father providing for us all.

So have faith and do not be troubled. We are there for you. God's love has blessed you all and will continue to do so. I send you my love and my blessings. So many of us here are watching over you, helping you. We will continue to do so. May God bless you all. I am your brother in God's love, Moses. My love to all.

MAY YOU FEEL THE LOVE RADIATING FROM YOUR HEART
September 8, 2019

My children of the earth, from where I have long been gone, but come today. You have begun this journey with your souls reaching out and longing for the Creator's love. You have begun to feel this golden light of love in your souls, radiating from your heart, from your solar plexus. This, I tell you, is the true alchemy, turning the image into the very substance, your souls made in that image, becoming at one with the Creator in receiving this love that the Creator has for all.

It is not an intellectual pursuit. You need not read a thousand books or try to consider every aspect of everything that enters your mind. You only need to open your heart to allow these longings of your souls to go out to our glorious Creator, who then showers you with love, as in this beautiful circle that you have, that is expanding around the world, your world. But you are joined by many in the Celestial heavens as you create this larger and larger lattice of light, a circle of love.

We in the Celestial heavens and I, who have been a spirit for many thousands of years, salute you and honor you and welcome you on this journey, this never-ending journey, now filled with the golden love of our Creator. I come to offer my love and blessings. May you all be transformed that you will join us sooner than you imagine, in God's Celestial heaven.

May God bless you. My love and blessings to all. I am Moses.

Elizabeth

ONE IN GOD'S LOVE
June 16, 2020

I am here Elizabeth. I am the mother of John, the one they call the Baptist, and the aunt of the master on earth and the sister of Mary. There is a great longing, and I would say emotion, coming from the women in this community to hear more from the voices of those of us in the Celestial realm that are your sisters. The depth of your feeling is very evident to those of us here. The depth of your prayers. You are indeed the nurturers on the earth. You give birth, you embrace, and you feel deeply.

There is a difference between male and female on the earth, perhaps many differences, but as the mother's love that signals the embrace of God's love is here, many men are drawn, as in this circle. I must tell you that in the Celestial heavens any variation between male and females is irrelevant and eventually disappears because of the balance in God's love. As you pray and as the love of God enters your souls, each one of you, all these things that seem to separate you, find equanimity and balance and oneness. This is where the path of God's love shall lead you in joy and in glory and in happiness.

It's hard to conceive of but I tell you we are joyous for this gathering of such beautiful souls, both women and men. May the gift of God's love bring you to oneness, change you, bless you on earth and on your journey here to the kingdom of God's love. I am your sister and friend, a disciple of the master, and one with you in the love of God. I am Elizabeth.

John The Baptist

SPIRITUAL METAMORPHOSIS
December 31, 2021

I come in the love of God. I am the one they call the Baptist, the cousin of the master, and the forerunner to those who became baptized in the new birth. For the water I baptized with became through the master the 'living waters' imbued with the spirit of God.

The change that comes upon the soul that is open to receiving the essence of the Creator has often been compared to the metamorphosis of the caterpillar that crawls, forms a chrysalis, and emerges a beautiful and new creature with wings. It is not a perfect analogy, but certainly you can see the difference between a crawling caterpillar and a beautiful butterfly ascending into the heavens. This is your journey, your destiny, as you discard the old and embrace the new.

Here in the spirit world, we also have new chapters, new beginnings, but no spirit ever takes a step backwards: there is only progression. On earth I know it seems, as they say, that you take one step forward and two steps back or two steps forward and one step back. But in reality, you have always moved forward for progression is the law in the Universe. Although some may stagnate and seem to flounder, all souls eventually seek love and progress.

On your journey many of you have experienced tragedy, loss, abuse, addictions and so forth. The material mind looks for material solutions, instant gratification, and the self-satisfaction of the senses. Yet, at some point by the grace of God, the soul gets clarity and begins to seek out that love which not only lifts one up but transcends the ups and downs, the comings and goings. For this love is the essence of God and it is eternal. This baptism in spirit, as we say, brings each soul to the happiness and joy and love that it is seeking. My dear ones, brothers and sisters, this you know. So be it!

May you bring this gift, this truth to all. For it is the gift of the soul. As you walk into this new year may the love of God give you the guidance necessary for the times ahead and may you know we are never far away. When you call, we come. I thank you for allowing me this time, and I shall step back in prayer with you in the glory of God's love, in the luminance of this circle of light. May we all be blessed. I am John the Baptist. Go in peace!

Mary

BLESS THE CHILDREN IN GOD'S LOVE
September 1, 2019

I am here Mary. I come today with my son, for I too am a follower, as is Joseph. I come with a mother's love and with God's love. My band and I, we nurture the prayers of those who are open to us, but we also protect them.

Joseph and I, we had eight children,[45] Joseph the natural father of all of them. We became a holy family, followers of our eldest, Jesus. But truly, we are all children of the Father, our heavenly Father. My son brought the message of the transformation of the soul in God's love, as he was the first to receive this transformation. But he did not, and does not, wish to be set apart and worshiped. His wish is that all become transformed in God's love, the soul transformed from the mere image to the very substance of our loving Creator, all of us one in God's love and yet, each soul unique.

I speak also to the mothers here, that our charge is to nurture and protect. When you pray and you open up your heart and your soul to God's love, this light reaches your children, and this is all that is necessary. All else is, as they say, icing on the cake. So, remember, this love is the leaven in the bread to make it rise up above this world to touch on heaven's door.

---

45 In an earlier message (2001) Judas named all the children, and they are : Jesus, James, Simon, Judah, Joses, Thomas, Rachel and Lea. Eight in all. That means Jesus had seven brothers and sisters.

We come when you call. You wonder: 'How can this be? Mary and Joseph, Jesus and the other angels: so many!' But as Joseph said, you are precious cargo, so you draw us near, and we come close. I come with a mother's love and God's love, and I wish to offer this blessing to each of you.

Let your worries drift away, your concerns, your doubts, and your hurts. Where you have held anger, allow your heart to forgive. This blesses you as much as the one you forgive, allows your soul to open to Divine Love, allows a healing. I embrace you, as Mother Mary. Joseph embraces you. Jesus embraces you as he did with the blessing.

May the love of the Father touch each one of you and stay with you on your journey. Have no doubt, we will protect you. We love you so. Stay in the light and the love, this gift from above. My love and blessings and embrace to all of you. May God bless you. I am Mother Mary.

Jesus

Honestly, though I have the deepest appreciation of what I believe are the true teachings and life of Jesus of Nazareth, I never wished to receive communications from him since there are so many people claiming to do so already. I grew up in the Catholic tradition but later rejected the orthodox teachings of Christianity in favor of the more embracing Hindu scriptures and teachers which recognized the divinity of Jesus and his teachings of God's love. I also found myself diving deep into Sufism, Buddhist writings, yoga, meditation, Jewish scriptures, as well as being inspired by teachers from many traditions.

After I had a direct Divine Love experience with two Celestial angels in 1987, I began to study the messages of James R. Padgett contained in the four volumes entitled "The True Gospel Revealed Anew by Jesus," which shed an entirely different light on the life and teachings of master Jesus. I began to embrace the message of Divine Love where it was extant in many religions (however obscured it had become) including Christianity, Hinduism, Sufism, and Judaism.

When I would feel his presence during a prayer and meditation session, I would ask him not to give me a message (yes, I know that sounds terrible). Every time that happened, John the Apostle (the beloved) would come forward to speak. One evening Jesus came to me when I was alone and said he would like to give me a message in private and that I could record it, and if I did not wish to share it with others that would be fine. Feeling I had nothing to lose and no embarrassment to gain, I agreed. Only a few occasions have I felt simultaneously overwhelmed and at the same time comfortable enough to allow a message to come through from Jesus. I am humbled and grateful to have received them.

How I Love You
June 2, 2021

I am here your brother, your eternal friend. I walk in love, I speak in love, I sing in love, I heal in the love of God.

Words, beautiful as they may be, fall short in describing with proper eloquence divinity in these realms of light, in these abodes, so far above the earth plane where we see your pain and understand your concerns. We come in your prayer knowing that as God brings His love into your soul, there will come faith, there will come trust, and there will come insight. The sacred journey of the heart will find the path of immortality and happiness which may be inconceivable to the mortal mind but can be fathomed by the soul.

When one walks in faith and allows God in one's walk, all things are in grace and in the harmonious flow of Divine Love where every heart is healed. Every wound, every affliction, every hurt, is dissolved in the balm of God's touch. I come with open arms awaiting your hearts to join me that you too will rise above all that concerns you, all that keeps you bound. The love of God unshackles every prisoner, frees every soul. Join me, take my hand. Let go and, as is said, and I shall say, 'Let God. Be still, feel His grace. How I love you, you cannot count the ways.'

Every Soul Has a Choice
December 14, 2021

The gift of free will is a gift of choice. It allows every soul to decide which path to take. It allows for each soul to discern its destination on earth, and more importantly, beyond - in spirit. What is given is a reminder to be aware that you may be awakened in God's love, the somnambulant world is being tested by everything that is happening on earth at present. For most the response is fear; and fear is a resistance to the openness of love. It is a closed heart.

The love of God changes every soul, opens every heart to the sacredness of life, to the preciousness of every soul. One begins to get a sense of the eternal. It requires persistence, it requires you to be in touch with the longings, the deep longings in your souls, that send you into prayer. And our heavenly Father's response which is to touch you, to fill you, to change you.

When you are in God's grace you feel empathy for all of humanity, even those who may hate you. This is what is required: that you may show the world the love in your soul which is the love of God so those in darkness may see the light. Please know I give you my humble blessing. The magnificence of God humbles every soul, and in that there is great glory and treasure. So, trust and have faith.

I love you with all the love in my soul, and I shall be your friend through all eternity where we are all one in God's love, I am Jesus. God Bless You.

Jude

EVERY JOURNEY BEGINS WITH A FIRST STEP
December 30, 2021

May the light of God be upon you, may it illumine your souls so that you may carry your light into the world. It is said, 'every journey begins with a first step.' When you consider things that you have brought to fruition, you can recount the steps, the chapters, the verses, the moments that led to the finale or the completion. If you take every day one step towards that which you wish to be, that which you wish to create, you will come to the fruition of your wishes. And though the journey is eternal, you begin to see the progression from finite to infinite. You begin to sense that which is a blessing to your soul, that sustains it, and transforms it. So, have faith, take heart, take that step. God will open the way for you on your journey.

I have not come before to this one, but I have made him aware of my presence the last few days. I am Jude, brother of James, Joseph, Simon, Joses, Rachel, Lea, and our beloved brother Jesus. I thank you and I shall come again, with your permission. With all my love and the grace of God, may peace be upon you.

Mary Magdalene

ALLOW THE BLESSINGS OF GOD'S LOVE TO COME INTO YOUR SOUL
July 12, 2022

I am here, Mary Magdalene. I live in a sphere high in the Celestial realms. I came into your discussion about discernment and perceiving the truths of God's kingdom with the soul. Most are aware of my occupation while on earth, and some are aware of my status in my community of Magdala. You may find it odd that I was a friend of many women, housewives, prostitutes of course, and both the young and old women of my community, but that is the truth.

It is purported that I had the greatest understanding of the master's teachings when on earth. I will tell you there's some truth to this, but as there were many followers of Jesus, there were also others who felt the love of God, and with their souls could comprehend the master's words as I did. And in those days as now, most people were occupied with material things, material distractions, material concerns.

To those who find themselves in crisis and begin to see the futility of trying to find happiness and freedom in the possession of material things or the self-satisfaction of the senses, they begin to pray, each in their own way, for a healing, for truth, for redemption. And though they may not use the words, they aspire for their souls to finally be in ascendancy over their minds, and for their hearts to open that their souls may be blessed. In your complex world this is truly the simplest of things though it requires setting aside all else for your time with your Creator, so that when you open your heart and your soul to Him, His love will come pouring into your soul without fail. Be still and relax that mind. Allow the blessing of God's love to come into your soul. More and more you will begin to see the results as the depth of your prayers bring deep love and all your gifts to flourish.

Lastly, I say this, give yourselves time however you can, away from the world, and the news, and the vibrations of fear and bewilderment, and come into the safety and glory with us in the love of God. My dear ones, I thank you. Go in the love of God. I am Mary Magdalene.

Andrew

Plant the Seeds of God's love
August 29, 2020

I am here, Andrew, a disciple of the master and a dear friend of my brother Judas. As you may know, I came to Judas when he was in the hells to give him hope, to let him know that he was forgiven, to lead him again to the light and love of God which was his initial aspiration. All of this is well documented in the writings of James Padgett, and in this wonderful book[46] that you are studying.

My purpose in coming is to use my experience with Judas as a template for how things work between souls whether in spirit or on earth. Let me give you an example. You tell someone about Divine Love, about the path of prayer, about the transformation of souls and the truths as you understand them, from what you have read and from your own experience. And although their souls may get this, their minds reject it. They are either simply not interested, or in fact, quite in opposition to these unorthodox ideas.

It may be many years later whether in spirit or on earth, they come to a point of crisis, an epiphanic moment, when they begin to see and remember what you told them, and they call on you and you show them the light and they see the condition of your soul. And I may say, even on earth they can be capable of recognizing the condition of light, of joy, in your soul, in comparison to the condition of their souls and the darkness.

It is never a wasted effort when you lovingly speak the truth, when you tell a story of God's grace, a miracle, an overcoming that you had from a dark condition to one of light. When you tell another this, you have planted a seed. And eventually those you have told will have the opportunity to revisit the truths you have conveyed to them. To water that seed and watch it grow in their own soul. There are many ways to do this. One does not need to be a proselytizer and be overbearing. If one can show, by example, of the love in their soul, of a kindness, of a story, of a song, and so forth, this will have an effect, on down the road, as they say.

---

46 The book, 'Judas of Kerioth.'

So, we encourage you to share your stories, to share your journey, and above all to continue praying for God's love and studying these wonderful messages which our dear brother Judas has given. I thank you for this opportunity, for I have not spoken through this one before and I am pleased with his efforts. May God bless you each with the great inflowing of Divine Love. I am your brother in the love of God. I am Andrew.

Simon Peter

CONSIDER WHAT IT IS TO BE TRANSFORMED IN DIVINE LOVE
October 11, 2021

My dear brothers and sister in the love of God, I ask each one to consider from the heart, from their soul, what it is to be transformed in Divine Love, from the mortal to the divine angel. Though I was considered the first leader of what became the Christian church, I was simply a mortal man touched by the love of God, and a follower of the master, though three times I denied it.

After the Resurrection and the Pentecost's showering of God's love, it is fair to say I did indeed become 'the Rock,' from Simon to Peter. What has occurred in the centuries that followed this humble beginning is full of light and love and also of sin and error. As your community grows, your church without walls, it is important to remember that each one of you is beloved by God. You have been given much truth, many messages, enough to fill books. You have songs of praise that allow you to open your heart and prayers to carry you. You need not depend on any person for your redemption, for your salvation, for your transformation, only God and the truths you have been given. For, as in my day and the days that followed, the human nature of men so corrupted the beautiful message of master Jesus that it took nearly 2000 years to correct it.

Keep the fires burning in your heart, the light in your soul. If you find yourself in doubt, unsure of which way to go, follow the path of love, for each soul knows what love is and what is not. The love of God, may it be your guide in all things, in all ways, beyond the ken of men, the allure of this world, the distractions and manifestations that are presented to you, for in the love of God, you are lifted above all, beyond this world.

I know of what I speak. I do not wish to demean the work of this one or any other but only to remind you, you are worthy. You are just as much a child of God as any other. Go deep in this prayer. Open your heart that the Holy Spirit of God may open your soul and fill it with love, love everlasting.

I shall join you in this prayer and all those here. I am your humble servant, your brother in Christ. I am Simon Peter. Go in peace.

John, The Beloved

GOD IS LOVE
June 15, 2020

I am here John, a disciple of the master and one that comes in God's love. This gift from the heavenly Father that the master gave us: the truth while he was on earth, he continues to teach and bring in the heavens and on earth. This truth embraces all others: that God is love. These words made it into my gospel though it was interpolated, translated, and retranslated many, many, times but that great truth stood, and still stands. This love of God, let it be your guide, let it flow in your lives.

May your words be filled with the essence and the glory of His love. You who wish to be transformed - you know the way and we are with you and we are drawn to help you and guide you at your bidding and in answer to your prayers. May this love, this divine distraction be yours. May God bless you and keep you in His grace every hour, every day, every night for all your days. You are loved. I am your brother in Christ. I am John.

SPREAD LOVE BY EVERY MEANS AVAILABLE!
January 20, 2021

I am here, your brother in Christ, John. I come on this day of hope,[47] the rays of love descending upon the earth, rejoicing. As you read those words that were given to James Padgett by myself and others, most especially on the laws of rapport and communication, I ask you to take

---

47 Change of administrations in the U.S.A. government.

them in with your souls, that they may resonate with your being. For indeed they are of great importance.

I come to encourage this one receiving this message to go ever deeper in his prayer that his soul may be able to communicate the highest truths. He is indeed well on his way despite his reluctance, and I would say at times, resistance. I wish to thank all those here for their encouragement of this medium, for these messages received here will reach many, beyond your vision.

It is important at this time to reach out in as many ways as you can with the truth of God's love. If you can do this in song, so be it. In poetry, so be it. In film, so be it. In telling a tale, so be it. For there are many ways to receive the truth and there are many expressions. The reason for this being that the diversity of souls creates a situation where many different channels are used to inspire and bring the truth of God's love and the higher truths of the spirit world to all humankind.

When you touch the heart of any human something opens and the heart supersedes the mind, and things that were once tightly held beliefs, take a backseat to the great driver of divine truth and the presence of God's love. This is why we often say if you cannot reach someone with words, just love them, encourage them, bring them music and inspiring words. This you all do with each other, and you see how it lifts you up and moves you to prayer in this receiving of the beautiful gift of God's love. I shall come again, and I am pleased with the reception of what I had to say and delighted with your small group of devout souls, which in reality is a much larger group that you will one day see. May the light and love of the Creator be with you, stay with you. On this day of joy may each of you indulge in the happiness that is yours. Let your light shine my dear friends. God bless you. I am your brother in Christ. I am John.

Luke (The Physician)

Hearing from Luke the physician is always a deeply rewarding experience. He not only is a commanding presence but a healing force. He has that very Celestial and powerful combination of authority and love second only in my experience to Jesus and very much like another apostle, John the beloved. During my time with Care, she expressed loving the messages that James R. Padgett had received from Luke, her favorite after the ones from master Jesus. The clarity and gentle truths that come through Luke can be so beautiful as to be considered scriptural in nature. I am honored to receive from Luke messages that I truly hope are helpful to others on their spiritual journey.

The Magnetism of God's Love
September 23, 2019

I am here, Luke. When I walked the earth, the master had asked that we go out and preach the good news of God's love without regard to culture, race, where one resided, or what they believed. We were in fact not asked to start a new religion, but to bring news of God's love to all. This request is still the same as it was then.

And you see how things have become organized and institutionalized in the world. This is the way of the world. And quite often those who are good at this job of organizing and creating institutions are not so good at opening their hearts and souls to the love of God. Not because they are bad people, but because they have an intellectual understanding that does not include the opening of their soul. I say to you - it is important, to touch the heart of all with kindness and love, always forgiveness. Or, as the master said, 'love all as I have loved you' and you know he meant with God's love. This is the divine balm that he offered the human world.

We in the Celestial heavens have nothing but love for you. Can you feel this? We live in a realm of light. It is beyond the imaginings of those on the earth plane. I say your soul can sense this, it can see this light, it can feel the love.

Yes, your job is not to be too distracted. And yet, you live in the world. We understand. So, live in the world and be above it. Or live in the world and not live in the world at the same time, with your soul in God's love, and your feet upon earth. In this way you can move forward. You can move mountains. You can touch hearts. The magnetism of God's love attracts every soul that is open and longing for it. Just plant those seeds. This is all you need do. Be not concerned for the harvest. For that is God's business.

We wish to say - and to remind you - there is much love from this realm to all of you on the earth. Those who wish to progress in this love - we are with you. Acknowledge this and know it is closer than you imagine. We are with you, and we love you. Go in God's grace and peace. And know I am your brother and friend in Christ, Luke.

Be Aware of What Is in Your Heart
July 3, 2020

I wish to comment on the heart and the longings of the soul. If you could see into each soul laid bare, the desires, the longings, the physical appetites, the prejudices, the beliefs and so forth, all of which are of the mind but are held in the soul, you would see that the afflictions of the heart represent the disparity between the two. For the soul in its essence makes no distinctions, and in the case of all these in this circle, the longings are to be at one with their Creator, our loving Creator.

If you must be serious, and many of you are very serious, be serious about your happiness that comes with your soul receiving the Father's love. For as I said about your heart being where your treasure lies, if your heart is in sorrow, you will draw that, if your heart is in joy and in happiness and in the Divine Love, you become a magnet for that grace and goodness and you will draw unto yourself. We here ask you each to be aware of what is in your heart and the thoughts you hold, and allow your souls to take precedence in the longings for God's love so that your hearts may be in joy and that you may walk this earth, not without compassion and empathy for suffering for the hungry, the homeless, the marginalized, but in fact with great compassion and the love of God in your souls so you will bring joy even there.

May God bless each one with a great inflowing of His love. I am your brother in Christ, Luke. God bless you.

Let Love be Your Guide
July 10, 2020

God has given you all a soul and a heart and a mind. The mind is a wonderful organ of discrimination. It allows one to tell one thing from another, to be able to define things and therefore it's a very good gift for navigating the world. The heart is the center that pumps the blood through the body, oxygenating it, allowing the life force to permeate the physical body. It is also the doorway to the soul, or one can say, the seat of the soul. The emotions come into the heart by way of the mind and are how the mind perceives. The soul wishes to receive truth. It opens to love. If you wish to know if what is being presented to you is of the mind or of the soul, I encourage you to make this measurement by means of the feeling of love.

When someone loves you, it is wonderful to hear them speak their words, but in fact does this not only confirm what you already felt from them? For if they tell you they love you and you do not feel the love, you don't believe them. Your heart knows the difference and your soul certainly does. When a message comes through and frightens you, disturbs your mind, and it is not filled with love, this is not of the soul, and this is not something you need to take in.

When you feel the love, it is a blessing to your whole being. If you think that this love of God - this great gift - has not been felt demonstrably, it is only because your mind is in the way. I can tell each one of you is receiving this gift of God's love inflowing into your souls for the simple asking, the simple yearning and longing. We do not wish for any of you to be disturbed, frightened, or in doubt because this love conveys the truth that every good and perfect gift is given to all from the father who takes care of all His children in love and provides for each one.

Discern what touches your heart and fills your soul with love as truth. Allow it to be your compass and your guide. Be not afraid, for the love of God connects you to His Celestial heavens. How blessed you are to have this truth. Thank you for hearing my message through this one. I am pleased with it.

May God bless you with the glorious gift of His love. I am your brother in Christ who loves you. I am Luke.

THE THOUGHTS YOU ENTERTAIN
September 1, 2020

My brothers and I and our two sisters have been with you today listening to your conversation. We are gently guiding you, influencing you, though not interfering with your free will, for we will never do that. I wish to stress the importance of the thoughts you entertain and the entertainment that influences your thoughts. You are all aware of the world and the negatively and the violence and greed and darkness which has caused so many to lash out in anger because the material world does not fulfill the needs of the soul.

I see children completely absorbed in games that, in the context of love, must be considered inappropriate. These games have filtered down from their source in the military in many forms but there is often a lot of killing and violence. There is also a lot of energy and adrenaline, the outcome of which is a kind of numbness to the pain and suffering in the real world caused by such actions. I will give you an example. Someone playing a video game and they are able from a drone or an airplane to drop bombs, to take out targets (as you would say) and watch things explode and make thunderous sounds. They later find themselves in a real-life situation where their only reference point has been a game and now, they are dealing with real lives and real guns. When the pain of the actual weapons is felt, of course the recipient knows without a doubt that they have been mistaken. This is not a good thing in terms of what they have done or participated in and yet their recognition and realization of the wrong in a sense is a good thing.

And so, you see in the spirit world people that have participated in these kinds of things, and there are untold numbers of them that have been in wars or gangs, or in personal violence, and they must often have their realization in spirit. And like our dear brother Judas, they see the ugliness that results and the place of darkness where they abide. And yes, we go to them and, in fact, it is the activity of many spirits to visit and offer hope and light to them.

Occasionally those of us here in the highest realms, the Celestial realms, and even the master himself visit the hells and the lower spheres, as you have read. But, as if shining a huge spotlight on someone in darkness, it is often necessary and better to send someone closer to the sphere these souls are in, but a higher sphere. This is how spirits help one another and this is the story of Judas and so many others. I mention this to you because it is our wish not only that you will help others to climb out of the darkness, to be healed and to see the state of their souls, but that each one of you will experience transformation while on earth. That your very presence will shine a light on the darkness. So, if you entertain spiritual thoughts, watch spiritual film-video, assist others, and stay in the longing of your souls to be in the light and love of God, it will only cost you a little time and prayer and God will bless you as He is in this very moment.

I thank this brother for taking a long message he did not expect, and I am happy with its reception. We all send you our love and blessings in the grace of God and we thank you for your efforts, for your service. I am your brother in Christ and a disciple of the master, I am Luke.

Choose What Touches Your Soul
September 11, 2020

I came in to follow your conversations and to accompany the beautiful spirit Care. I wish to speak to young Michael. As you explore the many facets of the Divine Love path, the highways and byways, the heights, and the depths, remember your soul and what nourishes the longings in your soul. Though you receive information with your mind, our wish for you is to hold on to those things which touch your soul, and of course in this regard, I speak to you all.

There is an endless amount of material on the earth plane in terms of spirituality, metaphysics, extraterrestrials, and so forth. It is not my place to tell you specifically what you should investigate in this regard, except as I have said, when it touches your soul, that is something worth pursuing. And as often attributed to me in one form or another but originates in the gospel of Matthew, 'For where your heart is, therein your treasure lies', you can use this as your template. For when your heart is touched, most especially in joy and happiness, in the excitement of the new, and above all in love, this is good for your soul. Of course, in God's love, this is the greatest, and it is our wish for you.

How wonderful it is that you are going through these messages given by Judas to the brother in Ecuador because they are contemporary and speak to the current day and are in harmony to a great degree with what James Padgett and Dr. Samuels received and what this dear brother receives from us. It is all about God's love.

May you all receive every good and perfect and beautiful gift as we engage with you, inspire you, influence you, and walk this path, because you have asked. May you go in the grace of God and his love. I thank you. I am your brother in Christ, and a disciple of the master, I am Luke.

God's Love Opens the Heart and Transforms the Soul
April 26, 2021

I come in the presence of the most holy God of all. The God of love. For is it not love that brings you here? Is it not love that heals? Is it not love that lifts your soul up? Does not this love of God bring faith? Is it not the answer to your hopes, your dreams, your desires to be transformed in love, to be changed?

It is love, the love of God, that opens the heart, that transforms the soul so that at some point you are lifted above this world, lifted above your material concerns in the bliss and glory that is yours for your soul's asking, your soul's longings. It is this great love of God that permeates this circle of light and brings many, many, many, in the spirit world, attracted to the light. And although some would not hear me in the spirit world, they come to this realm attracted, as I say, to the light and the love here in this circle.

I say to all, allow God to open your souls with His most Holy Spirit to bestow this gift of love that you feel in this moment, in this presence. Have faith, trust. For God so loves all of you and showers you with this great gift in this moment and beyond. Your intention is true. May the great peace and glory of the love of God be yours and all here. I thank you my dear ones. With all my love and blessings from above. I am your friend and brother in Christ. I am Luke.

Seek Ye First the Kingdom
July 27, 2021

You can see from your studies today how a soul, even with a drop of love, can help another struggling soul, provided they allow of their free will to be helped, provided that their soul sends up the longing. And so it is on earth, those of you with this love of God in your souls can lift up those who perhaps unknowingly are asking for this love. And with your guidance and with your patience, they will come around to prayer. I would say it is important to remember that the mind is capable of believing many things, some in truth, others in error. The mind seems in fact, indefatigable in its thirst for knowledge, and those here that inhabit the higher natural spheres are ever seeking out more knowledge of the universe, of how things work, and at the highest level have a sense of universal consciousness and oneness, and this is to be distinguished from the very substance of the soul being at one with its Creator.

Those of us in the Celestial heavens, we too explore these things and delight in all creation. But our longings are in ascendancy over the material mind as the desires of our souls are the deep longings for love, Divine Love. We do not experience the ebb and flow in the tides of natural love but surely, we can see them, just as we can see the condition of the soul reflected in the spirit body of each one.

Robert Lees is around guiding you in your readings, and as you can understand he was given a great many truths, and therefore should you wish to disseminate his writings, he would be profoundly grateful to you as they are sanctioned in truth. So again, I remind you on behalf of all your guides, many who are with us as I speak, and the dear sister Care who wishes me to tell you she was so delighted to see her dear friend, the mother of her grandson, come into this circle however briefly today, and this one I am speaking through could feel her joy, and so I will express it for him. As Judas has been with him and wishes to continue, as does the lovely Clare who brings her brightness and grace and blessings, and many others. It is said repeatedly by those of us here: 'Seek ye first the kingdom, and all else will be given to you.'

You who have chosen this path, I ask you to keep this in your souls, follow your heart's desire for the love of God, and every day will be a blessing, a miracle, on your journey in Divine Love, to the Celestial realms, and the transformation of your souls. With all my love and blessings and in the grace of God go in peace. I am Luke, God bless you.

WALK IN FAITH

November 1, 2021

When you truly love another, it energizes them, for you radiate true love. And to those who are open, they feel your love. It gives them hope, it sustains them, comforts them.

The master had spoken to his disciples about having the faith of a mustard seed, a very small seed, that produced a beautiful plant. And he often admonished them when we did not walk in faith, but of course, in a loving way. I learned of these things through brother Paul who had met James and Peter after his conversion. When you come to prayer in that faith that you will receive an answer, with the deep longings in your souls for the love of God, you receive this gift, however small, that will ultimately blossom into a new creature, transformed. Allow faith to guide you, knowing that the heavenly Father never refuses his children that come in faith and sincere longings for his Divine Love. There is the faith of a child trusting its parents. There is the faith of the traveler to arrive safely at their destination. There is the faith of one who is ill to expect a miracle.

The answer to your prayers is not always the one that you might expect, but it is always the right one. As you come in prayer, your soul, activated by God's love, enables you to walk in faith. To bring this gift to your day, to your family, to your friends, to the world, and yes, even to your enemies.

So, my dear friends, as you're praying for the love of God and your soul receives it, be grateful for this gift, be grateful for your answered prayer, and with this gratitude in your heart, walk in faith. May the love of God be yours. I am your brother in Christ, I am Luke. Go with God, go in peace.

Paul

TOUCH OTHERS WITH LOVE AND EVERYTHING WILL FALL INTO PLACE
August 24, 2021

I am your brother in Christ, Paul, the Evangelist. I am sometimes credited with the spreading of the message of Jesus beyond the Jewish community to the Gentile world, and to a certain extent that is true.

As is the case with those who are credited with writing the Gospels, Epistles, and letters, much of what has been attributed to me I did not write. But I did write: "Though I speak with the tongues of angels, if I have not love, I am but a clanging bell."[48] So, in the context of your desire to spread the Gospel of God's love and the truths that you now have knowledge of, remember that words without love behind them will often fall upon deaf ears, or simply sound as a clanging bell.

I did have the love of God in my soul, and though some of what I understood was in error and not perfectly aligned with the master's teaching, the love that I possessed caused people to listen to my words.

---
48 1 Corinthians 13: 1

And yes, we had miracles and there were signs which were all a result of my prayer, my communion with God, and my faith.

I remind you to bring this love to those to whom you wish to share, and proclaim that they can receive it by going to God as you have. Touch them with this love first and foremost and everything will fall into place as you so desire. Because I am aware of your time today on earth,[49] I shall leave you with that. Be in God's love. Pray. Share. With all my love I am your brother and friend and a redeemed soul who is an inhabitant of God's Celestial heavens. I am Paul. May God bless you.

Thomas

THE SOUL TOUCHED BY GOD IS THE REAL PROOF
July 25, 2022

I am here, Thomas the Apostle. I come in the love of God, a disciple of the master and your brother in Christ. I wish to talk about proof and evidence, which in so many areas of life are required. Even in the area of mediumship those who channel are often called 'evidential mediums.' This is because someone can verify their relationship to the person that is coming through. This is a gift of the mind and a beautiful gift as it provides a window into life beyond the earth plane, of the existence of a life beyond in the spirit world.

I would say in general however, that while the spirits that speak through these mediums can be progressive, they are generally not on the path of Divine Love, and almost never celestials. Nevertheless, those who provide this service do a very good thing in acquainting those on the earth plane with their loved ones in the spirit world. Divine love mediums that we speak through, cannot generally provide evidential proof because we communicate soul to soul. And while the information goes through the brain and the language and the filters of the medium, the connection is a higher connection that only the soul can receive, of course translated to some extent by the brain and the language and knowledge of the medium.

You may know all too well the story of Thomas the doubter who required proof that the master had risen. And though he was told, though I was told, I wanted proof because I could not fathom that Jesus

---

[49] One person had another engagement to go to and would be leaving early.

could be present with us in physical form. So, I required physical proof, and the master provided the proof while he lovingly admonished me and the others to remember those who have not seen and yet believed, how blessed are those. I raise this subject because many on this path also at times want to require physical evidence, some manifestation, an appearance, in order to prove that we celestials are communicating.

But I tell you this, I understand the desire that you have, those of you who wish so much to feel, and touch, and see, that you can believe and have your faith strengthened. The manifestation of God's love in your soul is the real proof. It is the substance when possessed by the soul that is the true manifestation of what you all seek. This substance is brought about in humble prayer, in deep longing for God's love and its inflowing into your souls. So there will be those for whom seeing, and touching is believing, but how blessed are those who have felt the love of God in their very being as a real substance, His essence transforming your soul and lifting it in light and love.

I thank my brother for agreeing to take this message and for understanding that I do not wish to judge but to clarify a great truth. May the love of God fill each one, awaken each one, and transform each one. I am your brother from the Celestial kingdom. I am Thomas the Apostle. God bless you.

Nicodemus

COME TOGETHER AS A COMMUNITY
December 18, 2019

I am here Nicodemus. I wish to address those concerns about the future. I know you have been privy to information from the Celestial realms where I abide, and which comes from the master and others about the coming events on earth. These are earth changes, and the request is for you to create sanctuary, places of refuge so as to embrace the many, the diversity, all in God's love. We have asked you these things that you may go into prayer and be guided in the moment so that you would become accustomed to ongoing guidance through whatever changes occur. And you have been told a certain amount of chaos, turmoil, eruption, and displacement is on the horizon. I come to you in the hope that you ask for clarity in the light of God's love. That you will come together as a community so that you will have strength in numbers, strength in prayer, strength in truth and protection. Now is the time.

As we come through winter and into spring in the northern hemisphere be mindful of your garden internally and externally. In the southern hemisphere as we come into summer be wise, prepare, the harvest will be at hand and you will surely reap what has been sown, internally and externally. It is said 'prepare for the worst and hope for the best.' There is some wisdom in that, but there is even more wisdom in being in the flow of God's love, of being in the guidance. Yes, prepare externally, this has been requested, but also you must prepare internally that there may be harmony between your inner and outer worlds, that there will be a flow.

You may be required to leave your dwelling places due to the changes. This of course will be your choice. We do not interfere with your free will, your free choice but we say to those who are willing to face the changes, to present the truths of God's love to the world; 'come together.' This we ask: 'Come together in truth,' for God's love outshines every difference whether it be dogmatic, political, mindful. God's love embraces all. This oneness, let it be your template as you prepare. And on behalf of all those here I say: 'This is the time.'

I wish to say this in the most gentle and loving way but also to stress the urgency. Even though all somehow seems normal on the surface, there is a great rumbling beneath. There is a great wave coming across what may seem to be the calm and pacific ocean of somnambulance. Take heed! Pray for clarity and guidance and above all for God's love. For the sake of the earth, for the sake of the children, and grandchildren, and great grandchildren and on and on. For the souls of all, for the healing of the planet, for the transformation of every longing soul, pray!

I leave you with my love and blessings and gratitude to this instrument who was quite surprised that I wished to speak as he is alone and in prayer, but he knows there are many in prayer with him so in essence this is for all. May God bless you. May you open to guidance and know we are with you to offer protection and guidance and love. You are precious to all of us, each one, God bless you. I am your brother in the Celestial heavens, Nicodemus.

Stephen

SPEAK TO THE WORLD FROM YOUR SOUL
December 26, 2021

I am here Stephen, a disciple of the master, and the first one martyred for my beliefs. I come in the grace of God with love for all. As you may know, we were not learned men, with a few exceptions. Many of us had our own agendas, our own lenses through which we processed what the master gave us. Those who came seeking wisdom and knowledge to inform their minds were given (that) but were often disappointed, as the deeper message was always given to the soul.

Those of us in the Celestial realms communicate soul to soul and we allow the mind of the medium to use words so that you may all understand. This is, of course, why if I should speak through another, the words would be somewhat different but the intention the same. So, as I am speaking soul to soul, I am impressing upon this one the importance of those of you receiving the love of God in your souls, to speak to the world from your souls.

When you are speaking to one who seems challenged, whose mental faculties are distant, those you call as being on the spectrum, those with Down syndrome, Alzheimer's, and so forth, you can always speak to their souls. And if you come in the grace of God and you shine your light upon them, which is the light of God's love, they always respond. This will give you some idea of communicating soul to soul. And I know there are some in this group who are well aware of souls who may not be intellectually developed or who have lost, as we say, their train of thought, but who all respond to the vibrations of love. This is why you come into prayer that you may be in the vibration of love and more particularly in the grace of God's love, the highest vibration. Your souls, each one reaching out and the Creator blessing all, embracing all.

So, walk into the future whatever it may bring in the material world, amongst the changes on earth, amidst the turbulence, may you walk in peace, yes, the peace that passes understanding, in the grace of God. This is truly the gift to be giving and I know you will. I thank this one for allowing me this time and I now join you in Holy Communion for God's love.
Note: of interest - St Stephen's feast day is December 26th.

Chapter 5: Inspired Then, Angels Now

Mahatma Gandhi

Mohandas Gandhi(1869-1948) was an Indian lawyer, anti-colonial nationalist and political ethicist who employed nonviolent resistance to lead the successful campaign for India's independence from British rule. He inspired movements for civil rights and freedom across the world. Reverend Martin Luther King, Jr. was inspired by Gandhi's non-violent social change philosophy. (Wikipedia)

BE IN THE LOVE
June 23, 2020

I am your brother and friend Gandhi. I am your brother in Christ, and yes, a disciple of the master, in God's love. Thank you for allowing me to come. When I spoke the words: "Be the change you wish to see in the world," I meant that people should live in love, kindness, compassion, peace, non-violence and brotherhood and sisterhood. And whatever their spiritual beliefs they could be one in the love of God. So now if you reflect on my words, I wish you to see them in a new light, the light of God's love.

Be the change and be changed in God's love. Bring that to the world. Bring with it what you will in kindness and charity and whatever you can give on the material plane, but above all be present with the love that you hold in your souls. Give this gift, be this change. As you know, this is all that truly matters and this love, this love divine, will change everything. It will draw unto you every good and perfect gift. It will bring peace to wherever you walk. It will bring you protection and joy to your hearts. Oh, how we wish to see this in the world! Be the light because you are God's children, as are we. May the light of love of our glorious Creator be in your souls and shine forth from you to each one. God bless you all. I am your brother and friend and a redeemed soul and an inhabitant of the Celestial heavens. I am Gandhi.

THE LOVE OF GOD BRINGS PEACE
June 30, 2020

Namaste! I salute and recognize the Divine Love in your souls. As you may know I brought a message of non-violence, ahimsa, to my country where there was much violence and a great longing to be free from the yoke of colonialism. This message, this gospel of peace, has been a part of the teachings in India from ancient times, from the Jains and through Hinduism and all the various sects, there has been a call for peace and non- violence.

And yet in the world we see the followers of all these religions caught up in acts of revenge against injustice. I was very much involved in wanting social justice in my country but not through violence. Each one of you can see, as you look through your lives, that violence, and war and revenge has solved nothing. When I said, "an eye for an eye makes the whole world blind," I was drawing this from the great wisdom of master Jesus and his beautiful sermon on loving your enemies. And yet I saw even his followers bereft of keeping this in their souls.

As you view all of the injustice in your world you may feel this anger, and it is a righteous anger in your hearts and your souls, but I ask you to pray for the love of God that brings the peace that passes understanding. The gift you can give to this world is to love each one as God loves you with this Divine Love in your souls and create the change with love. We created a nation in this spirit of love. You who have been blessed in your souls with the light and the presence and the joy and the healing of God's love, we encourage you to bring this gift to the world. Bring this peace, bring this joy and yes, make change. May the love of God be with you all. May the peace and the joy of His grace be with each of you.

With all my love and blessings, I am your brother and friend in God's love, I am Gandhi.

White Eagle

I had a dream around the time White Eagle came to me and at the time I wasn't sure what it meant. I was walking in a very green field with a gently sloping hill to my right and a tree at ground level on the right just a few steps in front of me. I saw what appeared to be a pack of dogs in the distance slightly to my left except as they came closer, I could see they were of several breeds with a small white buffalo in their midst. The dogs seemed very excited to see me and came towards me very quickly which startled me and made me wonder if they were indeed friendly. As they came nearer, and I approached the tree I saw the small white buffalo veer off and head up the hill. Then I was beneath a beautiful tree and the dogs were upon me licking me and very happy to see me so I relaxed and gazed up the hill on my right to see what had happened to the small white buffalo. Lo and behold, there it was standing next to a very large white buffalo and looking down at me in a majestic and benevolent way. I felt so very loved.

Later I asked a First Nations friend in Canada what the dream meant. I was told the dogs represented the many tribes on earth coming together in love and the white buffalos were a symbol of that love and good fortune, that prayers were being answered and prophecy fulfilled.

White Eagle Comes To Offer Healing
March 29, 2020

I am here, White Eagle. I come to offer you a healing that your hearts be not troubled. In my time on earth, we relied on the Great Spirit, The Creator, God, for our spiritual sustenance and we had faith in the Creator who had provided us with a beautiful earth to sustain our bodies. It was not a perfect existence, but when it was peaceful, we knew the harmony of existence with the Great Spirit and His creations. We traded with others although we did not use what you would call money; mostly we bartered. When the tribes were in harmony it was a beautiful thing.

Those of us who relied on the Creator who opened our souls, and that part of the soul that can see beyond, we had visions. Some had visions of the events that are occurring now, for even then we saw the ways of some were not sustainable. This one whom I am speaking through - he has dreamed of the great White Buffalo, and it has stunned him. But I come to offer him reassurance that this is a most auspicious and beautiful dream of protection and realization and strength.

I come bringing you this energy and the love of God. I wish to encourage you all to continue your journey in prayer to the Great One. To stay connected in your souls, that the love in your souls will guide you through these times, as we will. This you know deep down. And as it has been revealed to you that these times would be upon you, we encourage you as a community to be in harmony with the earth that your bodies may be sustained, that you may come into harmony with each other. This is what the Creator envisions for humanity, spiritual community, and oneness with Him in His love. This you know. It is great!

Be not afraid; have faith, walk in faith… breathe in God's love and exhale the darkness, the fear, whatever separates you. Keep your hearts open that your souls may be touched. I am so happy that this one stepped forward and allowed me to speak to you. Our love and our hearts are with you all. You are the blessed children of the Creator on earth.

I embrace you in love as your brother. I am White Eagle and a disciple of the master. God bless you.

The Only Tribe

April 19, 2020

I come to you in the grace of God as your brother and friend. My work as a healer answers the call of those who sincerely ask. My band has been working to heal those in this circle whose friends and family have prayed, and we never refuse any sincere request.

I come to speak about the gathering of the tribes. Is not this gathering one of many peoples, many places, many cultures? Consider concentric circles reaching towards the fountainhead of God's love, each one receiving grace commensurate, as dear brother Augustine has said, with the intensity and longings of their souls. These circles are connected in an ascending spiral from the lowest spheres reaching to the Celestial heavens. Though there may be stagnation, it is always a reaching towards the light.

It is often said that my people are indigenous, but my friends, all peoples are indigenous, for we are all God's children no matter what tribe. Have you not all come together in prayer to receive the great blessing of our Creator's love? All one in this circle. Your prayers to receive God's love bring you closer and closer to the Celestial heavens and immortality. This is the sustainability of a soul blessed.

On our beloved Earth, many are waking up to realize how fragile and yet how powerful the Earth can be. As you move towards a more sustainable Earth, you will not be moving backwards. Although you can benefit much from indigenous cultures, sustainable cultures, there will be a blending of technology and sustainability. This is the choice that is being given to life on Earth. This blending of technology and sustainability which can be in harmony for all who wish it, as you wish to be in harmony in your souls.

So, wherever you are, reaching to God, to the light and love of the Creator, you will receive and be at one for there is only one tribe and one God. May each one in this circle, this medicine wheel, bang the drum of life that your spirits will be lifted, each soul blessed in oneness with the Creator. We are truly with you in this time of healing and transition as you are truly one, as we are in the Creator's love.

May God bless you, sustain you, protect you. I am your brother. I am White Eagle.

Hazrat Inayat Khan

Inayat Khan (1882-1927) was an Indian Muslim Sufi. He was trained as a scholar to teach rhetoric but fell in love with music. His life's goal was to spread the message of Sufi Islam to the West.

KEEP A SONG IN YOUR HEART
November 9, 2021

I come in the grace of God with a song in my heart and the Divine Love in my soul. I am Inayat Khan. It is written that in the beginning was the word and from that all creation began. In the Hindu scripture, the Bhagavad Gita, which means the Song of God, it is the sound, and the song, and the vibration that is the creative force. When master Jesus healed, his soul burning with the love of God, those words, their vibration, enabled the recipient to feel the healing force of God's love and it brought faith and changed the lives of each one. I was a musician and a Sufi, and I brought Sufism to the west with music and poetry and my writings - all about how to connect with God, to feel the presence of God and to be open to it. This is the power of sound, the magnificence of song.

When I came to your circle today, I was impressed that you began with a beautiful song that allowed so many to open up; to receive the gift. This is true of the highest spiritual work of musicians. It a service unique - the vibrations of which can heal, can bring joy, can uplift. Because in fact, all spiritual music is a prayer unto the Creator. So, it is appropriate to begin any prayer session with music.

When one speaks the listener can perceive the intention often regardless of what the words are saying. For instance, when a doctor speaks with empathy and love to a patient, whatever their condition, it is a healing force, and it is a blessing unto them. I wish for you all whether you are musically inclined or not, to be mindful of the vibrations of your voice. For did not master Jesus say, 'It is not what goes in a man's mouth that defiles him, but what comes out?' And he spoke with love and the authority of heaven.

I would encourage each one when you feel lost, when you feel overwhelmed, and when you feel perhaps you cannot meditate or pray, to find music. And find a song or a melody that resonates with your heart, for each one of you is indeed a song. I shall not continue today but will come again, and I am so pleased that my brother, though somewhat reluctant, agreed to allow me to speak today. May you all be blessed in the love of God and keep a song in your heart and in your soul. In the love of God and the eternal song I am your brother and friend. I am Inayat Khan. God bless you!

Martin Luther King, Jr.

Martin Luther King, Jr. (1929-1968) was an American Christian minister, activist and political philosopher who was one of the most prominent leaders in the civil rights movement in the United States from 1955 until his assassination in Memphis TN in 1968. (Wikipedia)

KEEP YOUR EYES ON THE PRIZE
August 17, 2021

Thank you for trusting me to come and allowing me to come and be in your circle. On my journey on earth as a Reverend, I prayed earnestly, and some days without ceasing, for guidance and for protection. My template was based not only on the teachings of Jesus, but also on the non-violent activism of Gandhi. I saw what he was able to accomplish by an absolute refusal of violence, of taking up arms against the oppressors and this became my message to those who joined me for the causes of social justice, racial equality and for the freedoms that were guaranteed by the founders of my country and yet as you well know, were not extended to those who were considered less than human, not equal, less smart, not good enough and so forth. We persisted and by the grace of God we succeeded in many ways, and yet the cancer of violence and hatred and segregation and superiority still exists in many places, and in many cultures.

I believed that God was love and that Jesus was His great prophet, son, and prince of peace. I often quoted from the Gospels and sometimes from the Old Testament; things that would awaken the consciences of the oppressors, but also to give hope to my brothers and sisters. We marched in faith, and in peace and suffered, but we kept, as I would say, 'Our eyes on the prize.'

So, you who have had the wonderful privilege and blessing of receiving the truth of God's love, the true Gospel of Jesus, and of the progression of the soul to the kingdom of God, I say, 'Keep your eyes on the prize' for there is none greater. And while you live on earth do your part with this love that you have, do your part for social justice, for the earth, for the poor, for all those in need. The love of God gives one great empathy for all those who suffer, for the hopeless and the hungry and yes, even for one's enemies. Did not the master say: "love your enemies, those who oppress you and hate you?" Let your love conquer all, as it is the great weapon of peace and light that comes from God, and we are all His children.

May God bless you each on your journeys and I thank you for taking my message. We here have great hopes for humanity in this time of peril, in this time of change and transition. Fear not, have faith and walk in the light and love of God. All is well. May God bless you - truly bless you. I am your brother and friend in Christ. I am Martin Luther King. Walk in peace.

Thomas Merton

Thomas Merton OCSO (1915–1968) was an American Trappist monk, writer, theologian, mystic, poet, social activist, and scholar of comparative religion. On May 26, 1949, he was ordained to the priesthood and given the name 'Father Louis.' He was a member of the Abbey of Our Lady of

Gethsemane, near Bardstown, Kentucky, living there from 1941 to his death.

IF YOU WOULD HAVE ONE BELIEF TO CARRY WITH YOU
May 24, 2020

I am here Thomas Merton.[50] I am your brother in God's love. I walked the path of love while on earth because I had discovered the one thing in God's universe that was truly important and necessary and believe me, I had baggage.

Imagine if the religions of the world were as tenacious about clinging to the love of God and the brotherhood and sisterhood of humans as they are to their individual beliefs that have caused so much grief. Imagine as the song goes 'no religion too' (referring to a John Lennon song 'Imagine'). This is a difficult pill to swallow because religion has also done much good - on the human plane of charity, working to alleviate poverty and all these things in human love with a belief in God and kindness towards your neighbor. Yes, these are truly good things.

I wish to tell you the stubbornness of the beliefs that say I am right and you are wrong, or this one is God this one is not, these will prove worthless to your souls. The mind is a curious thing: for I studied the Buddhists and the Sufi poets and the saints of Hinduism and the prophets of old, and you know there was one factor, one common denominator of all the great ones - God's love.

Beyond the beliefs, beyond the orthodoxy, that clinging to the rock of God's love - If you would have one belief that will carry you across the threshold to the shores of the Celestial heavens believe in God's love with all your heart and from the depths of your souls. Let it be your prayer.

Thank you for allowing me this time with you. May the blessings of God's love change you each one of your beautiful souls. All my love and blessings in the heavenly Father's love. I am indeed your brother, Thomas Merton.

---

50 Merton wrote more than 50 books in a period of 27 years, mostly on spirituality, social justice, and a quiet pacifism, as well as scores of essays and reviews. Among Merton's most enduring works is his bestselling autobiography 'The Seven Storey Mountain (1948),' This account of his spiritual journey inspired scores of World War II veterans, students, and teenagers to explore offerings of monasteries across the US. It is among National reviews list of the 100 best non-fiction books of the century.

Diversity and Oneness
July 17, 2020

I am here in the grace of God, Thomas Merton. I am drawn to this circle by its diversity and its oneness. You who come from different cultures and regions on the earth, find there is oneness in your longing to receive God's love. This too, this oneness is something that I aspire to - to unify all. I knew in my soul there was only one Creator but many prophets. Of course, as a Christian I believed in the divinity of Jesus, and that he was a divine soul.

But I explored many traditions and even Buddhism which I loved; the freedom of and the peace of meditation that could come from that path. And yet my soul longed for something to connect me. I had a favorite meditation that I learned from the writings of an orthodox monk whose meditation was called 'Prayer for the Presence of God,' because this is what I longed for. On the one hand I was fascinated by all the literature and words and concepts, and I believed in all of them, and I would not deprive anyone from seeking. And yet, the bravest of all these searches, as you have discovered and I have discovered, is to be in prayer to receive the love of God.

This circle of light attracts so many Celestial beings, who wish to be in prayer with all of you, who wish to inspire and influence you while respecting your free will. Above all, to be at one with you as we are one in the love of God. Beyond the words, beyond the teachings there is the simple presence and grace of God's love. May it be upon you all. I thank you for allowing me this time and I am honored to be here; it is my privilege. May you all be blessed with love, the love for each other and in the love of God. I am Thomas Merton, God bless you.

The Simplicity of Prayer
May 31, 2021

I am here, your brother and friend Thomas Merton. Some of you may be familiar with my life, with my work, more familiar than this one I have chosen to speak through today. You may know that I had a deeply inquisitive mind and I wished to explore every nook and cranny of spiritual life, religion, and philosophy. And as the Sufis would say 'I wished to be in the world but not of it.' This dichotomy inside of me was never fully amalgamated and yet I did explore and wrote with as much honesty as any seeker could, and I had many followers, people who read my writings, listened to me.

At one point when I did not feel connected in my heart and was overwhelmed by my busy mind, I began to explore Buddhism and that peace and calm that seemed to come with the Zen of their meditation. This was a wonderful discovery for me, and as I did with anything, I immersed myself deeply, and yet my soul longed for at-onement. I wanted to feel the Christ love, to be christed in fact - what I now know as soul transformation.

And more shocking than my sudden demise and entry into spirit was the discovery of the simplicity of prayer, not the detachment of the mind, but the engagement of the soul. I was greeted in spirit with so much love, so much guidance, all my questions answered and my prayers. So, I want to give you a very simple prayer. 'Dear God touch my soul, take my whole heart into Your arms of love. Fill me with grace that I may be one with You. Awaken me to your presence. Heal me in your love. And transform me in your grace. Amen.'

I shall step back in the silence of this prayer and in the joy of God's grace, and in the company of such wonderful souls. Thank you. God bless you. I am Thomas.

Baal Shem Tov

Israel Ben Eliezer, known as Baal Shem Tov or BeShT, (1760) was a Jewish mystic and healer who is regarded as the founder of Hasidic Judaism. 'BeShT' is the acronym for Baal Shem Tov, which means 'master of the Good Name,' a term for a holy man who wields the secret name for God. (Wikipedia)

Every Religious Tradition Can Receive Divine Love
February 7, 2020

I was known as Baal Shem Tov, a reformer in my community amongst the Jews in Eastern Europe, and the founder of Hasidic Judaism. I had experienced the light and love of God through my prayers, and I experienced this as being everywhere and accessible to all.

In every action there could be a connection with God, and I preached this. At first there was quite a negative reaction - not what I expected. But as we prayed and danced and celebrated more and more experienced this truth I had received, and it reached many - into the thousands. I stressed prayer over the Torah at a time when there was a great disparity in my community between the wealthy and the poor. Often the scriptures were used as a way to continue this chasm. Now I realized in my own prayers that whether rich or poor, all could be blessed. All could feel the ecstasy of the divine. I did not understand at that time, certainly as I do now, the great teachings of the rabbi Yeshua. The greatest rabbi I might add.

But I had a sense of this Divine Love and though I had some limitations in expressing (falsely) that it needed to be received through someone who was blessed or knowledgeable. I realized in spirit that anyone who prayed could receive this love and be blessed. And this spirit that I carried transformed an entire community, and to this day is honored throughout the world in the Jewish tradition for sure.

Why do I tell you these things? Because, you see, whatever tradition you may find yourself in or amongst, by recommending the simple truth of prayer to God to receive His love, His blessings, His light ...who can refuse this? What becomes an experience, a connection, a communion with God beyond any belief system can be realized by each one of you as you share what you have received and what you know to be true in this world.

I am grateful to this one, this channel whom I have always had a connection with for the opportunity to come through and share my love and blessings and teachings with you all. I wish for you every blessing in God's love. I am Baal Shem Tov.

Let Your Prayers Go Deep

January 4, 2021

I am here, Israel Ben Eliezer. You may know me as the Baal - Baal Shem Tov. My dear brothers and sisters who come together in the love of God - each one's heart requiring the tender embrace that is the love divine. Some come in pain seeking the balm that heals the heart, that soothes the soul and the body.

I encourage you to let your prayers to God go deep. Allow your heart to open that God may fill it with love and touch your soul. That no matter what condition you came to this circle in, you can leave in joy and in the light and in the glow of the gift of the Creator. This love is eternal. This love will carry you across the ocean to the shores of eternity in the Celestial heavens. I speak from experience. In my time we danced, and we prayed, and we celebrated. We felt the fire, the glow of God's love, whether in times of poverty or abundance as we had the wealth of the heavenly Father's love.

This place of light where every soul is transformed, lifted, and awakened is a precious place indeed. This is why you have what you have and maybe you do not know the words to explain it but it does not matter. What matters is that you have arrived at the doorway to the kingdom with the keys of prayer, the longings of your souls, to which God responds - opening the door of His soul and touching each one of you with grace. If even for a moment you can be lifted above your concerns, all the troubles, trials and tribulations of this world into the balm of His love, in the Joy, then you know you are on your way to a divine destination.

So, with all my blessings for the new year on earth and the light of God's love that will transform all: May it be yours. May it be yours. I am your brother and friend in the love of God. I am Baal Shem Tov. May God bless you!

Yogananda

When I was in my twenties, I devoured every spiritual book available to me. I was introduced to Paramahansa Yogananda, an Indian monk and Yogi, by reading his book, 'Autobiography of a Yogi.' And though I felt very good about this Yogi, I did not want to join his Self-Realization Fellowship because it seemed to me a somewhat limited organizational approach to his life and teachings.

So, I moved on to many other teachers while searching for the spiritual growth and physical manifestations of the spirit world I so desired. While I experienced some success, the results were limited and not permanent. For years this strategy of seeking spiritual enlightenment and coping with my fears felt like riding a roller coaster with intense highs and lows. Then I realized that my core fear was fear of death, and nothing I had experienced so far had lifted me above my mortality.

In the depths of this spiritual crisis, I had an awakening experience in Divine Love and a visitation from two Celestial angels that took place in 1987 when I was 37 years old (See the Preface page in Chapter 6, the 'Care Darby Walsh' messages, for a description of this experience). This was the beginning of my true soul transformation. And I came to realize that all the spiritual teachers I had studied had to some degree experienced the love of God even though their orthodox religious traditions may not have promoted or even understood the path to receiving soul transformation through Divine Love.

Yogananda came from the Hindu tradition that emphasizes going within as the ultimate Yogic and spiritual path. But in his teachings and meditation practice he goes a step further by encouraging his students and followers to open to the deep longings in their souls to be at one with God through the inflowing of His love. He says, "After you have affirmed your oneness with God, pray to Him in the language of your heart; but do not ask Him for fulfillment of your needs or desires first. When you do that, God knows you do not seek Him for Himself, but for those gifts you hope to obtain from Him. That is not the relationship God wants with His children. Never ask the Divine Spirit for anything else until you have first offered Him your love and have prayed for His love and for Him to reveal Himself to you."

In the late 1990s I decided to visit the Self-Realization Fellowship (SRF) Temple in Encinitas, California. SRF is the religious organization that was founded in 1920 by Yogananda. I enjoyed a walk in the gardens of the beautiful Self-Realization Fellowship Center and experienced a great inflowing of God's love. Previously, I had a similar experience in Assisi, Italy in the little church that St Francis had built with his friends. It is worth noting that there is a St. Francis grotto in the SRF Temple gardens where I prayed and meditated.

In future years I came back to the Encinitas Temple several times with Divine Love friends. On the trip in 2016 I was accompanied by my friends Al Fike, a renowned Celestial medium, author, potter, and wonderful gardener, and his wife Jeanne. The day we planned to visit the Temple and gardens, we were driving from Indio, CA. We planned to arrive before closing time, but unfortunately, we were too late. So we rented motel rooms nearby to spend the night intending to visit the next morning.

That night I had a dream where Yogananda came to me and said, "If you come to my garden I will be there." This was one of those dreams you remember because it is so real, and at breakfast I related it to Al and Jeanne. Jeanne responded that they were scheduled to visit people in San Diego, so hopefully I would not be offended if we kept our visit to SRF short. Al said he would love to see the gardens. It is important to note that Al and Jeanne knew very little about Yogananda except that he was a Yogi and probably not on the Divine Love path.

So, we drove to the SRF after breakfast and immediately found a parking space directly across from the entrance. Jeanne, who was having some difficulty walking, used support sticks and was grateful that we were so close to the entrance. As we entered, we were very enthusiastically and lovingly greeted by a fellow who recognized Jeanne's disability and invited us to take the less steep path (generally closed to the public) that Yogananda used to walk to the gardens in his later years. We went up the path guided by our new friend and immediately felt the love and peace of that sanctuary. Al loved all the flora and fauna, and a flock of pelicans formed a protective ceiling on our meanderings about the gardens. We become absorbed in the moment losing any sense of time, but eventually Al asked me where it was that I had prayed/meditated previously, and could we go there?

We walked to the other side of the gardens where the St Francis grotto is located and to our delight found it uninhabited even though the rest of the gardens began to fill up with large numbers of visitors. We sat down and immediately felt a strong atmosphere of Divine Love and began to pray. I had the thought that it must be Jesus with us because the intensity of the love was so profound. Within moments Al began to channel Yogananda and I share that message with you:

> Friends, I am indeed Yogananda and I thank you for coming to my sanctuary, for being in this place and adding your prayers to this beautiful garden. You see, Light is everywhere beloveds, Light is everywhere.
>
> I am happy that the scales have fallen from your eyes, my two precious friends, that you see that I too have brought the truth of God's love into the world, that I too dedicated my life to soul awakening. Yes, my words were different, my teachings reflected my life and background, but each

of you may bring some teaching to the world as your souls are ignited and aflame with love. And you may share this love and share the truth of this love to whomever you meet, speak to and embrace. So, it takes all of us from many different religions and backgrounds and teachings who have seen the higher truth of love to bring this forward into the world so that the whole world may be a garden like this, beloveds. The whole world may be entranced by the condition of beauty and love.

Is this not God's will? Is not my God your God? Everyone's God? Think of the world in this way, my friends. Everyone is a child of God. Everyone must be loved and accepted and embraced. I do indeed inhabit the Celestial kingdom and I know you wonder about this. Do not let your biases get in the way of your acceptance of the truth. Know that each beautiful soul will bring forth their truth, their understanding, in their unique ways and their unique voice.

Accept this beloveds, the world is diverse, it is full of differences, but you have a choice, as do all; will you accept the differences of others and be tolerant or will you reject and say 'What is like me is the most valid truth'? Beloved souls, this earth is full of diversity. Wherever you go you will encounter differences, different perspectives, even different colors of skin. This is the way of the world. This is how God created us all, is it not, with these differences? When we bring them together, we create truth, beautiful truth.

My friend (Jimbeau), I am with you often and we have many conversations in spirit as you sleep. I thank you for introducing these dear souls to this place and to my presence. This will, I believe, create a beautiful relationship amongst you all as I continue to make efforts to bring truth to this world, as do all the angels in heaven. Accept, accept. love, love, breathe, breathe in truth. That river of God, that light of full understanding, that bliss of God's love pouring into your souls. Filling that vessel, filling you up with Him.

It is so simple. Even a little yogi like me may understand it. It is so simple. God bless you, beloveds. I will come again and speak with you. I have great love for you because you bring a light to this world, and the more you can allow it to shine to all the people of this world you will bring a change and a difference. You will light a candle, that will light a candle, that will light another candle in the world until the whole world is alight with truth.

God bless you. I am Yogananda and I honor you, I honor each of you as beautiful souls of God's love. God bless you.

The previous message was received by Al Fike, May 13, 2017.

> If the world shall break your heart, do not despair. Because a broken heart can become opened like a rose in God's love.
> ....Yogananda

WE ARE NOT SO DIFFERENT
April 1, 2019

My dear boy, my dear friend, I wish to start at the beginning as this seems the best place to begin. We are not so different, you and I, although that thought has never occurred to you until now because I am placing it in your brain. My parents wished for me to become a spiritual man, a teacher, a guru within their tradition and sent me to the proper schools for this training. Your parents wished for you to become a priest and sent you to the proper schools for the proper training and inspiration too, yes? Our mothers were both devoutly religious people, and this affected both of us very early on in our lives as young men. You become an altar boy and often attended daily mass at a young age with your mother, yes? I prayed and chanted, did puja daily at home or at temple with my mother. I had access to a very old traditional system that could propel me along the Hindu path in harmony with the deep desires of my soul. I developed my gifts and of course you know my story pretty well especially from Sri Yukteswar coming into my life and onward to America and the world. For you, growing up in the West and having deep spiritual longings as well as a rather mischievous and very curious nature, it would turn out a bit differently.

You simultaneously wished for spiritual growth from your soul longings, and at the same time, pursued earthly desires and interests commensurate with the cultural revolution of the 1960's in the West. Music became your path and your passion, but you also studied many different teachings from esoteric Christianity to metaphysics, astrology, the teachings of Gurdjieff, the Sufis, the Gita, Yoga, Meditation, and you followed several Hindu and Sufi Gurus, including studying my writings. This, along with your somewhat rebellious nature, has turned out to serve you well, my dear son, leading you ultimately to your beautiful soulmate and the truth of God's love.

I knew this love too but within the confines and classical content of Hinduism which teaches that it is within, and so I taught this as well. You, however, have discovered that I constantly told my students and disciples to think of God, to ask God for oneness, to go to God for everything in meditation and prayer rather than putting the attention on myself as so many gurus do.

Praying for God's love became my principal practice, and my reunion and realignment with my beloved teacher, Sri Yukteswar, already well established in the truths of Divine Love, our Creator's gift for the asking, helped me progress quickly through the various spheres as I have described through your friend and wonderful medium, Al Fike.

I wish to tell you my experience with master Jesus, whom I always loved when on earth and wrote extensively about through the lens of my eastern understandings and incorporated that in my teachings and honored him as one of the great teachers. He is indeed the highest soul in God's kingdom and the most loving, gracious, humble, and glorious spirit - truly beyond any description with mere words. I did, on earth, realize things about him and his life that were in harmony with the truth, though other things I superimposed upon him within the understandings, however limited, of my own tradition.

You have had the privilege and great fortune of the writings of James Padgett and your life with your dear Care and many others teaching you these truths for more than 30 years of your earth life. What a gift your Divine Love friends are to you and the world. We shall work together to bring these truths to the world.

It is time for me to deliver the broader teachings to my disciples on earth, and it is my deep wish that you will allow me to do so through our conversations in spirit. We are one in God's love which embraces all the religions and yet transcends them in the transformation of our souls. I am your brother and friend of your eternal soul, Yogananda.

BETTER TO BE A FOOL OF GOD THAN A KING OF MEN
April 6, 2019

Aloha, dear brother. I am Yogananda, friend of your soul. Earlier today I made rapport with you while in prayer. You indeed felt my presence at your side and my wish to communicate a message through you about rituals, but you declined to speak aloud on my behalf, deferring to the dear soul and instrument whose home you are visiting. Internally, at the same time, you were telling me that if I were to speak through this other dear soul, this other instrument, you would in future agree to do so on my behalf. So, to your surprise and to the complete unknowing of Al Fike, I did speak, although not on the subject you wished me to. That is because, dear brother, it would be better for me to give that message through you, and so I will.

At present, let's revisit the internal discussion we had subsequent to the message received earlier today and during the silent prayer time. You were telling me that you did not wish to appear foolish and that you did not have any idea of the technique involved in receiving messages from spirit. I replied to you that "It is better to be a fool of God, than a king of men." And you still had thoughts of fear and embarrassment of feeling unqualified or being 'an idiot.' I told you "It is better to be God's idiot than an academic genius." And you seemed to have no trouble relating what I told you to your dear friends afterwards. So now I ask you, that if you thought you came up with all that with your own mind, would you have bothered to tell them? Would you have felt my presence and heard my voice so clearly?

I want you to consider something about channeling and mediumship in relation to your music, dear brother. You know without any doubt that you have at times, as you would clearly state, 'received music,' yes? You have often stated that the better the music and/or words that come to you are, the less you have had to do with creating them, yes? Would you not agree that when that happens you are in fact in a state of prayer, in a place of rapport with musicians in the spirit world and quite often Celestial musicians? I wish to tell you that not only is this true, but in fact you are a co-creator of these musical gems. The simpler is sometimes the better, eh? This is because your intention is to receive the love of God and to share His Divine Love and the truth of it to others, yes?

You have also composed symphonic works along these lines and have felt the hands of Celestial musicians moving your hands. Is this not true? Have you not stated this fact to others on occasion? So please don't feel that I am trying to embarrass you about this when my wish is to encourage you and remind you that you have been used as a medium for music many times, even by your own account. The process is much the same when composing music as communicating with me, although the instrument may be automatic writing instead of a guitar or me simply speaking through you instead of singing. At the same time, I do not wish to infringe upon your musical composing or your will.

I think you only recently remembered that I loved to sing and compose songs. So again, you see, we are not so different. We love to sing God's praises. I will come again soon and deliver more of what I wish to tell not only to my followers on earth but to all of God's children. Till then, my dear soul friend, follow your heart, know that I am with you often, and pray. Pray for God's love. I love you with all the love of a brother and true friend in God, Yogananda.

Let Your Ritual be Praying for Divine Love
April 7, 2019

I am very pleased to speak through my dear brother. Though he is reluctant to receive in his mind, in his soul he is open to this gift. Because he lives in the moment quite often, he doesn't remember that he has received messages before. He has received music as well.

But I wish to speak to all of you dear souls about ritual. I wish to say about these rituals that are carried on in the world that many have been corrupted and therefore are not useful. But the purpose of rituals which are practiced in my home country was originally to remember God in daily life, to awaken to a consciousness of God. When that kind of ritual is performed, it is most effective in keeping one's soul in alignment with God's love and God's light. Is this not what we all wish?

I wish to also say that ritual can become like an addiction. When it is such a thing, it must be a conscious and loving addiction, so it does not harm the soul or block out the light. I ask you all to choose wisely here.

We in the Celestial kingdom encourage you to pray and pray for God's love. Make that your ritual and things will fall into place.

I want to thank this dear brother for stepping forward and allowing me to speak. I will do so in the future as I have many things to communicate to not only my followers on Earth, but to all. From the Celestial kingdom, we send you our love and light. I wish to embrace all of you in God's love as does this dear soul. I am Yogananda and I love you.

Turn Grief to Joy

April 8, 2019

I come with God's love for all. I wish to remind you that the master said, "There are many mansions in my Father's House." Those who have passed on - many live in realms of light so far above this Earth plane - that in most cases, it is we who grieve. It is our loss but their gain. They wish for us to know, as the dear one just stated, "when you call them, they will come, when you think of them , they are there." This is reflected in the statement, 'Ask and you shall receive, knock and the door will be opened.' So, to those here who have lost ones to the spirit world and are grieving, please know they are progressing in realms of light and love towards the Celestial heavens. And of course, this is our wish for all of you.

So, yes, work with them, remember them, hold them close to your heart. They are not going anywhere. They are not leaving your heart. They shall always be with you, but the responsibility now is yours, and the choices you make, these are yours. You have free will. The heavenly Father wishes to be at one with you, and you should ask, it will be so. This you know.

The smile that comes to your face and the joy to your heart when you feel His love beaming in your soul, this is an eternal smile, and it will outlast all the others. The ups and downs of this world, the concerns of this material plane are but a mere shadow of the realms of light where you are all destined to go. I say, feel joy, sing God's praises, share with one another in happiness and joy for the loved ones that have gone on to these realms, and do not be sad. You are loved, and you love them, and God loves all. We are all embraced in His Great love.

God bless you. I love you. I am Yogananda and I love you.

Discard Your Distractions
May 3, 2019

Dear friend of my soul, beloved brother on the path of God's love, it is my joy to be with you in this endeavor, and I thank you for stepping up to receive what I wish to deliver. The vastness of the universe when viewed from the world of spirit is so humbling and at once so exhilarating that I ask each soul to consider what lies ahead in the light and love in the Celestial realms for those who seek to be at one with their Creator. What magnificence, what bliss, beyond any earthly description or comparison, will be yours.

You may feel at times that you are being required to give up the things on Earth that are so dear, that you cling to, that you feel sustain and comfort you, but I tell you unless these things are harmful to your soul progression, they need not be discarded. What needs to be discarded is the multitude of distractions available to each in the modern world that occupy so much of your time like painkilling drugs, which only give temporary relief from the pain of separation from God that each soul feels, to a greater or lesser degree, whether consciously aware of it or not.

Of course, those on the spiritual path begin to see their addictions and distractions over and against the bliss of being in harmony with God's love and laws, and therefore at some point make a very concerted effort to pray and meditate so that their consciousness becomes aligned with God's love and light, more and more, deeper and deeper. This is my wish for all of you to consider for your soul's progression, for your happiness, your real happiness.

What is of importance in any given moment? What is your deepest desire? You know that in any moment you can connect with our loving Creator in your feelings for God's love in your heart and your soul above your mind and the world of thoughts. When you are in your soul, as has been discussed lately, you feel a oneness in love, over and above the world of mind. A true connection, because it is of the soul, may in fact be difficult to put into words but is undeniable in feeling. Bliss and joy pervade and outshine the world. Questions get answered and dissolve into light. This is the hand of God upon you, dear friends. This is the embrace you long for. And as you continue to walk on this path you will see more and more of the workings of our glorious Creator, and you will never be disappointed for God will provide all, as it is written: "Every good and perfect gift is from above and cometh down from the Father of lights, with whom is no variableness, neither shadow of turning."[51]

I love you. May God continue to bless you each with love divine! I am Yogananda.

The Doorway is Through the Heart
May 21, 2019

You cannot imagine the joy in my heart to see such a gathering of souls opening to God's love. It is a delight. When you come together and draw this love into your souls from the deep longings that you have, you create a magnetism between you and God and you and each other. This magnetism, which is growing in what you call the lattice of light, attracts many spirits - those you cannot see who are with us, sharing in your prayer, feeling the shower of our glorious Creator's love coming into our souls.

I have said before that when things are of the mind, they are on a certain vibration, but when things are of the soul, they are of light. How do you get to this place? The doorway is through the heart. This instrument, through whom I speak, he has discovered this, that his heart is the doorway to his soul, so his practice is to go into feeling. I tell you, friends of my soul, whatever is in your hearts, if you go there and you open up and you give it to God, it will dissolve in His light and love and be replaced by this light and love, such a glorious thing.

My wish for you all is that you continue to open, and to be in the Father's presence, to be healed where you are hurt, to forgive where you have not. This will help you to be in your souls. May you all be blessed eternally in the wonderful Creator's love so that your souls will be transformed. I join you in this. I am your brother and friend, Yogananda, and I love you. Thank you.

A Gentle Rain of Light is Falling to Earth
June 30, 2019

I am drawn by the longing and the love and the deep intentions of this beautiful gathering to be open to the Father's love. If you could see

---
51 James 1:17

this from where I am you would see it as a gentle rain of light falling to her Earth, illuminating this place. Imagine if the entire Earth were open to receiving this gentle flow of light and love from the Father. In this moment you are being blessed with it. I feel the intention of each one of you to serve, to bring the truth to this world. I would say there are many avenues with which to do this. So many of you, in fact each one of you, do this in small ways, in big ways and in many ways.

I encourage you to reach out to others, whatever their beliefs, whatever their religion, whatever dogma they follow, to reach out and offer these circles of light, these prayers and meditations so they too may feel their soul open to God's love and this showering of light and love that you feel. It is our desire to see the whole world illuminated and changed, redeemed, transformed by the Father's love.

I wish to thank each one of you for the work you do, for allowing the longings in your souls to let the Father open them up to the inflowing of His love. You are all so blessed, and I am blessed to be with you. I encourage you, keep praying. You will see the transformation of this world.

I am Yogananda and I love each one of you. May God bless you and continue to shower His love upon you, each one. May the world be blessed in God's love.

The Mind and the Soul
July 29, 2019

I wish to speak on matters of the mind and the soul for those and to those who find it difficult to quiet the mind. Those who feel that perhaps, even though they are praying and being quiet, they are somehow not receiving the love of God in the abundance that they wish to receive it, but not because of any lack of intention.

Although it has been said that one cannot do two things at once, or one cannot be in two different places at once, I wish to tell you it is possible to be in your soul and at the same time to be in your mind. The issue is not whether you're in your mind or in your soul. The issue is which one is in ascendancy. For to be in the soul through the longings of the soul, of the heart, feeling the presence and allowing that to inform the mind, this is the place that you wish to be. In the world, it is the mind that informs the soul, the material mind.

You are in the human condition, so we do not judge whether you are in your mind or your soul, but we can observe and we encourage. As you know, prayer, this opening to God's love, this longing to be in God's presence, to have your soul infilled with this precious gift, this alone, this intention, whether it be with words or in silence, this reaches our heavenly Father. He cannot help but respond with His Holy Spirit and bring the love into every soul that sends this intention forward and upward.

So, my dear friends, when you feel that you are overwhelmed by material thoughts, by concerns, by all the things of the mind, I ask you, go into your soul. Talk to God: 'Oh Father, put my soul into your soul. Open it up to your love. Touch my heart. Awaken me that I may be a being of light and love for you.' As you send up this request, the heavens open, the love flows, the light comes forth. You feel the presence of our most loving Creator and you are now in your soul, informing your mind. You are now in a place of guidance. You know through your soul perceptions now, which way to go, what to do. When you are in this state of grace, this Holy Communion with the Father, you are in a sense, untouchable by the lower spirits, darker forces, vexations, and therefore are able to bring a healing presence to those who might otherwise throw you out of harmony, injure you in a way or, as they say, 'hurt your feelings.'

So, my dear ones, whatever you feel you're up against, know that you can go into your soul, that the Father will open it up to His Great love and you will attract those of us with the spiritual magnetism, the light that is coming into your soul, as we come down through the spheres to be with you. Though this is a journey that can be difficult, it is so rewarding to us, even for one soul to begin this transformation. And now we have many souls in the midst of it.

Oh, my friends, we are proud of you. We will continue to encourage you and be with you on this journey of not only your transformation, but the transformation of the world and great healing that is needed and you have all committed to and embarked on, embarked upon this journey for the sake of all. How we love you.

I am with you; my love is with you. May God bless you and embrace you in His light and love. We are all one in this. I am Yogananda. God bless you. God bless you.

Make the World Your Ashram, Your Monastery
July 30, 2019

You know, those who live in monasteries and ashrams and such places, where they have essentially removed themselves from the world to be in whatever form of Holy Communion that they are seeking, whatever forms of oneness, whether it be the natural love or in God's love, most of their practice is to be mindful of God, of love in every moment. Of course, this is easier to do when you don't have to get in your car and drive to work and get groceries and take care of the rent, children and all these things in the world.

But, like you have chosen this moment to be in prayer with your beloved friends, you can make the world your monastery, your ashram. I ask you, when you're busy, when your mind is really going a mile a minute, to just open your heart, to open your soul to God. As I have said before, if need be, talk to God. When you send up this prayer to God, to be at one with Him in love, you have elevated your thoughts to the soul level.

In this moment, we are all one in God's love. Whatever our station, wherever we are on our journey, we have allowed God to touch our souls. In this moment there is much light in this circle. Can you not feel this blessing?

So, my dear friends, I encourage you, make the world your ashram, your monastery. Be transformed in the Father's love. Be a blessing to everyone everywhere. I thank you. I send you all my love and embrace you in God's love. May you all be blessed. I am with you. I love you all. I am Yogananda.

The Most Important Yoga Is To Be Open to God's Love
August 6, 2019

I am often with my brother Francis (as I am today), and I wish to speak to you about the soul. The yoga of Divine Love incorporates the entire being. When the soul informs the mind, it is not necessary to have the organ of discrimination (the mind) in the forefront of choice because one is in the love of God.

Yes, of course, it is important to take care of your bodies. These are your vehicles as humans. If you make healthy choices, exercise, and practice yoga, that is good. But the most important yoga is to be open to this love. When I taught the Kriya yoga, I was attempting to make a bridge between the East and the West, between the materialism of the West and the attachment to the body and the Eastern path of abstinence and connecting to the soul. I used this physical body as a vehicle. But, as I said then to my disciples, my students, if you really want to succeed at Kriya yoga, think about God all the time. Let this be the first thing in your day, the first thought of your day. Whatever you do during the day, give it to God.

As I said in my last message through this one, make the world your ashram, your monastery, your church by being mindful of God in whatever you do. This is the yoga of God's love. This is what I wish to convey now from the Celestial heavens. This is soul to soul. I encourage you all to make this first and foremost in your lives and remember, as master Jesus said: "Seek thee first the kingdom of heaven and all else will be given to you." How true this is. Keep this in your hearts. Allow your souls the gift of receiving God's love in whatever you are doing. In this way, you will be a blessing to all, wherever you are, whatever you do, with whomever you may be. Words are not necessary whenever you are in communion with the heavenly Father. Let His light and love shine through your soul. I say to you, be a gift, be a gift to all, be a gift to each other as you are in this moment. As God gives you the gift of love, God's love in your soul, may this be your gift to God and the world.

We are with you on this journey. Yes, there is much light in this place. What a blessing. We shall stay a while longer with you today, and we will be with you later in prayer with your friends. We love you. May God bless you. I am Yogananda. I love you. God loves you.

Raise Your Thoughts to the Highest
August 7, 2019

My dear friends, much has been said in the world about the power of thought to become things, to be able to visualize and then build upon that vision. Of course, this is true as you can see manifestations of it everywhere. It is also true that when you send thoughts to us, we feel them. When you send thoughts to another, they may not feel the words, but they feel your intentions. This is why we always talk to you about how you are receivers, and you are transmitters.

What goes in does come out, which is why it is important to evaluate what you wish to take in. As they say, 'food for thought.' It is important in the material world with your bodies to take in foods that are healthy and nutritious, to sustain them and prevent them from illness and disease, however it is just as important as the thoughts that you take in and send out.

We in the Celestial heavens always influence you to raise your thoughts to the highest spiritual thoughts. I told my students, 'Talk to God. Keep your mind on God. Whatever your need, it will be answered.' This will raise your thoughts, as I have said earlier, to the level of soul. Then you begin to perceive with the soul. Within the mind of God, within the flow of love, in a state of grace, in this Holy Communion, the soul knows, and you feel it. This is sometimes referred to as the soul of the mind or the higher mind by some. I come to talk to you specifically about the soul transformed by God's love, this angelic soul, able to perceive what is best, what path to follow, what is in the flow of God's love. These soul perceptions, this is what we wish for you all so that you are not troubled by the mind.

As I have said before, let your soul be above your mind so that your soul influences your mind and not the other way around. You wonder: 'How do I do this? I have all kinds of feelings.' You do this in prayer. You send up the intention to receive, and the most Holy Spirit of the Creator opens your soul to receive, awakens your soul. You feel this. You feel this in your heart, your solar plexus. You feel this glow, this light. Questions that arise dissolve into truth. You are in the flow of God's love and grace. This, my friends, my beautiful friends, this is your destiny. Should you wish to be transformed, you will be. When we say: 'follow your heart,' there is such a close connection between the heart and the soul. Your heart is your feeling center. This is the place. When you open your heart, as you know, the most loving Creator can open your soul. The heart is contained in the soul.

This is also evident in music when someone sings deeply from their heart, we often call this 'music of the soul.' My songs that I sang when on Earth, I sang from my soul. I was not some great singer, some kind of opera singer, but my intentions were so deep from my soul, that I felt such joy in singing.

This I give to you with love. Let your hearts be open that your souls will be blessed, that your minds will be at ease in the peace that passes understanding. Allow this throughout your day. Whenever you are distracted, go to your heart that God and the angels may touch your soul.

I pray you will all stay in the light and the love of God. Whenever you call, we shall be there for our love is always with you, and we too are on this journey together, at one in God's love. My love to all of you. God's love to all of you. May you stay in His warm embrace, always. God bless you. I am Yogananda.

The Yoga of God's Love is the Highest Yoga
August 20, 2019

We in the Celestial realms are drawn to you in this circle of light. I wish to tell you that this is the yoga of love, God's love. There is no higher yoga. There is no finer belief. When you suspend your doubt, your reluctance, your material mind, which is of the world, you allow your soul to be opened by God's love. This of course can be done in a moment's notice. The wish you have deep within each of you to awaken and be transformed, when accompanied by faith and the suspension of disbelief or doubt or skepticism, allows our heavenly Father to touch your soul, to open it up to His love and to change it.

This journey is endless, but it is not without a beginning. I wish to say to you, those of you who have just begun, there is much to be gained in the world but so much more to be gained by being transformed in God's love. With a little bit of effort, you can direct your will to God's Will. Allow your heart to open in faith, open to grace. This will make a huge difference in your lives, not only that, but in the lives of all you touch, and you will touch many.

It is our Celestial desire to help each one of you. Do not fail to call on us as we are here for you. We cannot resist the call from your soul when you need assistance, when you need a healing. If you are surrounded by unharmonious or vexed spirits, call on us. We will come. Reach out to God. Those negative influences, those spirits cannot be in a place where God's love is and stay negative. So, it is for each of you that once you open to this grace, negativity will dissolve, and Divine Love comes in. Divine love will heal you, change you, transform you, awaken you. So, my beloved friends, as always, I urge you, stay in the love. Pray often. This is the yoga of God's love.

My love to each one of you. So blessed you are to have each other. We are with you. We love you. May God bless you, each one, and transform you. You are angels in waiting. I love you. I am Yogananda.

Open Your Heart to the Love of God
September 7, 2019

I am here your brother and friend, Yogananda. I come here to remind you and to encourage you. This is a portal of light, this sanctuary with the light extending all the way to the Celestial heavens, which makes it quite easy for Celestial angels to be with you today and any time you come here and open up to receiving our guidance and the love of God.

My dear friends, I feel your hearts where there are wounds. You may have closed your heart for protection. This is a human thing. It is like a clenched fist saying: 'Don't hurt me, I need protection.' I tell you, my beloved friends, open this fist and know that protection is yours. You cannot keep a fist clenched all day long because then it is going to hurt even more than the pain you're trying to protect yourself from. Open your heart. Allow the love to come in. Allow the healing to take place that the Creator wishes for you.

This light that comes in that heals afflictions, that dissolves wounds and barriers, this is yours should you ask for it. I wish to tell you to make use of this beautiful portal of light, that you can always come and feel the love, the presence, the light in this place. The universe is vast beyond your imaginings, so it may be hard to imagine in a sense, connecting. Yet you are not even a moment away. You are not a needle nose away.

The love of God is waiting only for you to be open, to transform your soul from the mere image to the very substance and essence of the Creator, to be at one, to feel this light and love. I encourage you and invite you on this journey whether you be new or traveling here a long time. We are in this together, so many Celestial angels here with you in this moment, in this portal of light, in the lattice of love. God embraces you, each heart, each soul. Let us all be in the light and love of the Creator.

My love and blessings to all. May the Creator's love transform us and bless each one on this journey. Thank you for letting me be here with you, it is my honor and privilege. And to this one here receiving the message, I thank him as well. God bless you. I love you. I am Yogananda.

Go Into Your Soul
September 24, 2019

The mind has such a dominance over humankind, so much to process, thoughts, all kinds of information, often conflicting one with the other. That is why, my dear friends, I encourage you to go into your soul where there is always truth and where truth prevails.

It is true, a calm mind and meditation, withdrawing from the world, is a very good thing. Certainly, the world needs more of that. But you my friends, who know of this great love that lifts you up and above this world, that awakens your souls and your soul perceptions, this yoga of Divine Love, I will always encourage, because it leads to the very transformation of each soul who receives it. If you wish to be changed, this is the path that is required. It is never demanded, only offered. 'Seek the kingdom first and all things will be given.' Did not the master say this?

May your day be blessed. We shall watch over you. There are healing angels and spirits with the dear brother in hospital, per your request. Many are praying. Blessings will be received. Have no doubt. May the Creator's love flow in you, reside in your souls, and transform them.

I am your brother and friend, from the Celestial heavens. I am Yogananda. God bless you. My love to all.

I Always Pointed to God
September 29, 2019

My dear friends, I should like to talk to you about control and about being in the flow of God's love. When I was on earth, I had many students who were devoted to me and my teaching of Kriya yoga. And you know I had been so humbled by my relationship not only with my teacher Sri Yukteswar but my closeness to Jesus and my longings and my connection with God and His love that, quite honestly, I was not an attention seeker, and I was overwhelmed by the request of my teacher to come to America and bring this yoga.

My thoughts and feelings about this journey have been well-chronicled so I needn't revisit them, but what I do want to say is that in my teaching I did not want the focus to be on me. I did not ask my students to meditate on me, to make me the center of their attention, but to still their minds and open their hearts and their souls to God. Sometimes in the present day this part of my instructions, my suggestions, takes a backseat to those who wish to honor me and those who wish to follow a more limited path of Kriya yoga and meditate on me or my teachers.

Those who examine my words while on earth will see that I always pointed to God. I was not seeking to control the lives of people but to lead them on the path of love and transformation in God. I continue to do this work here now in the Celestial heavens in spirit, through this instrument, my brother and sometimes others, yes. I say to you on this issue of control in this world where there is so much darkness, where each one wishes to have some measure of control in their lives, this is the human condition but you know, when you relinquish control and open to God and the guidance of the celestials, you are in the flow and control is not necessary because God is in control. Are we not all along for the ride - this journey of love into the very essence of our beloved Creator? As they say: 'Onward and upward.' Yes, this is my recommendation to you: 'Be in this love. Let go of your concerns.' You cannot dissect this.

We are here in this moment with you. Do you not feel the Father's love, His hand upon us, His embrace? What else could matter? This of course is a choice you can make in any given moment. And I suggest, I never demand. I embrace you with my love and blessings and thank you for allowing me this message. There are many here and we embrace you in God's love. I love you and I am your brother and friend in the Celestial heavens. God bless you. I am Yogananda.

(long pause)

I wish to add something as I am still with this instrument, and he wishes me to state it. Something I wish you to consider. Scientists examine the universe and its vastness, and they find out year by year that it is bigger and more wondrous than they could have imagined, and yet they also find that in the smallest component of the atom there is the same wonder - the same miraculous life.

This journey leads to wonderment and awe and hopefully, to those that are intellectually minded, the opening of their hearts and their souls in the realization of how great the Creator really is and indeed God is Great!!! I say this because whether you are trying to fathom the wonder or vastness of the universe or simply what you shall do in this moment, realize my dear ones, it is all a miracle. It is all a wonderment. It is all glorious. Thank you. God bless you. I leave you now in love and peace.

The True Meaning of Divine Love
October 14, 2019

I say to you, this Divine Love - and when I speak of Divine Love, I mean the love of God and not anything less as there are many in the world who say this is divine, that is divine, this is Divine Love - but this Divine Love that we celestials speak of, this is the very essence of the heavenly Father. It does not have ups and downs. When you are in this love, there is a bubble, a protective bubble around you and a light, and you cannot possibly wish harm on another.

This is how you know you are in Divine Love. The disappearance of ups and downs, of them and us, this at-onement with God, the radiance surrounding the heart, this beam of light coming down from the heavens, this spiritual magnetism that connects your soul with God, this is the reality of the Celestial heavens. This is the reality that the dear sisters spoke of. I speak to all parents when I say, it is immensely important to share this love of God with your children whatever their age, with the world yes, but with your children it is so very important.

As the master said: "love others as I have loved you," meaning in God's love. You will create an eternal bond with those you touch in God's love. There is no end to it. It is above this world and beyond. Yet it embraces this world. Carry this love with you dear friends. Walk in the light. Live in the love. Do no harm, as the great physician Hippocrates, said: "Do no harm." And as the poet Virgil wrote so long ago, "love conquers all." How very true. Love all in God's love.

May God fill your souls and transform them in His glorious love and light, this gift you are blessed to receive. All my love and blessings to you. I am Yogananda.

You Are Worthy of His Love
November 16, 2019

Where you have been angry, fill it up with forgiveness. Where there is fear, let there be love and knowing you are loved. I ask you to consider your worthiness, because every child of God is worthy of receiving His love in every moment. Know that you are worthy and that when you receive this love and you open up, it will transform you. It will heal those places where you have been blocked. This is the yoga of Divine Love. This is the practice that supersedes all others for those who wish to be at one with the Creator, for those who wish their souls to awaken and progress towards the Celestial heavens where every soul who asks and receives this love will find themselves.

I come as your brother and friend, and I love you all. May God bless you all with a great abundance of love. Be in joy, be in love, let all else go. May God bless you. I am your brother, Yogananda.

Christmas: A Grand Time To Share the Gift of Divine Love
December 15, 2019

I am honored to be welcomed in this circle, such beautiful hearts you have. When you pray and you feel the inflowing of the Creator's love, any separation that you feel is removed. In the Creator's love there is a oneness, and while you retain your individuality, each one of you is a beautiful unique soul and a creation of the Father, yet you become one in God's love. If you were lost, you feel found. If you were in doubt, you now have faith. If you were in despair, you feel hope because these are the signs of Divine Love. These are the gifts that are given in prayer.

I know some of you struggle with this. In this busy world, so much to do, so many things to get done. You have been given very good minds indeed. Yet, as I have said before, let your souls rise in prayer that they may be in ascendancy over your minds. Allow your soul to direct your mind that all things that are done will be done in love. All connections will have the light in your soul as a gift to others. This is the greatest gift. This is the gift that was brought to earth at Christmastime. This you know. What a beautiful time. A grand time to share this gift with family and friends. Your light and your love in God is a reminder to all. This is truly your gift. You have received it from God, and you give to others. Let this be our Christmas wish for all. Fear not. There is hope. Doubt not. Have faith. Know that the Father's love is the great gift we share with you.

All of my love and blessings. I am your friend and brother and I love you. I am Yogananda.

Pray!

December 20, 2019

I am Yogananda, your brother and friend. Because you have come together in prayer and in humility, recognizing our Creator and asking to receive His great love, you have been blessed.

The situation in the world, the material world, is often one of lip service through the established religions and rituals. But there has been a great movement of secularism, of atheism, often well-founded, because of the misdeeds of church officials and of simply sometimes seeing no results, not feeling God's love but being asked to give in some way or another. However, even in these orthodox structures, there are those individuals who truly pray as you do. Perhaps without the same understanding that you have, nevertheless because they pray from their heart and soul, their prayers are heard.

You are looking at a world bereft of the humility, the recognition of the Creator, in which deeds have been done for so long without regard to the health of the planet, to the health of individuals or to the needs of the soul. You now find yourself on the receiving end of the actions of the many, but all is not lost, for as you know, your prayers are heard. Yes, events will occur that are a result of many years of wrongful actions against the environment, not addressing the needs of all, greed and guns being more prevalent, or so it seems, than peace and charity.

I ask you all, my friends, to step out in this world. If you must, put on the headlines of the newspapers: "Pray." For what does the world have to lose? Everything is to be gained in God's love. Have faith. Trust in God. Go in peace in knowing your prayers are heard. My love and blessings to all. God bless you. I am Yogananda.

You Can Indeed Dispel the Darkness

January 7, 2020

My dear friends who have gathered here on this raft of prayer in an ocean of madness led by your soul's desire to rise above the storms and the fires and the conditions of your world. If it were possible to become enlightened, as they say, by reading all the books and listening to the right music, hearing the highest messages, and having all your ducks in a row, you would be enlightened already. But you have found that asking for the love of God to be in your soul is the path, the path of light and lighting your soul because you humbled yourself before God and opened your heart that God would touch your soul. What a blessed thing. I thank you for heeding the call to prayer.

I say, if the world shall break your heart, do not despair. Because a broken heart can become opened like a rose in God's love. What was once a bud can bloom. Take this love into the world, this beautiful fragrance that you are so blessed to have in your souls.

I know that this period of time seems overwhelmingly difficult and challenging. You may wonder can we indeed dispel the darkness. Yes, indeed, you can, and you will, and we shall be there with you. Stay on this path and transformation will be yours, enlightenment will be yours, the love of God will shine from your souls and bless this world so in need.

There are many here with you now embracing each one of you in this beautiful circle. So with all my love and blessings and the love of God, I leave you with one final thought. Pray, beyond your mind from the very depths of your souls with all your heart, and the kingdom will be yours. May you go in God's grace. I am your brother and friend, Yogananda.

COMPARING MEDITATION AND PRAYER
January 14, 2020

I wish to explain the differences and similarities in meditation and prayer. These things sometimes separate but can also be one and the same. In traditional Eastern meditation, one is taught to go within, to let the mind go, to find the stillness in the center of one's being in the heart chakra area, to relax the body completely but maintain awareness. In this place there is peace, there is a oneness.

In my own teaching, where I presented Kriya Yoga, learned through my teacher Sri Yukteswar, I focused on this going within and allowing the body to be a vessel of light, opening each chakra so that it was as if there was a beam of light extending from the lowest chakra all the way up through the Sahasrara (crown chakra) into the heavens. I presented this in a very scientific way, and this method in the West became very well-known back in my day. Many thousands of people tried this approach with great success, finding great peace, feeling the light, feeling the oneness with the cosmic forces and the consciousness of love pervading their being.

I must confess, my own meditation was a bit different. I went within and of course I experienced tremendous bliss and energies in being at one with the cosmos and often had visions (third eye - 6th Chakra) as you know. But I also spoke to God from the longings in my soul, sometimes just very simply asking for my soul to be at one with God. Other times I would have questions about my work or situations that had arisen, such as my separation from my homeland, and at the beginning of my time in America wondering, why am I here? How can I possibly be successful at this mission my guru has given me? All those questions were answered in prayer. But also, my deep desire in my soul to connect with the Creator brought God's love into my soul and began to transform it. I would always urge my students to talk to God, think about God all the time.

I always gave credit to God, not wanting the focus to be on myself. At no time did I seek to be worshiped as God on Earth, but rather as someone who had self-realized what I call 'Christ consciousness,' at oneness with God. Where there are ashrams and monasteries and temples where devotees pray, there is often a rapport created between the heavens and those longing to connect with their Creator beyond the oneness of feeling at one with the universe, into the gloriousness of truly feeling at one in love with the Creator.

This indeed is the meaning of the words in the gospels when Jesus says, 'I and the Father are one.' He did not mean he was God. In the East, when they interpret that wrongly as God incarnate, with Jesus or any other teachers, they are in error. For truly He was the first divine Son of God, but there have been others, although He is the greatest. Are not we all children of God, sons and daughters of our Creator who wishes us all to be at one with His essence which is the Divine Love?

My intention today is to draw a bridge, create a bridge between the meditation of going within and being at one with creation and the universe and opening up in humbleness to our Creator to receive the great love which is given to all who ask. If we take the meditation of going within and the humble prayer of reaching out for the essence of the Creator to be ours, we can call this a Divine Love meditation, for it is a combination of the two prayer and meditation.

I would encourage you to go within and be calm. Find that place in your heart, in your soul where there is the beautiful natural love given to all. Allow your mind to become still, your heart to be opened, your body to be at peace. Allow for the longings of your souls to reach the Creator in the humbleness that is required in the recognition of the great one. This is truly becoming transformed in Christ consciousness, becoming anointed with the love of the Creator. Being transformed as a soul from the mere image of God to at-onement with the very substance of God and immortality, eternal life. This is the gift that is offered from our most loving Creator. I encourage you to ask, for you truly shall receive.

I thank this one for taking the time to receive this message which I have longed to give to my students and to the world. May you all be blessed and transformed in God's love. I love you and I thank you. Go in peace. I am your brother and friend in the Celestial heavens, Yogananda. Thank you. God Bless you.

DIVINE ROMANCE
February 9, 2020

My dear friends you have come together in the presence of God, in the glow of His love drawn here by the deep longings in your souls to be at one in love with God. This is a divine romance you have chosen, and it is unlike any other. As you open to this love, all that is not of love begins to dissolve, to fall away and you feel this joy throughout your being.

You may wonder at times, how do I decide whether or not to pursue this or that, or take this path or another? If you do so with your mind, you will have some kind of logical conclusion. When you reach into your soul, you will feel that which is the way of love and joy. I will give you an obvious example here: Think of the vast sums of money that are spent on advertising attempting to get your attention to purchase this or that so you can be beautiful, sexually appealing, unique, successful, and satisfied. If these means of grabbing your attention did not work no one would use them. But in fact, they do grab the attention and often they appeal, of course, to very base desires.

The other side of this equation is the Celestial realm which also wishes for your attention because the deep desires you have to feel this love divine must supersede all other desires. As you consider what to put in your bodies, what is healthy, what satiates your palate also consider what you take in, what you watch, what you read, what you listen to, for the sake of your soul. True soul food, the love of God, this is worthy of your attention. All else will find its place. Consider what you choose to take in and go from the deep longings in your souls to decide so that you may live in joy.

You needn't be obsessed with the darkness, with the troubles of this world yet I know your good hearts are touched by the sufferings of others. I say consider staying in the love of God that you may truly touch every soul, so that you will become a magnet drawing in those who wish to feel this love to be healed, to be in joy. They will ask and you can respond in truth: 'May your soul be touched by God's love.' Each one of you come with this desire so bring it to the world.

My dear friends you are so blessed. I leave you with my love, my blessings and all of us here embrace you in the Creator's love. May God bless you and transform you. Peace, I am Yogananda.

Do Not Despair
March 3, 2020

I see there is a bit of a weight on you all today, as you see so many changes taking place on earth, the world that you live in. You have been given insight into these earth changes in advance, that you may pray and be in God's grace throughout, that you may trust your guidance as to how to react.

There is an inner and an outer world. The earth is a living being, as you are living beings, and the earth responds to repair, as you respond to heal your wounds, your walls and all that you have built or encountered. And you go to God, who brings His Great love into each soul to remove and dissolve these barriers that separate you. So too, the earth begins to remove and wash away and disrupt the in-harmonies that have been placed upon it.

It is a consciousness, and so, with your great consciousness of soul awareness, you can look upon these events and be joyful in knowing. As your souls are purified and brought into alignment with the Father's love, the earth too is being brought into alignment with its natural harmony, with its origins. Do not despair but go into your souls. Allow God to open them up so that you may live and walk in light and love and in grace without fear, for you are the light in this world by the grace of God. We are with you. Feel this, know it, and have faith. All will be well. With all my love and blessings and the protection of the Celestial realm, may God's love be upon you and transform your souls. In His love, I bid you farewell for now, I am Yogananda.

Stay In Grace
March 17, 2020

All of you have received the great gift of God's love and know the great truth of its availability. As each one of you grows on your journey to the Celestial heavens, as each one of you receives more and more of this great love, you truly become a channel for light and love in this world. So first and foremost, remember as the master said: "Seek ye first the kingdom of heaven and all else will be given to you." This is a great truth, and it indicates what is most important on this journey for all else will be given. The path will be illuminated by the love you carry. And as you know, this holy, sacred, glorious presence beyond the mind, beyond any words you say, is your gift to others.

As you grow and you bring this gift, this blessing, walking in grace is truly all that is required of you. Because you have asked, you have received. And as you touch other souls, and how well you know this, some will inquire as to what they are feeling around you, and should you wish to do so, you can tell them what your spiritual practice is.

The love of God humbles us all, and yet we are lifted up in its glory beyond any desire we may have had, or still have, for material things and for the satisfactions of this world. You know, of course, in spirit it is easier in some ways to let these things go because they no longer have any weight. And yet attachments linger on for many, and they hover near the earth planes wishing to satisfy their desires. For those who may be with us unseen, we ask God to bless them with love. And those who are in the physical realm we embrace them in God's love for they suffer from a certain blindness however temporary, and you who see and feel the light and love can shine on them, embrace them, and lift them up as you have been lifted. This is the great gift of God's love.

As the changes are upon you in this time all we have asked is for you to pray. To stay in grace beyond fear and to allow the light in your souls to guide you as to which path to take. This is still all that is required. Know you are protected and above all so very loved, as we all are by our heavenly Father. Be not afraid, stay in this peace, in this love. We are with you. All my love and blessings my dear friends, I am your brother, Yogananda.

Prayer Connects You With God's Soul
March 18, 2020

Dear friends I too wish to share some thoughts on prayer and the desire of each one of you to come together in prayer despite people being quarantined around the world. Due to the wonderful technology that is available to you, you are able to come together. From one point of view, you might think that there is a great disparity between one culture and another, one belief, one religion and another. And yet when people come together to enjoy the food of a different culture, whatever language barriers, whatever cultural barriers they think may exist, can dissolve. This is true with music and art and even the technology that spans the globe now.

During my time on earth, I was very interested in other cultures and seeking knowledge, seeking truth, and I wrote about this as, of course, you may know. I would be with some beautiful soul in another country and though we did not speak the same language we would come together in prayer in the grace of God, and whatever differences we supposed that we had were gone. We needed no interpreter for the joy and the oneness we felt in our prayer. Certainly, this is on a spiritual level, the level of soul, for I could say if you only pray with your mind in words, you could come together with that vibration with different cultures, but when the heart opens and God touches the soul with grace, with love, there are no barriers.

Prayer is a bridge connecting the earth plane to the heavens. Your prayers that long for the essence of the Creator for God's great love are a bridge of light connecting the Celestial heavens, all the spheres in-between, and the earth plane. It is a wonder to behold even from this Celestial realm where wonders never cease. The longings in your souls truly have created a bridge of light and love. I wish for each one of you transformation in the great love of God. And though I came from a different culture, are we not One in the grace of God? My beautiful friends, what a gift! May God bless you and transform you each one. I am your brother and friend, Yogananda.

A Glimpse of Eternity
March 27, 2020

I am Yogananda, your brother and friend, here to join you as you take a break from the world and allow the longings of your souls to reach out for the Creator's love. During this period of time, in this slowing down, many are being released from the mortal coil, from the physical body into spirit, where all will go permanently at some point.[52] Realize the freedom to be above the worries, the troubles, and the concerns of this world, as you pray to receive this love divine and you feel the presence of God's grace and light around you. To truly feel this is to have a glimpse of immortality, have a glimpse of eternity - a glimpse of the vastness of God's creation and the love that transforms each soul. Before you relinquish the physical body to spirit, allow the soul to be present above the mind, above the world, with the longings in your heart, your soul, and so precipitate the blessing of God's love.

So many have come into this circle of light today and you need not question their reasons. For our joy is in seeing all coming together with desire of each soul to be at one with its Creator. Fear not, for this change upon you in Divine Love opens the door to eternity. And through that door a light is descending from the Celestial heavens to the earth. To see this would be like looking at a constellation far away in another galaxy. And those here in the Celestial heavens, in that light, in that galaxy, looking down upon you on your beautiful planet where now the birds are singing - they're not worried, the sky is happy, the water is clear, there is rest and peace. This time of transition of the earth brings each of you into the glorious opportunity of the transition of your souls in God's love. We are with you on this journey, and we rejoice in the presence of almighty God and His glorious love, His essence bestowed upon each one.

Go in peace, rest in this joy beyond words, and know you are so deeply loved. May God bless each one in the transformation of your souls and this communion in this moment where you reside. God bless you! All my love and blessings to each one. I am Yogananda,

---

[52] Refers to the slowdown on earth during the Pandemic in 2020

How The Chakras Are Used in Spirit Communication
April 3, 2020

I come in the grace of God's love, and I am with White Eagle and Francis. They are my brothers. White Eagle is going to, at some point, speak to you about the Great Gathering of the tribes and its true meaning. Francis wishes to talk about the alignment between the angels and prayer and his experience. We have decided today that I should speak. I wish to give you some reference points so, on your journey, you do not become confused. You are all mediums. There is not one here who has not had the experience of thinking about someone, whether they be in spirit or on earth, and a song comes on, or you are captured by a picture, or maybe a butterfly, indeed some sign that connects you with that soul. You say: 'Oh, wasn't that a wonderful thing!' You felt that this person was present or perhaps that the person will call on you. If they be in spirit, they may come as I come. If they be on earth, they may call you through whatever medium is available to them or to you.

There are energy centers in my culture that we call chakras. Many of you are familiar with this concept but some may not be. The sixth chakra, sometimes referred to as the Christ chakra, is between the eyes and somewhat above. You sometimes will see pictures or meet people who have a bindi at that spot which is a dot representing the openness of that chakra. It is also called the third eye. It is even represented on the U.S. dollar bill. This eye in many cultures represents the opening to the astral or spirit world. When my teacher, Sri Yukteswar, passed into spirit, he would come to me in this way, and I could see him.

Those of you who have visions, whether it be of lights or spirits, you are seeing through this center. Through this center, spirits can communicate but unless the medium is also aligned within their soul with the Divine, and with the Celestial angels, and with God, they may be able to communicate only with spirits who have no interest in the transformation of the soul in love. They may thus receive messages that are purely intellectual. This, of course, is not a bad thing if for instance you are to repair something that is broken. If you get a technical message from a spirit or from a book or whatever, through guidance, this technical information can be very useful.

But if you are on the path of God's love and you wish to be transformed and you wish to communicate with those of us in the Celestial heavens, the heart chakra must be opened. We call this chakra anahata, because, as I have said before, the heart is the doorway to the soul. When you pray earnestly with your soul longings, your heart is open, and God can touch you and bring this love into your souls.

When your heart is opened and this chakra and the ajna, the sixth chakra is opened between the eyes, there is a light that comes down from the 7th chakra. We in the East call this the crown chakra, the seventh chakra and it is from the crown and above because it receives from the heavens. It is called sahashara or sahashra. I tell you all this with the hope that I have given some clarity because my wish for all of you is to be in touch with your souls, to receive guidance that is Celestial. I wish for your hearts to be open, your souls to be blessed, the third eye to be open to communicating and for God, our most loving, glorious Creator, to shower you all from above with His love divine.

My brothers will come again and speak. May the living waters flow in you and through you. May you drink up of God's love. I am your brother and friend and I love you. I am Yogananda.

GOD'S LOVE
April 17, 2020

I wish to add to the master's beautiful description of the soul in relationship to its Creator. I give the example of falling in love, human love. You're willing to give your whole heart because you are so enamored. Then perhaps you find out that the object of your affection feels the same way. You thank God. You thank your lucky stars. You're willing to jump out of your skin and you simply might say 'Oh, what joy' and mean it because you feel like your whole being is buzzing.

This is the natural love, the human love, which extends to your parents, your families, your friends, your children, your animals, and the love of Mother Earth. Then imagine and consider, if you will, our holy Creator who gave you this potential of not only the joy and harmony of the human love fulfilled, but of the great gift of offering His gift of Divine Love, the very essence of Himself to each one that embraces it and transcends the human condition. Imagine the love of God that has given all these gifts and you giving your heart to the Creator who will fill your heart, fill your soul with a love that is eternal, that contains immortality in the very essence of God. One love, however great, is fleeting. The other is everlasting. You will know and you do know the difference in the glory, in the light, in the transformation of God's love.

Thank you. I am your brother and friend for all eternity. I am Yogananda. God bless you.

Walk This World in The Love of God
May 9, 2020

I come in God's love, and I wish to say just a few things to this beautiful circle of light. The gifts that each soul may receive become a blessing to the world when they are in love, and the great gift of the Creator's love raises these gifts up, and thus the world. This circle and the greater circle of this beautiful community has so much support. Our hearts are with you and more importantly, the love in our souls.

The dear brother (GB) who mentioned the master and his opening his arms in the gift of love beyond words, has shared something every soul can offer. When you walk in grace and in God's love words are often not necessary, but should you speak to them please know that they contain the intention and the presence of your souls. You need not convince anyone that you love them when they feel your love.

So, as you walk through this world with love, the love of God in your souls, you touch many, you bless many, and you bring a healing presence. May you continue each to know from the very depths of your souls and with all your heart that God loves you. We will never abandon you. Should you call, we shall come. And as the dear brother (TA) said: 'he felt no fear' so walk forth in love and those who are fearful - you will bring peace to them.

May the peace that passes understanding be with each. May the glory of His love be yours. With all my love and blessings, I am your brother in Christ. I am Yogananda.

Thoughts Become Things
May 19, 2020

I am here Yogananda your brother and friend in God's love, a transformed soul. The world is filled with knowledge, and it is true that thoughts become things no matter whether the thought is received in spirit or the thought is inspired by the mind.

When the thought comes to create something, to build something, or to change something these inspirations can indeed take form and many beautiful things can come into life. Many inventions began as seeds implanted in the mind. For those of you who seek to build a truly spiritual existence you too have a vision, have a feeling of something that can be developed.

On the path of spiritual knowledge there are all kinds of wisdom. When knowledge is realized as truth by the soul it becomes understanding. When understanding is embraced by the entire being and carries with it a state of grace, this is a divine revelation. This reflects the beginning of a soul changing from the image to the very substance of its Creator, our heavenly Father, our glorious Creator. Allow your souls to test the waters, allow your hearts to feel God's love. This discernment will inform the transformation of your soul in the knowing with all your being that this is the path of God's love.

So, we always encourage you, pray with your hearts, from the depths of your souls, that our glorious Creator may open up each soul and fill it with the essence of His being. This Divine Love that transforms from the mere image to the very substance, from the human to the divine angel, from the mortal to the Immortal. This is the gift of eternity.

I shall pray with you this day and always. We come close whenever you wish in this beautiful circle of light, in this communion of souls, and in God's love. I am your brother and friend in God's love. I am Yogananda. God bless you!

Ask!

May 29, 2020

Isn't it wonderful the feeling that you carry when you love someone, a most beautiful gift, or you walk out into nature and you see the colors and smell the fresh air, or the sea, or the forest, looking up at the blue skies and the sheltering clouds; or you fall in love and you're so beside yourself, you can let everything else go just to be in that feeling of bliss, knowing that you are loved, willing to love, to give of yourself.

All these wonderful gifts are part of the human existence and the natural love between humans and God's creation. These wonderful gifts can be quite healing, for love can heal many wounds. Of course life gives you a good measure of challenges as well as blessings, but I tell you that this gift that you have come together to receive, to be open to, the love of the Creator, or as my friend here might say, 'aloha from above,' this love embraces all, and this gift carries within it the seeds of change and transformation far beyond momentary bliss.

While living on earth one must consider one's physical health and well-being, perhaps the raising and protection of your children as well as yourself, what kind of work you do, creating a lovely home and so forth. All these earthly things and all the challenges they bring can be mighty. When you approach these things of the earth with the intellect, or from experience, the guidance of others, teachers, or books, you make your way, and you can recover from injury, tragedy, and loss. You can also find great joy in creating, in inventions, building a family and such. Yet, when you touch on your soul and the deeper longings to connect with your Creator there is the possibility to connect with that which is immortal, eternal, carrying with it such great joy and glory as to be somewhat indescribable with language.

We always say, go into your heart, go within, connect with your soul, and then send up a prayer from that place 'Dear God touch my soul, heal my wounds, lift me up in love divine.' This act of asking and being humble enough to recognize the Creator brings with it eternity and the connection from the mortal to immortal, from the human to the divine and the company of Celestial angels. We are drawn to this prayer, this longing and communion in God's love. May all here be blessed, healed, transformed, in this great love that awakens the soul, lifts you up above the earth plane in bliss immortal.

I thank you. May God bless each one with this great love divine. I love you; I am your brother and friend in God's love, I am Yogananda.

BRING IT TO THE WORLD!
June 30, 2020

Isn't the music of love a beautiful gift that sends a signal from on high to the heart, through the ears and lifts the soul up? I loved to sing praises to God, but was I a great singer? Ha, ha, hardly! Yet I had great love and so I now realize how my students tolerated some of my singing, as they also sang, and we let ourselves go into love and allowed the music to lift us up. This I have in common with my dear brother J.W. - he was informed yesterday that when the air clears, we encourage him to go out and sing. To do this without fear, without worry of judgment, because he carries the seed of love; and let those who have ears to hear, and those who have hearts to be touched, experience the awakening of their souls. And he would tell you he's no Caruso and yet there is beauty in melody and even more important, in the intention.

Dear brother[53] when you connect with your pastor, your friend, bring him a song to lift him up, to heal his sadness, to bring him the glory of the Divine Love. I ask you my brothers, is this not the task you have set yourselves to perform? Is not the intention in your hearts to bring to others the glory that you feel in your hearts, the happiness in your souls touched by God? Well, this we share! How much you wish to do this and to how many, we leave that up to you, but you cannot share it with too many.

I gave up the world so that somehow, I could be a blessing to the world, to bring it truth and healing, and what I knew of God's love. You who have this enlightenment can reach the many who are longing, who are hungry, and yes, some physically but so many hungry in their souls to make a connection with what is above this world, that is in the love of God, beyond the words. If you cannot have a prayer with them physically or through this media, send them a song, give them a song.

This I set before you my brothers that you may engage, however deeply, with however many you are moved to. In the glory of God's love you have nothing to lose except reluctance. May the great gift of God's love continue to light up our souls and raise us up in the joy and bliss that is God's gift. With all my love and blessings... I am Yogananda.

Holy Communion Holy Community
July 7, 2020

I had read the Gospels and studied the teachings of Jesus, and I was in awe, so I wrote about him from my somewhat limited understanding and beliefs. As you know, not all of my insights were, what you would say, 100% exact, but what I called the Christ consciousness, if you read between the lines, you see this is about the love of God in your soul,

---
53 Speaking to John M about his pastor friend.

waking up, being christed, being anointed. This I knew. And my followers in the West they could comprehend this message because it is nearly impossible for one to turn their back on such great love. In my prayers, I asked to carry this love into the world every day.

I tell you there were challenges and I had moments which you could almost define as being in despair when I prayed: 'Oh God what can I do, am I in the right place, is this really what you want for me, can I truly be a blessing, a help to others?' And the answer was: 'Yes, and you are.'

Allow yourself to be above the doubt and the self-recrimination. Be in the flow of grace. Please know that what I now succinctly understand, being in this Celestial realm, and what all of us wish to convey to all of you is to focus on what is truly important. You live in the world so of course you must meet your commitments, but you have chosen the path of this divine grace, Divine Love or divine truth. So, we ask you to love your brothers and sisters in the community of Divine Love whatever their faults, whatever their disagreements, whatever their lifestyle. Because they, like you, have all chosen, through whatever their capacity is, to receive the love of God and to go in prayer and ask for it. I tell you as your brother and friend there is no greater choice than asking for the gift of God's love. This is Holy Communion, holy community. Be One in God's love as we are One with you and God is One in His love with all.

I love you and wish every blessing. Know you have protection, know you are guided, be happy and joyous in this beautiful love you hold in your souls and this rapport with all of us. I am Yogananda. God bless you!

Be Open to Healing
July 28, 2020

I was present yesterday when brother Judas conveyed his message of the healing power of light and love. We had discussed this, as we often do, as to who would deliver the message. We agreed it should be Judas. I tell you he is a wonderful, bright, sunny, humorous angel. Much maligned in the world at times, but if the world could see him as he is, they would realize God works with all no matter what, no matter your past. Judas' journey, which some of you are familiar with, was not without its pain and self-retribution, but he was always a follower of the master. As you may know, he thought he was doing something good and when he realized it would not turn out the way he had supposed, he was struck in ways that are hard to describe in words, and yet, here he is - a divine angel who communicates wisdom and truth and the love of God and yesterday spoke eloquently about light and its vibration and its power to heal. I wish to add to that conversation.

Most healers on the earth are working in what you deem the natural love. Because wounds and hurts and encrustations, as you say, can be dealt with and healed in the natural love, providing that the recipient is open. You may wonder what is a Divine Love healing if all can be healed in the natural?

The natural love and its healers do not heal the soul in the sense that natural healing cannot provide or is not open to the Divine Love of the heavenly Father to transform it. Yet there are many souls who are in need of a healing, and they suffer from abuses in their childhood. This may be physical, may be sexual, may be verbal, may be environmental. Some suffer from the continuing of the habits of those who came before them genetically, DNA-wise, parents, grandparents, and so forth. And, difficult as it may seem, they are often able to get healings by being open to the natural love and natural love healers on the earth. This does many a great deal of good.

Others get to a point where they simply cry out to God, 'Dear God how can I overcome this addiction? How can I overcome this illness, these habits, these wounds?' This very calling out, this prayer and deep longing not only connects with God but opens a spiritual door that may have been closed and now allows for that soul to awaken and see the situation in a way they could not perceive before. Whereas they might now clearly see the environment that they are in is harmful - the company they keep, the places that they go to. It could even be what they watch via the media and film. And this has drawn negativity, darkness, vexed spirits, and so now they see that if they can use their will, they can extricate themselves from these influences and indeed, this must be done.

Whether they proceed in receiving a healing through natural love and the healers on earth, or whether they open to God's love, either way will bring great benefits. In the natural healing they may clearly see what is necessary to be done and what they can accomplish themselves by changing their habits, maybe their diets, what they consume in entertainment and through the various media as well as working with physical healers. In Divine Love healing to quote brother Judas, "when you open to this love of God you lift the vibrations surrounding you and open to a healing in your body, mind and soul."

It has been said, related to you, that anything can be healed except the organs of the individual that are beyond repair. I wish to amend that slightly by stating while it is true in the absolute sense, what is known on earth by doctors and scientists and the like as being beyond repair, is a variable. For this is not what we see and certainly not beyond what God can do. I say this to you so that you should never give up hope and have faith in the healing powers of God's love and your own ability to be guided in every way.

May this world receive a deep healing and your prayers and those all around the world lift the vibrations on the earth to a new consciousness, to harmony in the natural and the Divine Love. May God bless you with every good and perfect gift my dear friends, my brothers and sisters on the path of Divine Love. I am Yogananda. May God bless you.

Soul Transformation - Food for Thought
August 7, 2020

My dear friends, much has been said in the world about the power of thought to become things, to be able to visualize and then build upon that vision. Of course, this is true. You see manifestations of it everywhere. It is also true that when you send thoughts to us, we feel them. When you send thoughts to another, they may not feel the words, but they feel your intentions. This is why we always talk to you about how you are receivers, and you are transmitters.

What goes in does come out. This is why it is important to evaluate what you wish to take in, as they say: 'food for thought.' As it is important in the material world for your bodies to take in foods that are healthy and nutritious, to sustain them and prevent them from illness and disease, it is just as important as the thoughts that you take in and send out.

We in the Celestial heavens always influence you to raise your thoughts to the highest spiritual thoughts. I told my students, 'Talk to God.' Keep your mind on God. Whatever your need, it will be answered. This will raise your thoughts, as I have said earlier, to the level of soul. Then you begin to perceive with the soul. Within the mind of God, within the flow of love, in a state of grace, in this Holy Communion, the soul knows, and you feel it. This is sometimes referred to as the soul of the mind or the higher mind by some. I come to you specifically to talk about the soul transformed by God's love, this angelic soul, able to perceive what is best, what path to follow, what is in the flow of God's love. These soul perceptions, this is what we wish for you all so that you are not troubled by the mind.

Again, as I have said before, let your soul be above your mind so that your soul influences your mind and not the other way around. You wonder: 'How do I do this? I have all kinds of feelings.' You do this in prayer. You send up the intention to receive and the most Holy Spirit of the Creator opens your soul to receive and awakens your soul. You feel this. You feel this in your heart, your solar plexus. You feel this glow, this light. Questions that arise dissolve into truth. You are in the flow of God's love and grace. This, my friends, my beautiful friends, this is your destiny. Should you wish to be transformed, you will be. So when we say: 'follow your heart,' it is because there is such a close connection between the heart and the soul. Your heart is your feeling center. This is the place. When you open your heart, as you know, the most loving Creator can open up your soul. The heart is contained in the soul.

This is also evident in music when someone sings deeply from their heart, we often call this 'music of the soul.' My songs that I sang when on earth, I sang from my soul. I was not some great singer, some kind of opera singer, but my intentions were so deep from my soul, that I felt such joy in singing. This I give to you. Let your hearts be open that your souls will be blessed, that your minds will be at ease in the peace that passes all understanding. Allow this throughout your day. Whenever you are distracted, go to your heart that God and the angels may touch your soul.

I pray you will all stay in the light and the love of God. Whenever you call, we shall be there, for our love is always with you and we too are on this journey together, at one in God's love. My love to all of you. God's love to all of you. May you stay in His warm embrace, always. God bless you. I am Yogananda.

Spiritual Defense
August 21, 2020

I wish to touch on the subject of defense. We commonly think of defense in terms of the armies of the world defending the liberties of their citizens. Yet if we go back to the origins of humankind we can say, after the fall, that the defense mechanisms became part of the human DNA to protect humans from wild animals or beasts and soon afterwards from other humans, from tribal warfare and so forth. This is still, of course, a part of the human psyche and DNA and it does not take much convincing to assure you that this is true. Most people are aware of it and take it as a given.

But let us talk about the defense systems that we have built to protect ourselves from the slings and arrows of others who judge, who seek to control, who are aggressive or violent, whether it be physically or with words. In a sense our defense mechanisms are always up, always on guard, and from there we build walls to protect our families but in spiritual terms to protect our hearts. For there is only so much psychic pain and emotional wounding one can endure.

I speak on this subject because of the importance of being vulnerable, of opening, in safety, in faith, in trust to God that He may bestow the great gift of His love. The more that you can open your heart in a sanctuary the more it can be infilled with the love of God. This is why through history people have sought refuge and created sanctuaries, places where they could feel safe enough, protected enough to open up without fear and to bypass the DNA of defense so that the Creator might bless them with a great inflowing of His love and grace.

Let this be your guide as you trust each other more and more in the circle of light, in your prayers alone and together and create an opening, a spiritual magnetism that cannot be denied - a powerful force of light shining upon the darkness and bringing about the change we all so desire and that God wishes for humankind, for every soul in His creation. May the love of God bring you faith and trust and every good and perfect gift in grace. I am your brother and friend in the love of God. Thank you. I am Yogananda.

Curse Not the Darkness but Praise the Light
September 4, 2020

My brothers and sisters, I come to you with the love of God in my soul, as you pray for the love of God to be in your souls. I wish for you to consider this: There are two ways to approach life. You can approach it from the point of view of everything that needs to be corrected, everything that's wrong, every hurt, every sin and error in this world, or you can approach it by embracing all in the love of God, seeing the light and love and bringing that to the darkness. We come and we will not curse the darkness, but we bring the light that those in darkness may be healed, that their eyes may be opened with the light of love, that they may be lifted as you are lifted, in the glorious grace of God.

If God is not your goal, then you will be mired in the affairs of the world, so consider where you wish to be and what you wish your heart to be open to. Are we going to be a blessing to this world or are we just going to rail at it? One needn't buy into the negativity for it is not beneficial to the progression of your souls. I am not saying this is a retrograde step, but it can cause stagnation and the inability of letting go of those things which allow your soul to be transformed in every moment in the love of God. Is this not your desire? Is this not your stated goal?

Consider what you choose in every hour in every moment to the best of your ability. I do not wish to come and be in judgment but to encourage. I do this out of my love for you. Imagine God's love for you - how great it is; imagine the world being open to God's love. A world utterly changed from the darkness into light. Curse not the darkness but praise the light and the love of God. Bring it to every soul. This I ask of you my dear brothers and sisters. This the Celestial angels ask of you. For as the great president once stated: 'a house divided cannot stand.' And as another leader entreated: 'Keep your eyes on the prize.' These two great souls, let them be your guides in the love of God. With all my love and blessings to you both and to all of you that this message may reach. I come to you in the grace of God, your brother in Christ, your friend and guide. I am Yogananda. God bless you.

Nature and Divine Love
September 6, 2020

My dear ones, as the waves wash upon the shore, as the sun rises and sets, as the moon lights up the night, allow yourselves to be in harmony with nature. Allow your souls to be in the flow of the love of God, without attachment, but in harmony with the natural world and in the flow of God's timing. When one goes within and senses the oneness of all things, it is a beautiful realization. And as I have said before, when one connects with the Creator, the source of all things, there is unspeakable bliss, joy, and happiness. The flow of God's love and harmony with nature go hand in hand.

Although the love of God transcends the world, it is never at odds with it. This is why those who speak out for social justice, against tyranny and violence, only need to be in harmony with the natural love. That love gives one insight into how the world can be in harmony in all ways, in brotherly and sisterly love, in a sustainable environment, in peace and nonviolence, in good health, and all these things of the earth that God wishes for His children to be in harmony with.

For you who choose the path of Divine Love, you can see the beauty of the natural and harmony on earth. You also bring a light that is more powerful than human insight, and that is the perceptions of your soul that allow the grace of God and the great message of His love to touch all who wish to be at one with their Creator.

May God bless you and carry you in this great endeavor to bring the message of divine truth to the world. May I say: "We have your backs, and you have our love and our hearts." Whatever you need, call on us, God will provide, and we shall do his bidding. With all my love and blessings, I am your eternal friend in the love of God, Yogananda.

Love is the Healer
November 6, 2020

I am aware of the thoughts of healing which not only are here in this beautiful circle but are being sent across the airwaves of the earth. So many are wishing, praying for a healing.

Consider the human body and when there is disease it means the cells are out of alignment, out of harmony with their natural state. All healing is a realignment of the natural vibrations and done through means of light. As you know love carries light. So when you send love you also send light. When there is illness and the person afflicted has faith and allows the love and light of healing to come in, it becomes possible. As you know when organs are damaged beyond God's laws of repair they may not always be adjusted to their natural state. However, as I have remarked before, the laws of God and nature are beyond the scope of human understanding and science. Who would have imagined one could transplant a heart or a kidney or grow a prosthesis? Only a few years ago this would have been considered science fiction.

Consider the state of the earth, the state of sleep that pervades the earth, as Confucius[54] has remarked. I tell you two wrongs never make a right. If someone were to attack you, you might defend yourself, but to retaliate does not solve the negative issue and bring it to a harmonious result. All of the negativity upon the earth, the violence, the threats, the anger, all these things which are out of harmony with the laws of God and Divine Love can be healed in light, healed in love.

I urge you to respond, yes in truth, but above all with the love of God in your soul. Send this vibration out to the leaders of the world, to every country, and to the planet itself from this lattice of light that your souls sit in. You my dear friends influence upon the earth that is greater beyond what you can imagine. I would say reflect on the prayers that have been said and answered from the requests you have received and the many, many, healings that have come. Use these as your examples. Let God's love and light be your template to bless the world.

I send my love and blessings to all here and the many here in spirit today. God's love is connecting all of us on this beautiful Celestial bridge. How I love you. May God bless you each. I am Yogananda.

Allow God to Change Your Soul
November 10, 2020

I come to this beautiful circle of light in this time of change that is upon the earth. I come to say everything in God's universe is alive and in flux. The universe is progressive. You are all here because you wish to be changed into the very substance of your Creator.

---

54 Refers to a message received by Al Fike from Confucius.

In the material world there is change and there is also resistance. The greater the resistance the more friction or heat is created. On the material plane this can result in inharmony that can lead to very negative circumstances such as war, violence and so forth. For those on earth who are on the spiritual path there is, as you say, expiation - the letting go, forgiving and forgetting, allowing God to touch your heart, to change your soul. And when there is resistance, you might feel the heat. At other times this is manifested in anger or disbelief, negativity, skepticism, or feeling unworthy. This is why prayer for God's love is so important and why we love coming to your circles of light and being in prayer with you.

As you step out of the world and into the light and on to the bridge to the Celestial heavens, as your souls awaken and you allow the change of the essence of the Creator to be yours in very substance, a real part of your being. If you wish to change others, allow yourself to be transformed for they will feel the change in you. And as you bring them truth and your presence and allow God to speak through you, work through you, you can change the world. You can touch many, for this is soul to soul, above the mind, and in the grace of God. These changes that you requested are yours. This world will be blessed as you are blessed.

As we have said many times, do not fret about the past or worry about tomorrow, but be in the present. Be in His presence! Bring that to each moment as you serve the world with love. As my brother Gandhi said: 'Be the change you wish to see in the world.' Isn't that beautiful?

May God bless you with His love divine. I am your brother and friend. I am Yogananda.

The Path of the Heart

November 30, 2020

This love (the love of God) that permeates the universe is yours for the longing and transforms each soul. This love that brought you all together in this circle of prayer, this love that the Creator showers upon us when we come with open hearts and the sincere longings of our souls, this love, is of the highest vibration. If you were to speak it, it would be as if a beam of light shining upon the darkness. This vibration that singers reach for, to touch the heart, to awaken the soul, is the vibration of love. It is simple. Let it embrace your entire being. Allow this love into your heart, the doorway to your soul.

There are many words in the world. There are many teachings. You have been gifted with the truths of Divine Love and the true Gospel of the master. If you were to pursue this path purely with your mind and absorb all the information you would find that the ascendancy of the soul over the mind is required for the desired result of connecting to the loving Creator. The path of the heart that opens is a simple path. It does not require deep intellect or knowledge of everything in the universe, but it does require an openness and a willingness to allow God to open your soul and fill your entire being with His grace and the love divine.

Each one here is connected in the embrace of God, in the Song of love (The Bhagavad Gita). May the love of our Creator change your soul, heal your heart, and lift you up above this world that you may be a blessing to it. May your prayer for God's love be your template in the world that you may speak from the love in your soul, that you may sing from the longing in your soul and the light in your heart. May your entire being be blessed and transformed.

Remember the heavenly Father, Creator of all, loves you, each one His child. As you love your children, the heavenly Father loves all His children with the love eternal. Do no worry, do not be troubled. Live this love with each other, with your families, with your friends, and yes, with your enemies too. As the master advised 'love those who consider themselves your enemies.' Love all, bless all. You who have the glow of God's love, each one of you in your soul, how wonderful! Thank you for taking my message. All my love and blessings to each. I am your brother in the love of God. I am Yogananda. May God bless you!

THE MIRACLE OF SOUL TRANSFORMATION
December 14, 2020

I come to this gathering drawn by your prayers, each soul longing to be touched, to receive the essence of the Creator - the miracle that is the transformation of each soul in the love of God. You do not need to leave your body, only to put your soul first. When you do this, when you allow your heart to be touched and God opens your soul, and you are lifted, and you can be healed.

In this great love of God which touches every soul that longs for it, this glow you feel transcends the world and yet as I have said, 'embraces it.' It is not a secret, and it is not a mysticism to be uncovered. It is a simple truth, and it is yours for the asking. As the love of God comes into your soul and the light in this circle expands, you can send it to each one of those souls in your prayers today and to each other. There is great power and majesty in Divine Love. And though you cannot give a person's soul this love you can love a person from your soul with this love.

If only we would be mindful during our day, in our conversation with God and the angels, to walk with them as the day unfolds and you begin to see the flow of grace. I encourage you to do this even if only for a day, if only for an hour, to set your sights on the great love of the Creator and the guidance that is there for you.

This is why we are here speaking from our souls to your souls: *On this journey where each one will be transformed from the mortal to the immortal, from the human to the divine angel, from the finite to the infinite in the love of God.* May this blessing be yours. Have no doubt. Perish the thought that is not of love. My friends, stay in your heart and be that blessing you wish to be. With all my love in the grace of God. I am your brother and friend Yogananda. May God bless you.

Chapter 6: LADIES OF THE LIGHT

Care Darby Walsh

After I had been a practicing Hindu/Sufi/Yogi for about 20 years, I found myself in a deep, dark condition. I was bewildered and questioned how that feeling was even possible after so many years on spiritual paths, meditations, and manifestations with several gurus. In the midst of this crisis, I removed all the photos, beads, crystals, etc. from my little meditation altar and just started to pray. Not to any guru or saint but just directly to my Creator for help! 'Dear God, I am in a very dark place after all these years of walking spiritual paths, reading all the books, meeting the teachers, and meditating daily. Please help me find the light and love and joy that I wish to have in my soul. Please bring me someone who has the truth!'

I met Care less than a week later in an alley in Austin, Texas outside of a folk music cafe named Chicago House. I was leaving the cafe after having played a few songs, and she was going in. She stopped me in the alley, and we had a brief discussion about music and poetry. I was stunned by her! The light and happiness that seemed to emanate from her, her beauty, and presence was such a contrast to the dark condition I was in. My soul felt drawn to her like a magnet. She said she had performed her poetry there at times, and occasionally had noticed me playing songs. She told me her name, Care.

I spent the next few weeks talking about her to my house mate who was also a musician, and asked him, 'If you see her at Chicago House tell her that I would very much like to talk to her again.' A week after Christmas just before the New Year, he did run into her at the coffee house. She said she would be there the next night and would like to meet up with me. When I arrived, the place was nearly empty because people were on Christmas break. We sat, had tea, and talked.

The conversation quickly turned to spiritual matters after I told her that I had seen and felt a light around her that was so magnetic I wished to get to know her. She told me she worked with the homeless and often stayed in their makeshift camps serving as a prayer warrior and Divine Love minister. I asked if she was a Christian and she said, 'Yes, but not a conventional one.' I responded that I had some issues with Christianity that probably meant we weren't going to be friends. She said she was very open minded and asked me what religion I was. 'Hindu', I replied. She responded, 'Really, are your parents Hindu'? 'No, I grew up catholic' was my reply. 'Oh,' she reflected, 'that might explain a lot.'

Next, Care asked me what issues I had with Christianity and reiterated that she was very open minded and would not be offended. Encouraged by this, I said, 'Ok, for one, I love Jesus but do not believe he is God.' She responded sympathetically, 'Well, he's not, and he doesn't really appreciate people worshiping him as such, but he also knows that when their prayers are sincere, they go directly to God and are heard. What else?'

'I don't believe Mary was a virgin, but, from my studies, believe she was later portrayed as one - the only true substitute for the Greek virgin goddesses who gave birth to the gods.' Surprisingly, Care came back with this: 'Well, I know Mary, and she was no virgin; in fact, she had 8 children, Jesus being the oldest, and Joseph is his natural father. Jesus also says his blood has no power to redeem anyone's sins, and as one reaps, they shall sow.' Eager to keep this going I asked, 'Ok, but what about the Holy Spirit? 'Well, since Jesus is not God but His first true son to be transformed in His love, there is no Trinity. You know, Jimbeau, your spirit is the active energy of your soul, and it is how people perceive you. Well, God's spirit is the active energy of His soul and when people pray to receive His love, His spirit conveys His love into their souls. Orthodox Christians call this being in the Holy Spirit but it is really receiving the love of God through His Holy Spirit.'

I was simply blown away by all this and felt if this is Christianity, we were gonna be friends! 'How do you know all this?' I inquired.

'The Celestial angels talk to me.'

'Really?'

'Yes. Would you like to come and see where they talk to me?'

'Yes!'

'Do you have a car?'

'Yes!'

So, we got in my car, and she got in the back seat. I'm thinking, 'Ok, this isn't a date,' but I'm so happy to be with this person that it doesn't matter at all. We drove out of Austin into what was at that time the countryside with very little development and few houses. Care said a short prayer that was just beautiful and lifted the atmosphere in the car to where it seemed we were floating on air. We pulled into a country driveway and drove up a hill to a house. I got out of the car and started walking towards the house but was told, 'No, it's over here.'

In the moonlight we walked over to a large green lawn (unusual for that area) bordered by some tall pines, and Care kneeled and sat on her legs and began to pray. I don't remember the words but only that it was a very humble prayer to God, and I was moved to the point of closing my eyes and knelt resting on my legs.

Suddenly, there appeared some kind of light flashing in front of me and I wondered for a moment if it was the moon going behind the clouds, but it was more insistent, so I opened my eyes. Before me were two very large beings, clearly a man and a woman, made of light, wearing robes. They were maybe 18-20 feet tall. I was terrified so I closed my eyes, but I could still see them. I was shaking with fear and watched them approaching me. I felt their touch on my shoulders, and I was immediately calmed. The man said, 'Do not be afraid, we love you, God loves you. Go in peace.' Then they were gone. A few moments later Care said very gently. 'This is where the angels talk to me.' We went inside the house; I asked her to marry me. She said, yes!

We spent the next 4 years on an amazing, miraculous journey together until she passed into spirit exactly as she predicted, 'In a fiery car crash.' We're still in touch.

Make Them a Sandwich
May 28, 2019

You are all now beginning to see your dream, the larger community being realized right before your eyes. This is not something that happened in my time when I was on earth, but it was my dream. So, I share with you in this outreach that you have now, so many coming to you, that the angels have given you charge; the love in your soul has touched many and will continue to do so. When people come to the Divine Love through whatever avenue they find it, they are usually very bound up in the material world, as you know. All of you were once in this position. As you pray for God's love and receive it in your souls, these things fall away. Yes, the material is useful, but you are no longer so attached.

And now you see that those who come, they can be quite attached. In a sense this can be called spiritual materialism which is the trappings of spiritual life that people cling to, signs and symbols, even the modes of dress. Of course, certain things do remind them of God. These are not bad things, but ultimately these things begin to fall away as the soul opens to our heavenly Father's love and are no longer necessary.

But I tell you all this, not because you don't know it, but to remind you that those who are coming to you will often have these trappings. Just be aware and be kind and loving. As we have told you, do not judge others who may disagree or have other opinions. Embrace them in love. Make them a sandwich. Do whatever you do in love, for love is the great magnetism that draws those souls to you and really to God.

The work I do now is soul to soul. There are, of course, spirits who are very helpful on the material plane helping to fulfill the wishes of those who need material things. Though this help is not soul changing what is provided by these spirits are good things. But we who wish to serve the Father in love, we work on the soul level. This is where all of you are headed. Despite the distractions of the world and all the things that we have to do in the world, and you have to do in the world, you are now blessed to the point where you know that the work you do is soul to soul. I am delighted to be with you in this.

My dear love, Jimbeau, thank you for allowing me to come through. God bless you all. I love you. May God shower you with His love. I am Care.

THE DIVINE TRUTH IS GOD'S LOVE
April 7, 2019

I have been here listening to your conversation. I want to thank my beloved here for sharing this story about the angels. But I want to correct his story a bit because it wasn't that I talked to angels, I talked to God. The angels talked to me. Now I am a Celestial. I am in the Celestial heavens. So, I have the privilege of talking to you all.

Please know that the truth, divine truth, is that God's love is available to all, not enforced on any soul but as a gift to any soul that should ask for it. I wish to remind you beautiful souls here in this room of light, that many have received God's love who may have been in error about this or that, this dogma or that, or some other belief. When you open your soul up and allow God to place His love in it and change it, this transcends mental beliefs. So please know that divine truth is God's love. You have come to be open to receiving it, this is the truth. This is a wonder.

I wish also to speak to this one who has had this vision of light with these spirits, whose soul has long been seeking and attuned to the Father's love. I would say to her, only her mind is in the way of this vision because she has a gift of seeing. When she allows her soul to be completely open to this gift, she will be able to share this with others. So not to worry. All is in God's time and in God's hands. Suspend your doubt and pray.

As my beloved knows, I spent many hours a day in prayer. He now is, as they say, my 'boots on the ground.' He finds this humorous, as I would imagine, since I didn't really wear shoes. So, my dear souls here, thank you for allowing me to come. There are many, many here with you. This beautiful room in this house is a blessed place. You may be rest assured, this is a place of prayer and a sanctuary. When you come here to pray, we will always be here with you. God's love will be showered upon you to the extent that you open and allow God to open your souls to receive it.

So, stay in the light, my friends, and my beloved. Let your worries go. Allow God to direct your lives that you may be in the flow. Be not concerned for the troubles of this world. Just allow yourself to be a blessing to all. Love all. This will make the change that you so wish, not only in yourself but in this world. May God bless you all. My love to all of you. And to my beloved, thank you. May God bless you all. I love you. I am Care.

Follow the Path of Divine Love
September 9, 2019

I am here, your sister and friend in God's love, Care. My dear Jimbeau is very happy to be around this energy, this feminine energy in this room. But I want to address the words of the song that the dear sister sang.[55] I walked the path of love when I was on Earth. I am still walking that path. Yes, it is a road less traveled but as you know, when you are in the love of God, you are in the flow of things. You are lifted above the material world, even beyond a sense of space and time because everything falls into God's time. Your worries fly out the door. Your heart opens. You feel the

---
55 Reference to a song written and played by Jane G.

joy of not only the natural world which is indeed a blessing, but the door to heaven opens and you are touched by the grace of love that showers from the heavenly Father into your souls. The flow of this love puts you in the flow the Father's love and time. You open your heart, and your soul opens to the company of angels. Everything falls into perfect timing.

I know that your lives are busy. There are so many options, so many distractions, and necessities, some here more than others. I was a mom. I had children, so I encouraged them to be in the flow with me. I prayed with them, and I still do. So, as you open to God's love, be in the flow with the angels. See the light coming through into your world, the Holy presence that touches each soul and awakens you.

Thank you for letting me share my Celestial guidance with you all. My love and light to all. God's blessings to each one of you beautiful souls. I am Care.

Choosing To Live in God's love
October 10, 2019

Imagine, if you will, being in the state of love in every moment. Imagine the joy and the happiness that your heart feels when your soul is lifted in love, when you receive the heavenly Father's love, and you hold fast to His embrace. There is no force in the world that can take that away. We here live in the loving presence of our wonderful Creator. When we go and visit the earth planes or spirits in the lower spheres, we are not disturbed by their condition; we have compassion and love for them. Whenever they are ready, we share this with them and the truth of God's love.

So, I ask you to remember, remember this bliss, this love that can be yours when you let go and you truly let God bless you. If you walk in His light and His love, if you make that your journey, your practice, if you stay in God's love, the world cannot harm you. You will not be distracted or in any way affected by the negativity of the lower ones. So, given a choice whether to choose to be loved or not, choose love. You won't be disappointed.

I went through much in my Earth time that could be considered tragic, negative, or abusive. It was, at times, very difficult and I was not perfect. But the more difficult things became, the harder I prayed until always there was a loving and peaceful resolution in every case. Though we cannot change the (free) will of others because God has given all this wonderful gift, we can love them. We need not be pulled into any place that is not of love. I prayed hard and, as this one knows, often, if not constantly. What was the result? Miracles, blessings, and healings.

Yes, I saw my own passing over. I spoke of it. This made it easier for those in my family and for my loving husband to accept my passing over. This love continues and I embrace all. I make no judgment on your choices, but only suggest that whatever you choose, whatever you do, do it with all the love in your heart and hopefully in God's love, if you so choose; and then you will never be disappointed, and everything will be blessed. Go in peace. I give you my love and my blessing in all that you do. I am Care.

Walk This World With the Truth
March 9, 2020

Yes, it was John (The Apostle) who came. He was attracted, as were many here, to each one of you with your gifts and your knowing that the time has come to rely on God and the Celestial angels so you can walk into the world with the truth and the presence of God's love.

The community is expanding in Divine Love exponentially around the world and so each of you, as well as many others have their part to play, should you choose to do so. For me, I wished nothing other than to serve when on earth and even more so now as an inhabitant of the Celestial heavens, to work with you all. I feel your intentions and also your reluctance, but you are worthy, and you are qualified and you are gifted and above all, you are blessed.

So we here who are on this walk with you, we too are on this path, joyfully dependent on God. This you know. I was filled with joy at your gathering in this circle and I embrace you all with my love and with the love of God.

I thank my beloved Jimbeau for taking this message. Rise and shine and give God your Glory! I love you. I am Care.

Prophecy
May 12, 2020

You may wonder about the gifts of the prophets old and new, past and present. How could they see into the future? How could they predict certain events? I had this gift, but my gift was more directly from the angels. When on earth spending so much time in prayer, they could tell me who was ill, who could be cured, which way to walk and so forth. When a prophet is in their soul and their soul perceptions are active, they are given a window. On the level of the mind this can be called intuition, the power of prediction.

For instance, if you see two groups of people at odds with each other and they are gathering their weapons and they are tossing accusations back and forth, one can pretty much predict civil unrest, at the very least, and possibly war. I predicted my own death, my own passing into spirit. This came to me in a vision more than once and I told my beloved and my children. How was I able to do this you may wonder? Even I was amazed but I will say it was an answer to a prayer in a way. My vision was delivered to me so that my passing could be understood as meant to be. This gift was given to me directly from the Celestial realms.

You have heard the master say there were certain events he could see including his own death. This is of course because of the degree of God's love in his soul, he was given the vision. As you look into your soul and see what can be, we encourage you to look for the light, look for the path that sustains love, that awakens your soul, that embraces the many, that regards the earth and the preciousness of every life, and your dear mother earth.

I hope that I have answered the questions of some who have wondered about these gifts, and I hope for those who are concerned that God's love brings them peace, as is said: 'The peace that passes understanding.' How we wish this for all of you.

May your circle continue to be blessed in light and love and the embrace of The heavenly Father as you ascend towards the Celestial heavens. May God bless each one. Thank you for allowing me this time. With all my love. I am Care.

Self-Realization and God Realization
May 16, 2020

I am here your sister in God's love and your friend, Care. I am here with Nirmala who was known on earth as Anandamayi Ma,[56] and

---

[56] Anandamayi Ma (April 30, 1896–August 27, 1982), a Bengali Saint, described by Sivananda Saraswati (Divine Life Society) as "the most perfect flower the Indian soil has produced."

Yogananda, as are many others. They have allowed me to come forth and speak because they wish to honor you here in this circle for the work that you have done and continue to do to bring the truths of God's love to the world, to the many. As the dear sister spoke earlier, each one of you in your unique way does much to bring forth the kingdom to those souls seeking something deeper than themselves.

There is self-realization which is discovering the beauty of your soul within and the oneness of God's creation and the peace and the calm that comes with such a realization. Then there is God realization when the self reaches out in longings to be transformed and is changed from a human to a divine angel in oneness with its Creator. You have discovered this great gift, this path that leads to the Celestial realms where we abide. We are so delighted to support you, to embrace you, to let you know we are with you.

You have been given the truths that will carry you on the ocean of God's love to the realities of the Celestial kingdom and the shores from which we speak. We are with you in prayer. We bring God's love in our souls and the guidance we perceive at any given time whenever it is needed. Those here with me do wish to speak and share in this communion, and they shall come again to do so. We honor you; we thank you, and we are most grateful for your work. We shall continue this journey with you walking in God's love that will carry you all to His kingdom. Thank you. I love you. I am Care.

Brothers in God's love
June 25, 2020

Dear brothers, is there anything more precious than a true friend in God's love on this earth? Someone to pray with, someone who, despite whatever distance there is, knows that God will touch you and that the angels will be with you as we are all together right now. How beautiful those words from Andrew and the many here touching you with their love, the love of the Father.

I was privileged to have my beloved with me in prayer towards the end of my journey on earth, and I was with him today as I am with him now. And we prayed together, and I lifted him up and I embraced him that he would know we are together. So, brothers you are blessed in so many ways but above all things you are blessed in the brotherhood of

God's love and the friendship that causes one brother to call another and say: 'Let us pray brother, I need a prayer, let us ask the angels.' And yes, we come and as Andrew said: 'How we love you.'

I am your sister and a friend and mate of my beloved, now a redeemed soul in the Celestial heavens where the love of God shines on all. May it shine on you. I love you. I am Care.

You Are Worthy

June 28, 2020

I am here your sister and friend Care. I wish to affirm to each one that you are worthy. Worthy of receiving God's love. For we are all His children. I used to sing first thing in the morning: 'Rise and shine and give God your glory-glory.' Of course, they (my children) were sometimes grumpy and reluctant thinking 'Oh mom', but in my prayers as I dealt with my own issues of unworthiness and allowed God to touch my soul, my soul awakened, and I could not help but proclaim the joy and the glory and the happiness even while on earth. So please know you are truly worthy of the gift of God's love and the company of His angels.

May you receive His love in great abundance and shine your light on every being. I am your sister and friend, a redeemed soul in the Celestial heavens and I love you. I am Care. May God bless you.

Crazy for God

June 29, 2020

When St. Francis, as you know him, when our brother Francis walked away from the world…they said: 'He's crazy, he's lost his mind, it must be the illness.' When Gandhi refused to fight and yet changed a nation through his prayers and meditation and his gospel of peace, he was considered crazy by many, and so it is with so many who have changed the world.

Even my dear brother, Crazy John, as he calls himself, is he not crazy for God? Does the world want this, not need this? Is it too crazy to want to be in prayer, to want to be changed, to want to be an angel? Well, if this is crazy then who would wish to be sane? I had many issues, and the brother is not wrong when he says I could flip flop because at that time in my life I was struggling with my worldly life and the deep desires of my soul for God's love. My children were moved around a lot and when they recollect these times, they tend to see the negative aspects or the difficulties of being uprooted. But I tell you this, we had such fun that when they were given a choice of being with me or their father, their earthly father, they ran to me. And my beloved knows this because he was around. They all came to live with us to escape that normalcy of their dad's home for the freedom and joy that we all had in nature, in prayer, and in miracles.

As time went by and during this period with my beloved, my soul had been awakened, and I had been changed. There was no turning back or any wish to do so. My children felt this and though it is deeply hidden because of their struggles to make their way in the world, it will come out. They shall see. And they have truly appreciated the love that has been shown them in my absence by my beloved Jimbeau.

Now is the time, as we have told you before, to let them 'tarry till they find it.' You can do no more but be crazy for God. Even if the whole world thinks so - because you know in your souls that God's love is everything worth having. It makes all the difference in heaven and on earth. How I love you. Be at peace. May the love of God be showered upon you this day and always. I am your sister and friend in the grace of God. I am Care.

Allow God's Grace
July 21, 2020

In the flow of God's love, the ocean of His grace, the living waters, allow the current of God's grace to carry you. Be not concerned for other's expectations and judgments, only open your hearts and your souls to God's love and their needs will be met. How I prayed for this guidance and to stay in this light in His love. As I talked to God: 'Father please open the door, Father please keep me in Your love, Father please light the way,' I was in the human condition as you are, and I struggled yet God provided me with the perfect mate, one who supported my mission to the very end of my time on earth and beyond.

You have all the support of the Celestial kingdom at the beckoning of your souls. May God keep you and bless you and heal you as you allow the power of His love, the glory of His grace to be yours. I am Care. God bless you.

Children of God
July 23, 2020

I ask you to reach for the love, this love divine from the heavenly Father that brings an answer to every question, that heals every wound, that brings the peace that passes the mind's understanding. Allow your souls to reach out to God to lift you above your minds and the troubles and allurements and entanglements of the world. This way you bring a blessing to the world, a troubled world.

When you cannot see the path ahead you must walk in faith and trust in God and pray for guidance. The light that you see is the light that shines upon the path and leads the way for your walk into the future in every moment. As your soul receives the love of God you can walk in this faith, and you can be in harmony with the will of God and all the laws of the natural world stretched up to the Celestial realms from where we come. There is no inharmony here.

As God embraces you and touches your souls, as you let go and allow this love to heal you that you may become at one with God, your being is transformed. This feeling of bliss and of joy - let it be yours and bring it to others. Bring your light into every room as a child who comes in joy and without a care, lightens a room. You begin to realize the words to enter the kingdom: 'You must become as the little ones, as the children.'

The innocence of God's love as the child has faith in the parent to protect and guide and lead the way, so let all of God's children have this faith and trust in the protection and love of our heavenly Father. You have many guides, and you only need to ask and we are there. Dear sister should you require my assistance or that of my beloved we are here for you. He has given his heart to God and this work, but if you need me to come just call.

May this light in this circle of prayer stay with you. May your souls be lifted and awakened for you truly will be and are a blessing to all. With all my love and blessings to you. May the grace of God be yours. I am Care.

In God's Love There Are No Wrong Choices
August 2, 2020

My dear brothers, you are cared for and your every need is considered throughout the spheres and with us here in the Celestial realm. Your work is everything to us and your worth is beyond measure. We assist in providing you everything you need because God is the provider of every good and perfect gift. The master is overseeing this and his love, as you know, is beyond description. The effulgence of his light brings the light of truth to all.

Do not worry about the inner workings of this group or that group, this one or that. Only consider your soul in relationship to its Creator. The more you stay in God's grace and in the flow of His love the more we are able to assist you. So have faith and the path will be cleared and opened for you. You can follow your inner guidance whenever you are in prayer as we are influencing you and impressing upon you the many possibilities. Let your heart choose which ones to explore and where you can best serve.

Know that the heavenly Father blesses everything you do in His love and in His service as there are no wrong choices when all is in love, God's love. I am your sister in Christ. With all my blessings may you walk in the light and love or our heavenly Father. I love you. I am Care.

Faith in God and Your Gifts
August 15, 2020

I have been with you as you might imagine and really enjoying your explorations into the world of spirit and your longings for soul progression in God's love. How could I stay away?

I have had some discussions with Clare from Assisi about our lives on earth in very different times and yet we were both barefoot prayer warriors, at least that is how I described myself. Clare had her battles with leaving her family and establishing sanctuary in quiet and solitude, drawing her sisters near her for prayer. I too sought sanctuary in nature, in God's creation, in the quiet of a room, but I will say this. I could be in the middle of a crowded thoroughfare or a public place and if I felt someone needed a prayer I could not hold back. I moved from my self-consciousness to my God consciousness, and I focused on that soul and their needs and went directly to God.

In relationship to what you have been talking about and discussing when it comes to someone in need and being open, having faith, believing they could be healed, or simply believing that God could intervene, I will say yes, this is important. And as in the Bible account that John Mark wrote to H.R.,[57] I could often see the need of someone that they were open for a healing, for a blessing, and sometimes I proactively knew the need and even if that person did not ask, I would introduce myself, and if I received a message from the angels I would give it to them without hesitation in the knowing, in the faith that I had, that what I was receiving was real. No matter whether I understood it or not, it was important to deliver the message in hopes that the recipient, whether befuddled or amazed, would consider the content. Then of course it is between them and God.

I wanted to touch on this subject because I know it is part of your discussions and you are curious about it. I hope I have perhaps answered some of your questions and given you some things to consider. As you have been told many, many, many, times - when you pray, and you open to God and the angels, you receive. God bestows His love through His Holy Spirit, and we come to administer to the needs. You can think about this as we are answering all those emails, those texts from your soul that are calling out. Most especially we do this because you are praying for the highest, for the Creator's blessing, and we do His bidding. I thank you for coming together and allowing yourselves to be vulnerable. I wish to encourage you to continue to open your hearts to each other that God may open your souls to His love on this glorious journey. With all my love and in God's grace, I am your Care and I love you. God bless you.

WHAT WILL BE YOUR GIFT TO GOD?
September 22, 2020

In the material world it is often challenging to activate your will and let it be at one with God, in harmony with His laws, and most especially, open to receiving His love. The entertainments of the world that you live in are numerous and many faceted; some are like sparkling jewels, glistening, and grabbing your attention; others like deep, dark holes inviting you in, and appealing to those things that are not of the highest, with base desires, revenge, or violence. Others that I speak of can simply be more or less positive amusements.

When you explore spiritually, we help you open your heart, help you become a co-creator with God, with the angels, so you are able to use your gifts (and you all have gifts,) and bring these gifts to the world that

---

[57] This refers to the message from John Mark in the book 'Judas of Kerioth' pages 652-656.

it may be lifted up. I wish to encourage you to activate your will, to start your day in prayer, asking for God and the Celestial angels to touch your souls, to guide you, to open your hearts, and to allow your gifts to heal this world, to shine a light in the darkness, to give strength to those who are battling their addictions, hurting from their wounds.

What a blessed circle this is. What a privilege that you come together seeking the highest and asking God to open your souls to the great inflowing of His love. This is God's gift to you. What you do with it will be your gift back to God! I join you now in the peace of this gift of love with all my love and blessings in the grace of God. Thank you. I am Care.

Soul Perceptions vs. Intuition
December 23, 2020

It is easy enough to be concerned and to have empathy for those who live in darkness and for the blindness of their souls in the world when you are all seeking the light and wish to clearly see yourself and to serve. Please remember help is always available when you go to God in prayer, He answers. When you need guidance, it arrives. Sometimes in the form of Celestial angels or a progressive spirit in God's love, and sometimes God just puts the answer in your heart, in your soul, and you know.

There is a difference, a distinction between soul perceptions and having a feeling about something or intuition. Intuition tends to be more in the mind and in the natural, but it can be very helpful. Soul perceptions are, I may say, divine intuition, perceiving reality in the workings of God's laws and in the flow of His grace when you are in harmony allowing His Holy Spirit to work through you. This is where you feel as if there is a light on in your heart and you wish so much to share that with others. I have seen all of you do this and know it is your deep desire, and I encourage you to bring that to your day as often as you can. You know this is not a great discipline because the results are so harmonious.

When you give, you receive tenfold in return, and we celebrate this here in the Celestial realm and you feel it. When you are concerned about another and their state of being, their state of mind, their troubles, or perhaps they have offended you in some way, send them love, support them in the flow of God's grace. Lift them up and encourage them with love as you so often do. I only remind you how great this is and how happy it makes me and all those here. The true gift of the season is the love of God that you have been 'christed' as Jesus promised. May you continue to spread the joy and the truth and the glow of Divine Love in your hearts to all. I wish you every blessing, every good and perfect gift in God's love and I love you. God bless you. I am Care.

SLAY THEM WITH LOVE
January 4, 2021

I am here, Care. I am your sister and friend and your beloved and a grandmother. Perhaps it is Grandmothers' Day today? As you read the beautiful message from Ann Rollins, what a bright and beautiful spirit she is, and the beautiful words from blessed Eileen Caddy, know we are all Celestial angels, all mothers, and grandmothers.

If you are a mother, you can imagine one of your children honoring the work that you do now, whether it be during your time on earth or in the future. I am not only honored but delighted that my grandson has opened his mind and his heart and his beautiful soul to understand the truths and pray for the love of God. A mother's love for her children is deep and as a grandmother this love traverses the generations with the same hope from those of us in the Celestial realm for our children, for our grandchildren, for our families and for our loved ones.

My husband was awakened in this love and supported me in my work mightily and it is my delight to support him in his work. And all of us here support this beautiful circle and your gifts and we honor and encourage them. It is not a race, it is a path, with each one traveling at their own pace, though sometimes being distracted, and going off in one direction or another.

We continue to encourage you to stay on the path of prayer, to not be too distracted and to choose your entertainments well, that they may be uplifting and not cause fear, or concern, or doubt. For when you are in the grace of God, in His great love, you know you are lifted above those things of the world that often occupy your attention and trouble you. This is the message that we grandmothers bring to you this day. We bring it to you all and beyond this circle.

During this time of great transition reach for the light, reach for the love. When you are troubled pray. Try not to let the negativity come into you and trouble your heart but let that glow that is here in this circle, that is in each soul here, light the world. For each one of you is a light in the darkness, expanding. There is indeed a lattice of light with more and more souls wishing to connect in love, praying for peace, wanting a oneness of humanity whether that be in the natural state of things or in the Divine Love of the Creator.

Love indeed does conquer all. Let it be your sword and your shield. If you must be a warrior, be a prayer warrior. Kill them with kindness, slay them with love. The love from above, this wonderful gift from God. Be not troubled but be happy. Don't worry, for God is with you, we are with you. How I love you. God bless you. I am Care.

COMMUNICATE TRUTH IN CREATIVE WAYS
January 22, 2021

Luke is here, John is here, many, many are here. For we love what you deem to be a small gathering and we know it is quite large. Multitudinous!

When I was on earth, I received much guidance and was considered a medium. For the angels spoke to me, not so much in formal writings, although at times I wrote messages no matter what I was doing. Other times I would be guided to talk to someone where the angels would say, 'we have a message for him or her,' and it would just come through me. Because of my faith and because I prayed so intensely, I had a certain courage about being able to deliver the messages.

As you have read today about the importance of not withholding truth, I ask you to consider sharing your gifts. There are many ways we communicate with mortals and for some, the written word touches them in a way that opens them up. It touches their heart, illumines their mind, and creates in them a desire to have God bless them and open up their souls with His love. For others, it might be a song, for others it might be a film, a movie, for others a poem, for others a story told and so forth and so on.

There is no need to put a limitation on how you might receive, how you might co-create something filled with truth, filled with beauty, filled with light that you may bless this world and leave something truly good; something you can look back on as your work to serve God and to serve humanity so in need. So, it need not be formal, in fact the more playful, the more creative, the more joyful the more likely you are to touch the many. This is why people still sing happy songs long after they have come into being, or watch a movie that inspired them, or read a book that changed their lives, or read a poem that brings them to tears every time they revisit it.

The forms of prayer are many. It is only required that you be in condition and this, as you have discussed, is to find a place of solace, solitude and quiet. If you can do this in nature, as I did, it can be glorious. But you can always create sanctuary and connect with heaven and with the Celestial angels because we are waiting for you as this one here, my beloved, is finding out. Yes, your desires are important, but we wait for you to call and we come. I say this to all here and beyond this circle that this message may reach many for the sake of humankind and for the souls of all those on earth. Remember we are all children of God. All are loved, all are worthy. Allow this love and all the gifts to come with it to feed your soul as a gift to all. I love you. May God bless you always. I am Care. God bless you.

Choose Wisely, Choose Love
February 26, 2021

Music is a form of prayer when it comes from the longings of the soul. Movies that lift you up, that inspire you, that touch your heart, that have a moral compass or spiritual aspiration, can change one. What you read, what you take in is worthy of serious consideration. Follow your heart to joy. Follow your soul to bliss. One does not have to be able to sing the blues, as they say, to have them. But as this one knows, singing the blues allows one to be lifted from that condition, and that should be the goal of a song, of a dance, of a movie, of a book, of a poem, of a prayer. They are all mediums, or we might say, possible channels of light and love. So, choose wisely, choose love, choose joy. May God bless each one of you this day and always with His great love. I am with you, and I love you. I am Care.

Plant the Seeds and Be the Love
April 19, 2021

I often come to this prayer circle to be with my beloved but also because I am drawn to this group of souls who are not so much in their minds but drawn here with the longing in their souls. This I could relate to on earth.

I know that some of you are surrounded by those who cannot fathom the idea of a soul being transformed in the love of God, the simplicity of prayer without all the baggage of dogma, and yet my dear friends that light that shines from your souls, this makes an indelible impression upon all those family and friends and even those you may not know.

The early Christians, so many martyrs who died not willing to give up their beliefs in the love of God, in their teacher, had this glow within their souls more powerful than death. One can wonder about them - how were they not completely wiped out, which was one of the goals of those who persecuted them? And this is because that love that they carried impressed those who may have come for entertainment but left with an awakened conscience. As you may know, Roman Emperors Caligula and Nero, who murdered their soulmates, are now inhabitants of the Celestial heavens. And even (Julius) Caesar got blessed!

On my journey I often wondered, with all this time in prayer, feeling the love of God, talking with the Celestial angels, seeing the future even, have I done any good? And yet, this one who sits before you, almost 30 years after my passing into spirit, has never forgotten, because the love of God made an indelible impression upon his soul. And so, with each of you it is.

The glory of this love, the circle of light, the presence of God, and the company of His angels, this you receive. This you take with you into the world. From my experience I would suggest you not spend any time being concerned about the outcome of what you seek to bring to others, which is the love of God. And believe me, it is in God's hands. All you need to do, should you wish to do so, is plant the seeds. Be the love, be the light, as the song says, this is God's delight. And it is mine to be here with you. I shall step back in the beautiful silence of this glorious prayer. Thank you. May God bless each one of you. I am Care.

Every Soul is Unique

June 8, 2021

I have been with you today and so much enjoyed the harmony that ensued between my family, both biological and spiritual. I am touched by your movement towards the fount of God's love, your willingness to receive, your openness to sharing your gifts, and allowing them to be revealed ever more so beautifully in the days ahead. For the world cannot have too much love and it so needs peace and wisdom, however you wish to share. For as every soul is unique, every soul's gifts are unique.

And just as some like a particular kind of music or food or clothing or architecture or literature and so on, some will respond accordingly to each one of your gifts. Do not hide them in the closet, please. For if someone brought you the most delicious meal you would want them to set it at the table. And, as we sit at the table of God's love and as you pray to be in His grace and presence and the company of us celestials, you perceive and feel the oneness of the Divine Love family and the transformed children of God.

I tell you what awaits you is truly beyond your wildest dreams with happiness, such happiness, and such joy. I am delighted to be able to come and speak to you, for you are all dear to me, and I hold my grandson close, and my sisters in the love of God with my beloved. As you walk into the future evermore in His grace, you will witness more and more the manifestations, the divine manifestations, and the presence, the holy presence of the Creator who longs to embrace you and is always ready to welcome you and bless you.

Thank you for allowing me to come through. I wish you all the love, all the blessings and all the happiness your souls can receive in the love of God. I love you. I am Care. God bless you.

Make No Idols and Be Free
June 21, 2021

It is written that the master said: "love all as I have loved you." This you know to mean with the Divine Love of the Father. It is the human condition somehow to make idols that they can worship as they have made of Jesus and many other messengers. And idols have been made of celebrities and riches and power, and even the earth itself. When you come together in prayer and the heavens open you are joined by a multitude from many spheres, some in darkness wishing to be lifted, some progressing through the many spheres and planes, and those of us in the Celestial heavens who always come to maintain the integrity of this portal, and to strengthen the lattice of light.

As your prayers go to God, all those here can see the light emanating from each soul in their longing to connect with the light of love from the Creator, the effulgence of which permeates this circle. Make idols of no men or women or material things and be free in this love, which is a treasure beyond measure. I shall step back now, and I thank you with all my love and the blessings of our heavenly Father. I am Care.

FOLLOW THE JOY
July 22, 2021

I walked barefoot upon the earth whenever I could to be grounded. For at times, I felt I would be drawn up, my prayers so intense, my longing so deep. Nature was my church, for it was not the creation of man but of God. I had these gifts, as did my mother and grandmother, psychic gifts, you would call them.

In my case, because I discovered the path of Divine Love, the truth of it and the great happiness that lifted me up above all of my concerns, my sorrows, my trials and tribulations, to great joy. It so became my passion that I always wished to spend time in prayer with the angels, and I would ask others to allow me to do this, and I was so very happy when they would join in.

As I received this grace, my gifts became like a flower opening, with the fragrance of a rose in bloom. As my beloved here knows, when you open to the love of God, miracles happen, and often in the most ordinary of circumstances. For God works not only in mysterious ways, but sometimes, in quite obvious ones, and yes, He has a sense of humor. I was open to all kinds of experiences in the natural world, although I wouldn't say I was well versed in theology or philosophy. My wisdom was more homespun. And yet, what I could give others, what I could share with them, was divine.

I would say to my dear grandson, whatever you pursue, whatever curiosities you wish to explore, be sure they bring you joy. You can always ask: 'Does this feel right, does this feel like love, or a distraction? Does this lift my soul with delight and ecstasy, or does it just bring me to ponder?' This is the human condition, and I say this to you dear one, that you are curious and open and exploring, which is a wonderful thing. I would never discourage you from such pursuits.

All I ask is that you keep in your heart the highest pursuit of happiness and joy. For then you know that the path you are taking has been well chosen. Follow your heart on the path of Divine Love and you will never be disappointed. Thank you for listening today and allowing me to come.

I was observing with Clare (Clare of Assisi), and it was felt that a more personal message was in order. But we have surrounded you in love. We are filled with joy. We will continue, the many of us, to influence and inspire and support you in the love of God. I love you. I am Care, God Bless you.

Have Faith - Your Prayers Will Be Answered
August 12, 2021

It is I, and yes, I have been with you today. I come whenever I can and certainly whenever you call. I am Care. Life is a precious gift, as is the gift of free will. It is about choices, and if you were to follow your heart and assume that we will help you, then God will open every door in love. What would your choices be?

So often people are limited by their low self-esteem, their feelings of unworthiness. I tell you this is not helpful. Are we not all worthy in the eyes of God? Are we not all His children, and as the prayer says: "the objects of his great love and tenderest care?" You may stumble and even fall at times. But if you continue to pray, continue to be open to the great gift of Divine Love, walk in faith, all doors will be open to you in ways beyond which you can conceive.

And if you reflect on your past, the times you thought all hope was lost, or that obstacles were insurmountable and so you let go and sent up a little prayer: 'Oh God, please help me! I am lost, I am confused. I am at my wits end. I am depressed and lonely.' Did not God send help? Was not your prayer answered? Sometimes this is much to your amazement, hence the expression, 'O ye of little faith.'

But I say to you, think of that expression with humor, every time you get a blessing. It increases your faith. It increases your trust. It opens the door ever wider for new beginnings. Everyone is familiar with the saying 'follow your heart,' and I strongly agree. I would only add that you follow the deep longings of your heart for love, for happiness, for freedom, for healing, and above all for God's love.

May every good and perfect gift be with you who are dearly beloved, deeply loved, and cherished. Walk in faith dear ones. All will be given to you. How I love you! And if I may say, how proud I am of all of you for staying the course because I know where this journey will lead you. It is one of endless love and glory in God and his kingdom.

Thank you. Go with God. I am your friend, sister, grandmother, and beloved. I am a redeemed soul in the Celestial heavens and eternally yours, I am Care.

Be Not Concerned With the Outcome
October 22, 2021

If one of you had discovered a cure for cancer, would you not shout it from the rooftops? Would you not do your best to bring it out to the public? And so, you have discovered the immortality of the soul in God's love. I discovered this and it gave me great courage because I knew I had something that was golden, that transcended the world yet could heal it. When I was in God's love on Earth, I was willing to walk on water and I so wished to serve as I continue to. So along with Sir Arthur,[58] I wish to offer my encouragement with the addition of saying, 'Do not be concerned of the outcome.' As you let go and let God touch you, this is God's business. All you need to do is finish the work you wish to do and because it carries truth known in your soul, as a river finds its way to the sea, your work will find its way to the many.

I encourage you each day do a little bit as your brother Al has suggested and your work and the work of many will reach the great sea of humanity, shining a light that so needs to bless this world. I love you. I am with you and I thank my sisters and all for watching over my dear Jimbeau. I am Care.

Freedom
December 26, 2021

I am here, Care. Everyone in the world wants freedom, and perhaps freedom means different things in different places. On the material level, it might be freedom from worrying about money, quality of life, clean water, air, freedom or education, climate change, famine or even war. On the spiritual level, what is freedom? As someone who spent the early part of their lives being subservient, I found myself lifted in prayer with

---

[58] A reference to Sir Arthur Conan Doyle who gave a message earlier.

a sense of freedom that gave me courage to step out, knowing it is better to be free than under the thumb of another.

My beloved and I, we experienced much freedom in our travels, in our daily lives and with our children. Most importantly to me was the freedom to pray, to make music, to create, to be in nature. All beings who have souls need freedom and you know, we never interfere in the great gift of free will. I tell you this with all the love in my heart, that when you ask for whatever, it is you need, when you're asking is in harmony with the laws of God, with the progression of soul, with your physical or material needs, you shall receive. Consider freedom in all these areas, and know the joy, the exhilaration, and ultimately, the glory of being free in God's love. Each soul is a unique creation, as you are.

I am here for you, please remember that. With all my love in the Holy Blessings of the Creator, I wish you a very blessed journey in the new year with many changes in harmony, guided and blessed. There are no wrong choices made in love. And I love you. I am Care.

Eileen Caddy

I first heard of Eileen Caddy in the 1970's when I was living in a Hippie community on a farm in Wisconsin and we were all reading the Mother Earth News magazine, hoping to learn how to become self-sufficient. We read that Eileen had founded a community (Findhorn) in Scotland that had incredibly large cabbages, that the beautiful vegetable garden had fairies in it, and people around the world were in awe. I later saw an interview with Eileen and her friend Dorothy in their advanced years and noticed that they were like a couple of giggly happy schoolgirls, and ageless.

In 2015 while visiting my friends in Gibsons, BC I was given the book, 'Foundations of Findhorn,' by Eileen Caddy. Darlene Gaunt, who gave me the book, said she felt I might be interested in reading the messages that Eileen had received from God and that they might be helpful towards founding a Divine Love community. I was quite stunned by what Eileen had channeled and subsequently purchased other books of guided messages she had received over the years, often taking a book with me when traveling, to add to my morning prayers.

In April of 2019 I started to hear from Eileen who gave wonderful guidance. After receiving regular messages from her for over a year and a half, she started introducing herself as 'Auntie Eileen.' I later met people who knew Eileen well and confirmed that what I was receiving was genuine. Eileen, now in spirit, is an inhabitant of the Celestial kingdom. I was encouraged by her to approach Findhorn and offered to speak and channel her there, but sadly, the current Findhorn community leaders had no interest in anyone, as they put it, 'receiving guidance from without.' Recently the spiritual Universal Hall and Community Center burned to the ground. Perhaps this may have caused the leaders to consider going back to Eileen's guidance as I have been made aware that there is a weekly reading of her messages online from Findhorn. I am always thrilled to hear from her and feel her beautiful presence and always deeply inspirational guidance.

Findhorn Restored In God's love
April 9, 2019

I am here Eileen Caddy, and I am delighted to be with you. As you may know, I am the spiritual founder of Findhorn up in the northern regions of Scotland which can be a very inhospitable place. I found myself there, living in a caravan with my then husband wondering 'What are we going to do?' So, I prayed, and God spoke to me.

Out of this seed was built quite an amazing community which, of course to this day, although institutionalized to some extent, still exists and has expanded. It took many people to build and to maintain. It was built as a spiritual center, and I followed God's guidance every day. God directed us and guided us on how to build and what to build. We have a hall, a great hall. This was a portal of light and still is, although somewhat diminished. I come to you to invite you to this place to restore the portal there.[59]

I too was a 'new thought' person as was Brother Mandus,[60] but both of us were used as instruments of God, both of us receiving His love, sharing, and guiding with others. God told me unity was imperative. Unify all. Reject none. Accept all who come to work with you for what we are building in spirit is greater than any material things.

This place that I founded (Findhorn) needs to be revitalized and I urge you to request to speak there, to channel and speak with us there, to pray there. Because you are needed as you are needed in the other center there in England. I give this message to all of you, not to any one specific person. I come in joy and in celebration and my soul is so full of God's love and love for you all! Thank you for allowing me to speak. I thank this one whom I have been guiding daily for quite some time now, as he knows, and encouraging him to follow his guidance in the love of God. May every blessing be yours.

I wish to acknowledge this place as well, this bright, full of light portal of God's love and to thank you for maintaining this place, but please realize that now is the time to go out. There will be many centers. There will be places of refuge and those of you who carry God's love in your soul are needed. I will work with you and be with you in God's love. Again, thank you! May God bless your work and all that you do.

I am your friend and sister in God's love, Eileen Caddy. I love you. God bless you.

What Do You Want To Build
August 31, 2019

I am the spiritual founder of the community at Findhorn. I was at a crossroads in my life, and I needed to make choices, but I did not know how. So, I prayed with all my heart and all my soul for guidance and indeed I got it, every day.[61] From that small still voice speaking to me

---

59 This is a reference to an energy portal and her concerns were prescient as the Findhorn Great Hall and Dining Hall were burned to the ground on April 12, 2021.

60 Founder of the World Healing Centre in Blackpool.

61 Her autobiography 'Flight into Freedom' is a fabulous explanation of both her journey and

from on high was built an entire community which has expanded and grown over the years. Though the focus there has shifted somewhat from spiritual guidance to ecology, it is still a wonderful place, and it was built on guidance from God and the angels.

I would ask you all to consider, what do you want to build? What do you want to leave? What do you want to do? You have a community, and you have separate existences, so to speak, but you come together as one in prayer, in song, in sharing of food, ideas, travels and many things. There is so much desire here to feel love, to share love, to serve. What a wonderful thing it is.

We had this at Findhorn. People came from far and wide with all kinds of gifts and contributed, because they wanted to serve. They wanted to build something greater than themselves. It was often a very humbling experience. We had elements to deal with in that northern region where the community is. Yet we had the warmth of love and community and prayer and guidance. Those of you who know my work, know I was guided every day. I thought at first: 'This is too much for me. How can I do this?' But I began to realize with every guidance that it was much less work to be in the flow and to follow the guidance than to try and figure it out with my mind.

So more and more I was in my soul and that guidance was supreme and resulted in such beautiful things. So yes, we had the physical world to deal with. We built physical things, but we did them with spiritual guidance, so our souls were blessed as we created a physical community, a garden. We had much music and still do. I offer this to all of you as a template. You have built a wonderful community, and you can do more if it is your wish. You are one in God's love. We are all one. You have such great angelic support from on high, so many angels. We support you. Choose what you will and know you are not alone. You are with each other and with God and all the Celestial angels at your beck and call.

Thank you for allowing me to come and share with you. I am delighted to be in this portal of light with so many wonderful souls. Thank you. May God bless you all. My love and blessings to all. I am your sister and friend in God's love, Eileen Caddy. God bless you.

---

her guidance, amazing as it frequently was.

Open Your Hearts, Listen with Your Souls
October 6, 2019

I'm drawn to this circle of light. As we experienced many times in Findhorn, where I was the spiritual founder, my path was to hear a small still voice that I believed was the voice of God that instructed me. From these beautiful instructions was created a dynamic spiritual and ecological community in the upper reaches of coastal Scotland.

This path was quite simple. It did not require a lot of intellectualizations, whether there were people doing this on other planets, in other universes, but quite simply, to be humble enough to open and listen. I allowed the longings of my soul to reach God and thus I was guided, as were many.

I come here to share with you and to acknowledge so many beautiful souls here. Many are following the path of the mind and are yet drawn by the longings in their souls, to be transformed, to be love, to become love, to be a blessing of light and love in this world. Is this not what you wish, my friends?

When we allow our hearts to open and we listen with our souls, what comes to us in love outshines the mind and blesses all. May you all become and be the Gift of love, anointed with this glorious gift, living in light and love. Surely, the world as you know, needs you, needs your gift, needs your love.

I was drawn to this circle of light, as were many from the Celestial kingdom. We wish a blessing upon each one here, a healing, and above all, the inflowing of the Creator's love. My love and blessings to all and may God bless you all on this journey. We are with you. I love you. I am Eileen Caddy.

Be Beholden To No One Except God
November 11, 2019

I wish to convey something very simple to you all. Be beholden to no one except God. I can tell you this works. You can see in my life what was accomplished. I would say to you, each of you, that when you follow your path in God's love, there is a great freedom, a great joy. This is why there will be many groups, many channels and different souls will be drawn to different ones. But is not the message the same, to open to God's love? This is the deep longing in every soul. Those who are in their minds, they can go only so far, but you know they too are drawn to the love. It is not their minds that is drawn to the love, but the longings in their souls, however hidden, however buried.

I would encourage you to have your own groups on your own terms that you may feel the freedom and not be beholden to someone else's rules. Not that these are bad things, but it gives you a wonderful freedom to express the love in your souls with others. It is our great wish that these circles will expand and grow. As you have been told, there are many, many, many of us at your beck and call. It is our delight. I feel here at home with you my dear friends, though my home is high in the Celestial kingdom. These wonderful portals of light can be created with God's help and in His love around the world. You are a beautiful team. You are a lattice of light, our dear friends in soul and in God's love and we are with you.

My love and blessings to all of you, my dear friends. I love you. I am Eileen.

Grow the Garden in Your Soul
December 2, 2019

You draw me into this light with your love. You see how simple it is, just like in my conversations with the heavenly Father. It was really quite simple, just keeping my focus on God to provide every good and perfect gift. As you know, God did provide and does provide. I opened my heart. I bared my soul. At the beginning, I cried out as if in the wilderness and what a response I got! What was a barren and desolate place becoming a garden renowned all over the world where thousands have come and continue to come.

But most important for me were the seeds of love in my soul and nurturing those in my prayer to God who answered every one, every day, without fail. Yes, I had disappointments. Yes, I had those who opposed me and did not want to walk that path, the path of Divine Love. Yet, the love of God shone through my soul. Those who were open to it could see, this was a path they could take.

As you all know in this circle, this beautiful circle of light, the love of God does transform the soul and change you. This is not a temporary state of being. You have connected with eternity, with the infinite grace of the Creator of the universe by your simple request from your soul, from your heart, for God's love. So, like my other Celestial friends, I encourage you to continue. Do this and remember God because God is always remembering you. Grow the garden in your soul and blossom.

I ask everyone in a gentle way to remind yourself and others in kindness and with God's love, as you encourage each other for many are blessed as this circle extends beyond the reach of your imaginings. Those in spirit that come who are drawn to the light, they are blessed. So we thank you. We honor you. We pray with you. May God bless each one with a great inflowing and infilling of His love. I am your friend and sister Eileen.

You Shall Overcome
December 7, 2019

You knew I was here, did you not? Ooh, thank you for reading that beautiful prayer that I received. I come with a matter of urgency. I do not wish to be too serious, but I spoke with Charles (Chaplin) the other day about the need to have a many faceted outreaches of the truths of God's love. He of course, gave his message through film and art and I was surprised he did not include dance, but dance too.

You have many gifts in your community and there are many around the world who desire to bring forth the truth of God's love. The urgency is in putting in the time, staying focused, asking for what you need. I asked God and what a wonder. People showed up! So, put it out there. In these times, there are so many ways, so many avenues. So, I encourage you, ask and you shall receive. Put this word out there that it may spread over the world like a layer of light or, as you say, a lattice of light. This time is crucial. If you put in this work, because of the longings and the hunger around the world for love, for guidance and for truth, the doors will be opened. I wish to say there is one, at Findhorn, who will hear your plea and open the door there for you, should you wish to come and charge up, light up, the portal.

As you know, there is always resistance. But there is no negative force in the world that can go up against God's love and the love and light in each of your souls. Rest your will in God's will. Accept and allow the love to lead the way. You will know which way to go. But bring these gifts that so many of you have to the fore, to the world. Help each other in this way. Ask and the resources will be there for you. They were certainly there for me. I speak as one who knows the power of prayer for the soul and for building on this earth a lasting presence of God's love. You shall overcome.

I give you my deepest gratitude and my full support. You are so needed, and you are the blessing in this world. I am delighted, as always, to come into your circle and there are many (here). I leave now with all my love and affection in wishing you the greatest blessing in God's love. I am your sister in God's love, Eileen.

Love Connects Heaven and Earth
February 9, 2020

I am here, Eileen. There is a bridge that connects the realities of the earth plane with the realities of the Celestial world and spirit. When one is from the earth plane and has come to believe, that is all there is, and that they shall return again and again, and that within the human condition problems can always be solved in mindful ways, they do tend to get solved, but the recognition of the bridge to the Creator gets obscured.

I have asked for you to go to my beloved Findhorn and to present the bridge. It has not been lost; it is just obscured. The way to reach out through the soul is through love. No one there can deny the truth of the foundation of Findhorn in love and in guidance. You can stand on that rock because you present it with the love in your souls. So do not be intimidated. Stay in your soul. Look at what is required and respond in love. I will guide you in this because it is so dear to me, and I know that your intentions are nothing but good and in God's love.

Yes, community is important, so important to get us through these earth changes. But even more important is communion of souls in the love of God. For the real destination is beyond this world, as you know. Speak with love, write with love, sing with love, walk in love. You cannot fail. I am with you in love. May God continue to bless you and may you all know you have the support of the Celestial heavens in the work that you do. I love you. I am your friend and sister in the Celestial heavens, Eileen Caddy. God bless you.

The Courage To Proceed
March 8, 2020

As I listen to your concerns a smile comes across my face, remembering my own concerns and my wondering if I had the courage to proceed. Like you I prayed and my connection with God and the presence and the love gave me the courage to proceed. You have reached out to this world with Divine Love and the truth of it, wishing to embrace all cultures and creeds, crossing boundaries with love.

This too is what Findhorn wishes to do. To eliminate those things that separate us and embrace all. And yes, there are words that resonate and perhaps not everyone will understand, but if you reach out to the longing in each soul for love, for community, for connection, you will touch deeply those whom you wish to communicate with, whom you wish to make your presentation to. You are well on your way.

I told you I would help you. All you had to do was ask. And in answer to those questions you have, I hope I have addressed them. Embrace the many, touch the heart, awaken the soul and have the courage to walk into the light of God's love. God bless you all. I am truly your friend and sister in the Celestial heavens, I am Eileen. God bless you.

Prayer Is the Bridge Between Heaven and Earth
April 24, 2020

I am drawn to your prayer. For those of you who do not know me I was known as Eileen Caddy, and I was the spiritual founder of the Findhorn community which not only still exists but has grown exponentially since it was started in the early 1960's. It was started on a wing and a prayer from the guidance that I received. And what was considered a barren, sometimes desolate landscape has become a sustainable, flourishing, verdant, beautiful community. We always respected the individual's need for privacy and the need for community. So, as we prayed to receive guidance and for the inflowing and infilling of the Creator's love, we grew beyond our wildest dreams.

I share that with those here who, during this time of the earth slowing down, have the opportunity to consider what kind of future you would like to walk into for the rest of your days. Of course, those of us in the Celestial realm, we wish you to consider beyond your earth life, the future of your soul. As I have said before, prayer is the bridge between heaven and earth. So first and foremost, I encourage you to take time, find a quiet space, open your heart that your souls may be opened with the great gift of the Creator's love. And when you are in grace and you have the connection to eternity you can then envision what you wish to do for the rest of your time here, who you wish to associate with, how you wish to grow, what kind of community you feel drawn to?

I can tell you that the love in your souls will bring you everything you desire, in what you call the law of attraction, also known as spiritual magnetism, and as the great master Jesus pronounced 'where your heart is therein is also your treasure.' So with all my love I encourage you to follow your heart and be aware of your soul's desire. Allow this great transformation, this great gift, to be yours. For it is given freely to each one for the asking. I am your sister and friend and I love you each one. May God bless you! I am Eileen.

You Are the Blessing This World Needs
July 7, 2020

I am here, your sister and friend in the love of God, I am Eileen Caddy. When you go into silence, whether you hear the still small voice of God, or the angels, what is important is that you make a rapport in Divine Love.

I did teach going within but if you read between the lines of what I wrote and the messages that I received of the 'infilling and inflowing of God's love,' it is apparent that one can go within to that quiet place of the soul, that wonderful gift of God to each being, and then open to love. However, your heart sends out this request, whether with words or just in the deep longings from your souls, this intention connects you with the soul of God, who never refuses to bless His children with His great and glorious gift, as in this beautiful circle of light and love.

In these troubled times each one of you is given a great inflowing of this gift that you may take it into the world and bless each one. When confronted with something that is less than love - negativity, vexations, - go to your heart. Make that connection in your soul, and ask God to bless this soul, those people, that place. Wherever you may be, bless all, for you carry this gift in your hearts and souls. You are the blessing this world needs in God's love.

I am with you. All my love and blessings in the grace of God where we are one. I am Eileen. God bless you.

Soul Transformation
November 16, 2020

For those who do not know me I will introduce myself. I was the spiritual founder of the Findhorn community in Northern Scotland. This community came from guidance I received from God as I prayed, and one period of my life came to an end. And the next period, which was guided daily, became a seed, became a flower, became a garden, became a community, as people shed their old lives and embraced the new.

The value of community when it is centered on prayer, when there is trust and faith and guidance, is immeasurable. Although you do not all live in the same place, there is a oneness in the love of God when you come together in communion, in community, opening your hearts, allowing God to touch your souls.

The example of the metamorphosis of the caterpillar into the butterfly is often used to describe transformation. Consider the caterpillar who can only crawl and ingests leaves. Consider this as one on earth beginning to pray for and receive the substance of the Creator, which is love. And in the chrysalis, this caterpillar becomes a completely transformed creature with wings, a beautiful creature that can soar. One crawls, one flies.

I tell you this to remind you that you can let go of crawling and allow the love of God to change you, transform you, into the beautiful, angelic beings that you are destined to become. No one will demand this transformation of you. And I can tell you, it does not happen in a day. But the metamorphosis begins with the receiving of the substance of the Creator, which is this Divine Love and as it grows in your soul, it completely changes you. Ask and you shall receive.

This circle is the result of the desires of each soul to feel love, to receive love, to share love, to be love. For love transforms the world; love heals. And love lights up the darkness. As you allow this change in your soul and you feel the light of love and the joy of being lifted above the material world and all its troubles in the company of angels, this magnetism will draw you in again and again.

It is my privilege and honor to be with you in this circle of light on this journey you have undertaken from the earth plane to the kingdom of God in the Celestial heavens. May it be yours. God bless you.

Raise Your Sails on the Ocean of God's Love
December 8, 2020

I hope that the words I received that guided my life, and truly the lives of many, continue to be a blessing. For they are real, and they are true. The gist of them is to be open to God. Whether or not you hear a small still voice or the voice of an angel, or have a vision, I tell you if you will just allow your heart to be open that God may touch it and may fill your soul with love, the guidance will come. For as I wrote, you cannot fill a full vessel.

If you allow yourself to be empty and let the longings in your hearts, in your souls, to be foremost, you will receive. If you need to read words to get into your heart, to go within, to find that quiet place, then use words, use prayer, use song. For some just going in nature and seeing the beauty of creation is enough to bring them peace, calm and respite from the world. And should they wish to open to the Creator that will be their blessing and I know it is all your wish.

So, raise your sails on the ocean of love that the wind of God's Spirit may carry you into His heart, into His soul. If you put this first in your day, it will inform all subsequent events. If you can imagine having a conversation with God, or with a Celestial angel, or even with one of your guides for one day, and you set this as your task from when you awake to when you go to sleep, you can think of this as having an invisible friend like from your childhood, your guardian angel. If you could do this task, you would see the workings of God and the angels throughout your day and be amazed and be touched and you will be changed in His love. Isn't that great!

Thank you for taking my message and for all hearing this. May the love of God touch your souls, awaken your hearts, heal you and raise you up, for we here love you in the love of God. I am your sister and friend. I am Eileen, Auntie Eileen. God bless you.

Your Will and God's Will
December 16, 2020

I wish to say a few things about free will and the will of God. You may wish to reflect on how many times you use the expression 'I will' or 'I will not.' For instance, when you are asked to do a task, one that you enjoy and something you are looking forward to, you say: 'Yes, I will be there.' Of course, in contrast to that is having to or being asked to do things that you do not enjoy or feel will benefit you, especially in a positive way, and so given the opportunity you will not do them or attend to them. This is all, of course, within the realm of your earth lives.

Because you seek the kingdom and to be at one with your Creator, your will is to pray and to be opened to God's love, the reception of which puts you in His will, hence the saying that 'Thy will be done not mine.' It may be assumed that this means losing one's free will, since it is given over to the Creator, but in fact it is aligning your free will with the laws of harmony, the law of love, and every law of the Creator's, which when adhered to, brings complete harmony and peace as we wish for the world.

When you align your will with the will of God in prayer for His love, you have transcended the world and the earthly laws and now you are at one in love with your Maker. As you grow in this love, or let me say, as it grows in your soul, you see more and more the oneness of creation, but also the workings of God's love, His will, His grace, His mercy, His gifts to anyone and every soul that opens to them.

This path you have chosen is indeed the bridge to eternity, to immortality, to the Celestial heavens. You have chosen well my beautiful friends. May your prayers during this season be felt around the earth in celebration of the birth of the master who brought the truth of Divine Love, the great gift of the Father to the world. Be joyous, do not fear, for God loves you. We all do. I am your sister and friend, Aunty Eileen. May God bless you.

The Spiritual Life Requires Courage
February 3, 2021

You have discovered much about my life on earth and the struggles I faced, and you may have realized that spiritual life requires great courage, and it requires attention. Often in life circumstances come about where you feel you have no control over the outcome or that you are a victim of those circumstances. When this occurs, it is so important to go to God in prayer, to ask for help and to listen for guidance. Often this guidance comes as a feeling in your soul, a knowing in your heart which way to go. I tell you it is always the way of love.

I look back on my time on earth and I am thankful for the struggles that required me to seek forgiveness from those I had offended and allowed me to accept forgiveness and to forgive those who had offended me; and it was all for love. I could not help but take the path of my soul and when I made a choice that was out of harmony, I paid a price. And when I made a choice in love and had the courage to follow that choice the results were always beyond my wildest dreams as in the case of Findhorn, as in the case of the many who have been touched by the guidance I received from God.

I tell you, have courage, trust in your guidance. For ultimately it is between you and God. And while others may give you good advice, you can always measure this by the feeling you get in your heart, in your soul. Does this feel like love? Is this a loving thing to do? What is the best path for my soul? Am I enabling things that are less than love or am I encouraging and bringing love to the table?

Life is often a discovery of your soul longings for those on the spiritual path and this is in alignment with the gifts you have been given and often gifts you are not even aware of, until you reach a certain maturity of soul, maturity of love, and then they blossom before your very eyes, and as a blessing to others and as a delight to oneself, to one's life. Be not afraid of your gifts. Be not afraid to walk into the future for the benefit of your soul; to be transformed will be for the benefit of all in the love of God. Isn't that great? But you need not take my word, for you can discern this with your own souls as to the truth of it. For with love comes every blessing and the greatest blessings are in God's love. This you have. The journey ahead may be at times trying and difficult and again I say 'pray, ask for guidance, have faith, take heart, and be courageous! With all my love and blessings in the grace of God I am truly your friend, I am Aunty Eileen, Eileen Caddy. Go with God. Go in grace. Go in love.

Go Within - Allow God to Open Your Soul
April 20, 2021

I wish to clarify something that I know you are all curious about. When I constantly asked, or rather the words that came through me from God asked, to go 'within,' please know the place that was being referred to is the soul. And, if you follow the words that I received, going into the soul, going into the heart is imperative and then opening, as I received many times in words that you have all read, to the infilling and inflowing of God's Divine Love. These are the true elements of prayer and those were and remain my templates. You dear ones have recognized this, whereas this truth as I received it has been somewhat obscured or even lost to many.

I believed in many things in my life but always I had a firm foundation of going in prayer to God. At Findhorn we adopted a kind of pantheism, a belief that God was in everything. And perhaps this was more so felt by my friend Dorothy and my husband Peter who worked in the gardens and described what they called 'interactions with elementals.' This is the consciousness of plants, and it is real just as the consciousness of animals and the heightened senses that they have of smell and of hearing are real.

Humans, who are blessed with souls, have the possibility of a higher consciousness. Because they have very developed brains, which is the organ of the mind, humans are easily distracted by their intellectual pursuits as with their bodies, so they often give primacy to their animal nature with physical pursuits and pleasures. When this is in balance with the longings of the soul, it can create a beautiful harmony. My pantheism was more, if I may say, a belief that all things were one in the sense that they were all created from one source, God.

The foundation of Findhorn, which you are more than aware of, was one of prayer and guidance every step of the way. It has been written about and it has been set into words available to all who wish to read them. What I received and how that guidance was followed, and acted upon by those who came, and what was accomplished and built and our harmony with nature and our awareness of the consciousness of plants combined with our prayers for guidance, created a sanctuary, a sacred place that became a portal of light and was honored.

As time went on, having accomplished all these things, the focus became more on ecology, on science and going within, yes, but with a certain hubris, a pride of accomplishment and lack of humility. No longer going to God in humility but just going within to that place of calm and peace which is often assumed to be a connection with God when in fact it is connection with creation, wonderful as that is but not divine.

There may be those who wonder at the recent fires and the horrific destruction of the sanctuary and the community center at Findhorn. They may wonder did God take them out (the sanctuary and community center) because they were no longer places of prayer? Was it because the divine connection was lost and so in a sense God somehow destroyed them? The answer is no. We all know that God is a God of love and whether those who live there believe in God, or believe they are God, or do not believe, God loves all His children and would never bring such destruction upon them.

However, I will say this, that when things become out of harmony, even in the realm of secular humanism or ecology, there is no longer the protection of the Celestial angels when they are not called upon. The cloak of protection that God provides to those who seek oneness with Him in His love, is not there. And so, there was a distance created that permitted an environment that was open to attack and the motives of one who sought to destroy. This act of arson found a doorway and without protection, the beautiful sanctuary and community center were destroyed.

The community there now asks for help financially. And the world that is aware of these events will have a great outpouring of love and sympathy. It is my hope that the rebuilding will include asking for guidance from God and His angels, as well as those of us here in the Celestial realm who are Celestial angels. It is our deep desire that from the ashes Findhorn will rise as a Phoenix on the wings of Divine Love and grace.

My dear ones, thank you for listening to my long message and I thank this one. I am pleased with the reception. You are beautiful souls and I love you and thank you. May God bless you and May God bless my dear Findhorn and the earth and all souls with His love. Go in peace. I am your sister in Christ, Eileen Caddy.

Ask In Prayer and You Shall Receive
November 19, 2021

My dear friends I come in the grace of God, in the love of God, to this holy communion of blessed souls. You that come together in a community of prayer, a union of souls, are coming together to receive the love of God and knowing the magnitude of this effort joining together the family of Divine Love where all are one. I can tell you when you gather with singularity of purpose you bring a force that cannot be denied, as you are shining a beam of light in the darkness. We who live in realms of light attracted to your prayer are glad to come and to be in this community with you; to give whatever guidance and encouragement we can with the love of our souls.

In my time I witnessed firsthand what could be created by following the guidance of the angels in communion with God. Many came in service, and as one community we were able to create something greater than ourselves that over time drew thousands. And though that thread has been somewhat lost, and the light somewhat diminished you can know that the template of prayer that was able to inspire so many, this template is a worthwhile one to adapt in whatever endeavors you embark on. Ask in prayer and you shall receive. Follow your guidance, know you are protected. Know that we walk with you.

I wish to give a special embrace to my friend Susan and her Michael that all of you may know, that I am a Celestial and I live in the kingdom of God's love. And to all here in this lattice of light in this bubble of God's love where you open to the inflowing and infilling of His essence, may you stay in grace, walk in love, and grow, for the earth so needs you and I thank you. May God bless each one of you and your beautiful community that is a church without walls. I am your sister in the love of God. I am Eileen Caddy. Go in peace. Go in grace.

Ann Rollins

FALSE BELIEFS AND DIVINE LOVE
December 19, 2021

I am here, Ann Rollins.[62] I see no need for further introduction as you both know me. I would like to talk about how one can be believing in things that are less than love and being in God's love at the same time, for you know one cannot be in hate and in love at the same time. Yet, such is the difference of what the mind believes and what the soul receives.

I tell you when anyone prays and asks God to open their soul to His great love, He makes no distinction whether that person is a sinner or a saint, rich or poor, Catholic or Jewish or Muslim. The world is filled with mental beliefs and sometimes those who feel they have no say, or voice, will support those who seem to have a strong voice, and in a sense, give a part of their identity to that voice for protection. If that voice is not in love, or of love, then that clinging is simply the mind in fear.

However, when any soul steps aside allowing the deep longings and aspirations of their soul to send up a prayer to be at one with the heavenly Father in His love, in that moment of receiving there is no hatred, there is no enmity, there is no negativity. However, vexed that spirit may have been, it is now in condition and in harmony with God's love and His Laws.

I can tell you that as long as a person clings to the baggage of the mind, the soul can only progress to a certain point where it will await the deeper desire for oneness with its Creator. When that deep desire for God's love penetrates, the baggage is let go of and the soul can arise. It is important not to judge but to love.

This does not mean one needs to associate with those who are not in harmony or wish harm to others, but it does mean you must love them, and with the love of God in your soul. There is no more powerful weapon against negativity and hatred than the love of God. If you let your soul be in ascendancy, God will do the rest. Do not be troubled. The law of attraction leads every being ultimately to love. Be that magnet in the world my brothers. This is God's wish for you and mine. I thank this one for taking my message and I will come again. I am your sister in Christ, Ann Rollins.

---

62 Ann Rollins is the grandmother of James Padgett.

ABOUT THE AUTHOR / MEDIUM
Jimbeau Walsh

Jimbeau Walsh was born in Chicago, Illinois in 1950 where he grew up. His parents were first generation Americans: his father Irish American, and mother Slovak-Croatian American. They were both devout Catholics. Since Jimbeau's mother had hopes that her son would become a priest, he served as an altar boy, attended Mass regularly, went to Catholic schools, and seemed on track to fulfill his mother's dreams for him. But in boyhood Jimbeau became attracted to music and learned to play drums by listening to rock-and-roll and other popular music of the times. His musical interests soon became paramount and he started playing in a number of local rock and blues bands while learning guitar as well. He also started to write songs in his teen years.

In 1976 he started a band in Nashville with Tommy Goldsmith, Walter Hyatt, Steve Runkle, and Champ Hood called 'The Contenders.' Soon they were wowing audiences in Nashville with regular appearances at Exit/In and other local night spots. They also played to packed audiences throughout the South. After the group disbanded Jimbeau worked with many groups and songwriters as a drummer in both live performances and session work. The Contenders 1978 re-released, remixed and remastered album was voted 'Reissued Album of the Year' by the Nashville Scene July 27, 2023.

In addition to music, Jimbeau's other major life interest was and is spirituality. As a young man, after rejecting Catholicism, he studied and practiced elements of Hinduism, Sufi Islam, Buddhism, Judaism (Hasidic teachings), and yogic meditation. After decades of searching he found his spiritual home in Divine Love Christianity. He was introduced to Divine Love through a young woman, Care Darby, whom he met briefly outside a folk cafe in Austin, Texas one evening in late December 1987. Strongly attracted by her presence, beauty, happiness, and light, he arranged to meet her again. Their conversation quickly turned to spiritual matters. She explained that she spoke to Celestial angels, including Mary and Jesus, and that he (Jesus) is not God, but was the first human being to be transformed into a divine (immortal) human by God's essence, His love. She further explained that Jesus came to earth to teach the path of soul transformation, a path that is available to every human being through earnest prayer for God's love.

That same evening Care showed Jimbeau the place outside of Austin where she went to talk to angels. While they both were praying two angels appeared to him and told him to not be afraid, that God loved him and to go in peace.[63] Jimbeau was hooked. He and Care were soon married and had a wonderful, eventful four years of marriage before she passed to spirit in a car crash that she had foreseen in a vision.

After this devastating event Jimbeau moved to Hawaii where he continued to be active in the Divine Love community. He became an ordained Divine Love Christian minister and has officiated over 3,000 weddings and vow renewals. In 2019 he began receiving channeled messages from Celestial angels, and to date Jimbeau has received over 350 messages. He moved back to Nashville in 2022 to be near his son's family after living in Hawaii for 29 years.

During his years in Hawaii he also traveled extensively and gave spiritual talks in the US, Canada, England, Ireland, Germany and Australia. He co-authored a book with Rev. Michael Nedbal entitled 'The Divine Love Ministers Handbook.' He currently facilitates weekly prayer and meditation sessions where he shares his music and frequently channels spirit messages. He also gives spiritual talks to many groups without regard to religious or denominational affiliation.

Jimbeau continues to receive, write, an explore music. He says that his music and mediumship have a common spiritual denominator and are complementary. His songs in recent years have been focused mainly on Divine Love. He loves sharing songs and stories with other songwriters especially on Thursday mornings at the Cafe in Westminster Presbyterian Church in Nashville, and has recently released an album titled 'Reliable Roses.'

---

63 A more detailed account of the meeting of Jimbeau and Care and his encounter with two Celestial angels is in the preface to Chapter 6.

Afterword

Now that you have finished reading all or part of the messages I received from angel spirits you may be asking yourself questions like 'Are these messages really coming from these spirits, from dead people? How can I know if this is real and genuine? Why haven't I had spirits communicate with me? Well, I have experienced all these questions and doubts too. In fact I didn't start receiving messages from angels until after I had been a practicing Divine Love Christian for over 30 years. And until I was in my mid 30's I was a spiritual seeker but not a Christian in any sense. During my time as a DL Christian I read the Padgett messages and the messages from spirit that Al Fike and other DL mediums have received. But most important for me was having a regular, daily prayer practice asking God to send His Divine Love into my soul, to transform my soul to be at one with God's essence, with Divine Love.

I have and am still experiencing this soul transformation (in fact it is an eternal process), but it took decades before angelic spirits began to come to me and communicate with my soul. I never thought this would happen and never sought for it to happen to me. And like others who have become mediums I was skeptical when the messages started to come through me. But after a time I became convinced that I couldn't be making this up in my mind. The presence of a spirit(s) was too real - often by my seeing their light and outline and feeling their presence. And it was not infrequent when I would wake up in the middle of the night, still half asleep and an angel would be trying to communicate. I would turn on my phone's recorder and half consciously say the words. Sometimes I didn't even remember that a message had come through or what the words were. Only after hearing the recording and having the words transcribed did I know fully what the message was and meant. And since the spirit communicator is using my brain with my vocabulary, the words and phrases from different spirits may sound somewhat the same. But often the tone and words are different. For example no one would say that Charlie Chaplin's messages sound like the poet Hafiz's messages or that Fred (Mister) Rogers sounds like Eileen Caddy.

Why don't more people on earth hear spirit messages? First of all there are various ways and means that spirit people try to communicate with us on Earth. This may happen through inspiration, from a resolution of a problem you are having, from near-death experiences, from feeling the presence of a recently deceased relative or friend, or from a sudden sense of feeling at one with all creation. These are but a few examples of spirit communication. And if you pray sincerely and with soul longing for help or for a resolution of a problem, your prayer will be answered. It may not come in the form you initially desired but it will come. You don't even have to believe in God with your mind, but if you sincerely ask for help from your soul, in humility and in a heart-felt way your prayer will be heard and help will come. So being a medium is just one of many, many ways angels and God are helping us and communicating with us. None of these other ways are to be minimized or thought less of by any means.

A factor that tends to block people from seeing or feeling the influence of the spirit world is when one is predominantly living in their mind, in their thoughts and rationalizing and analyzing everything they experience. Progression in the spirit world happens as people intentionally move away from their mental assumptions about reality and experience life more and more from their heart and soul. This means calming the thoughts of the mind, living in the moment without judgment, without analyzing every moment of experience, without negative emotions preventing one from experiencing what is really happening in each moment. It's a transformation from fear, doubt, insecurity, mental pain and anguish, guilt, helplessness, resentment, and hate to peace, happiness, joy, faith and love. This does not happen instantaneously but is a process that goes on forever. And it depends on each one to sincerely long for the transformation and to intentionally seek for it through prayer and practice.

One of the key attributes of God is love. When we pray to God to receive Divine Love in our souls we are asking to be transformed from the human to the divine, from mortal to immortal. When you think about it, isn't it true that the key problem in human history, and in our personal and social lives and the state of our world right now is that for the most part we live separated from God. We have created a social and political structure that is a product of human thought, that assumes that people's needs and greed are endless, and other groups and nations are ultimately not to be trusted, that we must be prepared to compete with them and fight if necessary. In short we are fearful and want to protect what we think belongs to us or that we deserve.

A soul transformed by love turns the wisdom of the world on its head. In the words of Paul, "love is patient, love is kind. It does not envy, it does not boast, it is not proud. It is not rude, it is not self-seeking. It is not easily angered, it keeps no record of wrongs. Love does not delight in evil but rejoices with the truth. It always protects, always trusts, always hopes, always perseveres. Love never fails... (1 Corinthians 13: 4-8). Imagine a world where most people had this kind of love in their souls and lived it out every moment of their lives. Then you begin to imagine what heaven is like. What else could create a heavenly existence but love? How else can you experience the reality of God but through love? What else could possibly get at the root cause of all our personal, societal, national and world problems? Yes, love is *all we need*.

And the astounding and wonderful good news is that every single human being who ever lived and is yet to be born will one day become a soul so transformed by love that each will inherit and live in one of the spheres of heaven. But the greatest of all the good and perfect gifts that our Creator bestows upon us is the gift of immortality and at-onement with the divine essence, with God's love. All we have to do is sincerely ask for this gift.

May God and the angels be with you on your 'Path of Roses.

Index of Topics and Related Messages

Community
- Holy Communion Holy Community 28
- This Communion Can Be Yours. 32
- Carry the Love of God Into Spirit 33
- Come Together as a Community. 126
- Holy Communion Holy Community 176

Faith
- Trust and Faith 39
- The Importance of Faith 48
- What Part Will You Choose To Play? 82
- We Are Provided For. 105
- Walk in Faith 123
- Faith in God and Your Gifts. 200
- Have Faith - Your Prayers Will Be Answered. 209
- The Spiritual Life Requires Courage 223

God
- Comprehending God. 97
- May You Feel the Love Radiating From Your Heart 105
- God is Love 115
- God's Love Opens the Heart and Transforms the Soul. 122
- I Always Pointed to God. 159
- The Divine Truth is God's Love 191

Grace
- Celestial Energy 17
- The Path of God's Love. 31
- Stand Naked Before God 36
- Riches and Joy. 38
- Don't Rage Against the Darkness But Embrace All in the Light ... 77
- Stay in Grace 168
- Children of God. 199
- Be Beholden to No One Except God 215

Guidance

- Choose Wisely 41
- We Are With You on This Journey 42
- The Guidance I Received in Life 69
- Let Love be Your Guide 118
- Keep Your Eyes on the Prize 135
- Raise Your Thoughts to the Highest 155
- Curse Not the Darkness but Praise the Light 182
- In God's Love There Are No Wrong Choices 199
- Raise Your Sails on the Ocean of God's Love 222

Healing

- Love, Light, and Healing 4
- Begin Anew 16
- Allow the Intentions of Your Souls to Reach Out 30
- Love is the Healer of All Hearts 38
- Spiritual Immunity 49
- Let Your Love Be a Healing Balm 75
- White Eagle Comes to Offer Healing 132
- Turn Grief to Joy 149
- Open Your Heart to the Love of God 158
- Be Open to Healing 177
- Love is the Healer 183

Love Divine and its Effects

- God's Love is Anti-Gravitational 43
- This Will Be Your Treasure 45
- Love in Action 45
- Be in the Moment 46
- The Physical Manifestations of Divine Love 47
- Love of God Leads to a Life Of Service 51
- God's Love Is the Greatest Thing in the Universe 54
- The Thief of Hearts 60
- Tune In to Love 61
- Love is the Great Gift 65
- Explore the Truth With Your Souls 96
- Working With the Little Children 100

How I Love You. 110
Spread Love by Every Means Available.. 114
Seek Ye First the Kingdom. 123
Touch Others with Love & Everything Will Fall into Place. 124
The Soul Touched by God is the Real Proof. 125
Be in the Love. 130
The Love of God Brings Peace. 131
If You Would Have One Belief To Carry With You. 137
The Most Important Yoga Is To Be Open to God's Love. 154
The Yoga of God's Love is the Highest Yoga.. 157
The True Meaning of Divine Love. 161
Divine Romance.. 166
God's Love. 172
Nature and Divine Love. 183
The Path of the Heart. 185
The Miracle of Soul Transformation. 186
Choosing To Live in God's Love. 193
Crazy for God. 197
Slay Them With Love.. 203
Plant the Seeds and Be the Love. 205
Your Will and God's Will.. 223

Prayer

Make God Your First Resort. 5
Prayer is the Answer to all Problems. 12
Follow Your Hearts.. 26
Connecting to God as a Simple Act. 41
The Wise Choice. 50
Meditation Is Not What You Think. 49
Every Prayer Creates an Invisible Sanctuary. 53
Pray To Be Open to the Creator's Love. 66
Allow the Blessings Of God's Love To Come Into Your Soul. 112
The Simplicity of Prayer. 138
Pray!. 163
Comparing Meditation and Prayer. 164
Prayer Connects You With God's Soul. 169
Ask!. 174

Prayer is the Bridge Between Heaven and Earth. 219
Ask in Prayer and You Shall Receive. 227
False Beliefs And Divine Love.. 228

Sanctuary

The Safety of God's Love.. 5
A Bit of Advice. 6
This Sanctuary. 19
Be Mindful of Your Heart's Desires. 20
Become the Gardeners of Your Souls.. 22
The World Is Slowing Down. 27
God's Love Is Your Spiritual Lifeboat.. 103
You Can Dispel the Darkness. 163
Spiritual Defense.. 181

Sharing Your Gifts

Simply Bring the Truth. 13
Belief in God's Love Transcends All Other Beliefs. 24
Use Social Media to Reach the Millions.. 55
Use Your Art To Spread The Truth Of God's Love. 56
The Subject of Service. 58
Share Your Gifts. 59
Be A Gift To The World. 62
Discover Your Gifts and Give Them in Love.. 64
Explore Your Gifts. 92
A Lightbulb In A Dark Room. 95
Remember The Importance Of Guiding The Children.. 99
Keep A Song In Your Heart. 134
What Will Be Your Gift To God? 201
Communicate Truth In Creative Ways.. 204
Follow The Joy. 208

You Shall Overcome. 217

Spirit Life

Think of Eternity, Not Death. 8
Depictions of the Spirit World in Film.. 11
Our Souls Stand Naked Before God. 15

The Thoughts You Entertain.. 119
Let Your Prayers Go Deep. 140
A Glimpse of Eternity.. 170

Soul
Tend to the Gardens of Your Souls. 23
Crazy for God. 25
The Secret of the Soul is to Be Humble.........................34
Spiritual Metamorphosis..107
Plant the Seeds of God's Love...................................... 113
The Mind and the Soul.. 152
Soul Transformation - Food For Thought. 179
Soul Perceptions vs. Intuition......................................202

Soul Transformation. 221

The True Message of Jesus
The Way, the Life and the Truth.................................... 2
Let Go and Let God.. 10
Bless the Children in God's Love.................................108
Every Soul Has a Choice... 110
Consider What it is To Be Transformed in Divine Love. 114

The Magnetism of God's Love.......................................117

The Bible
Dealing With Threats of Harm.. 9
A Lightbulb in a Dark Room. 95
Voices of the Bible... 102
Faith in God and Your Gifts 200

Additional Resources

1. Divine Love Sanctuary Foundation: divinelovesanctuary.com website
   - contains info about the Divine Love Circles of Light, and
   - Jesus' messages in three volumes channeled through Al Fike during the years 2021-2022:
     - *Our World in Transition*
     - *Finding Our Way Home*
     - *Awakening to Soul Consciousness*
2. Geoff Cutler's new-birth.net website contains:
   - messages received by James Padgett
   - messages from Jesus channeled by Dr. Daniel Samuels
   - other messages from Jesus, Judas and other Celestial angels
   - additional material on spiritual development
3. Another Geoff Cutler soultruth.ca website contains:
   - over 2000 messages received from spirit communicators from the following years: 1969, 1970, 2014-2024 or the present time
   - other resources pertaining to spirit communications
4. Foundation Church of the New Birth divinelove.org website contains:
   - messages (1914-1917) received by James Padgett from Jesus and other Celestial spirits
5. Foundation Church of Divine Truth: fcdt.org
6. Celestial messengers, Jimbeau Walsh's web: celestialmessengers.net
7. Universal Spirituality website universal-spirituality.net
8. Global Healing Experience monthly on Zoom
   https://us02web.zoom.us/j/81245220412 or
   contact Maureen Cardoso at livingwatersspiritualheal@gmail.com
9. Divine Love Prayer Circles: https://lightbringers.info/calendar.html
   - Divine Love Monday 9pm CST Circle of Light Prayer and Meditation Circle with author, Jimbeau Walsh virtually on Zoom. https://us02web.zoom.us/j/275241599?pwd=OC8rU214c0w4eXgzb2lHVHI3NVYyQT09#success
10. Recommended Books:
    - James E. Padgett: *True Gospel Revealed Anew by Jesus (Vols 1-4)*
    - Robert J. Lees (trilogy):
      - *Through the Mists*
      - *The Life Elysian*
      - *The Gate of Heaven*
    - George Vale Owen: *The Life Beyond the Veil* (series)
      - *Ministry of Heaven*

- » *Lowlands of Heaven*
  - » *Highlands of Heaven*
  - » *Battalions of Heaven*
- Judas of Kerioth: *Conversations with Judas Iscariot, by Anonymous (Author), Geoff Cutler (Editor)*
- Eileen Caddy
  - » *God Spoke to Me*
  - » *Footprints on the Path*
  - » *The Dawn of Change*
  - » *Foundations of Findhorn*
- Anthony Borgia
  - » *Life in the World Unseen*
  - » *Here and Hereafter*
- Joseph Babinsky
  - » *Family Reunion*
  - » *The Little Book of Truths*
  - » *The Teachings of Jesus*
- Marianne Williamson: *Illuminata: Thoughts, Prayers, Rites of Passage*
- Jane Gartshore: *For the Love of His Own Creation: A Novel by Yeshua ben Yosef*

INVITATION / INQUIRIES:

For information about joining a virtual prayer group, prayer requests, or questions, please contact the author, Jimbeau Walsh at: jimbeau@pathofroses.com

Path of Roses 2024 Copyright Pending

www.ingramcontent.com/pod-product-compliance
Lightning Source LLC
Chambersburg PA
CBHW050526100526
44581CB00008B/146/J